T0384294

BEHIND THE SEARCH BOX

THE GEOPOLITICS OF INFORMATION

Edited by Dan Schiller, Amanda Ciafone, and Yuezhi Zhao

A list of books in the series appears at the end of this book.

BEHIND THE SEARCH BOX

Google and the Global Internet Industry

ShinJoung Yeo

1 2 3 4 5 C P 5 4 3 2 1
∞ This book is printed on acid-free paper.

Cataloging data available from the Library of Congress
ISBN 9780252044991 (hardcover)
ISBN 9780252087127 (paperback)
ISBN 9780252054174 (ebook)

For Yeo Dukyong and Bae Yangza
부모님에게 바칩니다

CONTENTS

ACKNOWLEDGMENTS

It's not an easy task to claim my authorship for this project considering the collective nature of its development. I have deep gratitude for Dan Schiller, who offered me not only invaluable intellectual advice during my graduate studies but also persistent encouragement throughout the years as I struggled with self-doubt. His words—humble, yet confident—always echo in my ears. Thanks to my friend and colleague Richard Maxwell, who kindly read the draft manuscript, offered feedback, and has been generous with his time during our weekly chats.

There are many friends I need to acknowledge for their academic support. Great thanks to my writing partners Morgan Ames, Megan Finn, and Lilly Irani, whose daily writing support was invaluable. In particular, thanks to Morgan Ames, who organized co-writing sessions for many years and never hesitated to give a hand to anyone who needed support of any kind. Her thorough and insightful comments and suggestions on my work have been invaluable. I've greatly benefited from her generosity.

In the same vein, Kyoko Sato, friend, neighbor, and academic colleague, helped me break out of my routines by brainstorming, sharing meals, and walking with me to Korean grocery stores in search of roasted rice and much-needed breaks for comfort food. Thanks to Matt Crain for being an intellectual comrade and for his much-needed critical scholarship in the field, and to Chris D'Arpa and Ellen Riordan for their unwavering friendship. On the other side of the Atlantic, my Turkish sister and loyal friend Burçe Celik always boosted my mood as she laughed at all my jokes and blindly praised the quality of my work even though she should have questioned it.

Many thanks to my San Diego comrades Anita Schiller, Jim Jacobs, and Mary Lou Locke for all the years of discussions and shared meals. Anita Schiller is no longer with us, but the hand-ripped *New York Times* articles she gave me are sprinkled throughout this work like delicious breadcrumbs. I know she would have been very happy to see this project come to completion. Susan Davis supported me through her delicious homemade biscotti and jams, which added sweetness during writing struggles. Indeed, I'm extremely fortunate to have as friends Nancy and Fred Jacobs, who always welcomed me into their family with smiles and love.

Many people were involved in the actual production of the book. I don't know all their names but at the University of Illinois Press I'm grateful to series editor Daniel Nasset for his patience and support and to Jane Zanichkowsky for the superb copyediting work that helped improve the project.

I don't have the capacity to express my gratitude to James Jacobs, the most important person in my life, who stopped me from quitting this project and academia many times and corrected many wrong prepositions, semicolons, Oxford commas, and more that I have never figured out after living in the United States for more than twenty-five years. There is no way I could have finished this book without his love, patience, and humor through the years. I wasn't able to accept his title suggestion, *Unboxing Search*, but I'm happy to relinquish the royalties from this book.

Finally, I credit this work to my parents, whose unconditional love and bravery allowed me to explore the world. Without them, I never would have questioned the world in which I live.

BEHIND THE SEARCH BOX

INTRODUCTION

The search engine is a ubiquitous and vital tool that assists us in our daily lives with seamlessly instant results; however, this plain search box, used by billions of people around the world, also conceals the most complex changes in the global political economy and geopolitics today.

Google (which is held by Alphabet, Inc.), one of the most popular entry points to the Internet is one of the leading Internet companies and an emblem of the "new" economy. For simplicity's sake, I will refer to it as Google in this book. Search as an entry point to the Internet has become a nexus of the power struggle among state, national, and transnational capital, labor, and other social actors as the Internet has become a new transnational marketplace and driving force for capitalist development and expansion. The goal of this book is to unbox search and show the broader structural changes that are occurring in global capitalism, dynamically intertwined with the political economy of the Internet.

In 2021 Google generated more than $257 billion in revenue, with $76 billion in net income, trailing just behind Apple and Amazon and ahead of Microsoft and Facebook. At that time the company held over $139 billion in cash reserves.[1] To put this in perspective, a $25 billion investment can produce enough COVID vaccines for all low- and middle- income countries.[2] If Google were compared to a country, based on its revenue, it would rank fiftieth in the world in terms of GDP, tied with New Zealand. How and under what conditions was the search function on the Internet able to generate this enormous wealth, drawn from basic daily information-seeking activities around the world, and restructure existing global information and communication domains?

Since its initial public offering on August 19, 2004, Google has been Wall Street's darling for reinvigorating the market after the 2000 dot-com bubble burst; at the same time, the company was also beloved by the public, academics, librarians, and politicians, who saw the search engine as a tool for the democratization of information and empowerment of citizens. Many believed in the compatibility of Wall Street and democracy because Google seemed a harbinger of a gentler and more benign and democratic capitalist system. Less than two decades later, however, Google has turned from being the "people's company" to being a new corporate behemoth and a symbol of a modern-day robber baron infamous for exercising political economic power around the globe, exploiting massive amounts of private data mined from its surveillance business model, using a profit-biased algorithm, destroying journalism and gentrifying local communities, with an undemocratic corporate culture and labor exploitation that relies on union busting and a large number of contract workers.

In response to these developments, domestic policy makers, scholars, and the public have increasingly demanded social responsibility and called for reining in the swelling concentration of power and wealth of Google and other tech companies, urging the federal government to increase regulations on those companies and across the sector. A bipartisan group of legislators has introduced several bills including the American Innovation and Choice Online Act[3] and Open App Markets Act,[4] aiming to curb the power of the tech giants and create a more competitive market. Legal scholar Tim Wu, who was named by the Biden administration to the National Economic Council as a special assistant to the president for technology and competition policy, has suggested creating a new regulatory body and breaking up large portions of the big tech companies.[5] Outside the United States, Google, along with its US competitors Amazon, Facebook, and Apple, is under fire for controlling the Internet, as alleged in a series of antitrust investigations by multiple nation-states including the European Union (EU), while the company has struggled to gain a foothold in China—the largest Internet market. These intensifying geopolitical tensions are reshaping the Internet.

As the search engine has become the major gateway to the Internet and the main mode of daily information seeking, there has been growing interest among journalists and scholars from a range of fields in its implications of the social, political, and technical functions. A significant number of scholars have rightly questioned and refuted the popular belief that the search engine is a neutral medium or a new democratizing force that makes room for new and diverse voices. They point out that search engines often reinforce dominant cultures, political power, and social hierarchies, drawing attention to the growing power of search engines and how they function in and have consequences for social, cultural, and political life.[6] In the political economic field are several works that focus on Google, addressing issues concerning ownership structure, surveillance, monopoly, and algorithm use.[7]

The purpose of this book is not to be redundant but to build and expand on this existing work by extending questions about how and under what conditions basic human information-seeking activities have been commodified and subordinated to capital in the first place, how search has transformed into a global industry that has accelerated the commodification and commercialization of the Internet and the accumulation of capital, and how it was turned into a new geopolitical focal point of the Internet. I hope that such a political economy of search will offer a broader understanding of today's global capitalism—which is absorbing and predicated upon digital technologies to an ever-increasing extent. I begin with situating search, represented by Google, within its political economic and geopolitical contexts. Although Google dominates the global search market, it is important to note that the search function is no longer exclusively taking place through the traditional search engine. Besides Google, Microsoft Bing, Yahoo!, Baidu, Yandex, and Naver, there are numerous vertically integrated search engines such as Amazon and Facebook, as well as mobile and voice search. Moreover, the search giants intersect with every media and internet business, and increasingly, sectoral lines have blurred as the Internet giants have extended their businesses across the Internet and beyond. Search is about more than the search engine per se; it is about a focal point of controlling and shaping the Internet as a marketplace. Thus, while this book is about search and centered on Google, it also covers the intersection between search and the major Internet sectors that drive the dynamics of the political economy of the Internet.

Political Economic and Geopolitical Context

As of January 2021 there were 4.66 billion Internet users around the world, representing a penetration rate of 59.5 percent of the total global population.[8] Google is the most popular site on the Internet with 86.9 billion total monthly visits, with YouTube (also owned by Alphabet) coming in second at 22.8 billion visits.[9] In 2020 the digital advertising market reached over $378 billion, accounting for over 50 percent of total global advertising.[10] In that same year, Google's ad revenues amounted to almost $147 billion, and its search advertising revenue was over $104 billion.[11] Microsoft Bing was second, garnering a little over $7.7 billion, followed by Yahoo! and the Chinese search engine Baidu.[12] Google remains the largest digital advertising seller, with a whopping 30 percent or more of worldwide ad spending.

Google handles millions of searches per minute on average as people search for everything from how to avoid coronavirus infection to how to apply for unemployment, where and for whom to vote, find jobs, items to buy, entertainment, health advice, research for work and school requirements, and information to fulfill myriad curiosities. The search function has wired and rewired our fundamental social, political, and economic lives. The search engine industry has turned the Internet into the most profitable capitalist marketplace, as it is strategically woven into the political economy of the Internet and reaches across economic sectors. Thus, if we are to understand the industry, it needs to be situated within the broader capitalist political economy, in which global capitalism's developmental growth increasingly hinges on the growth pole of the Internet sector. This was made clear in the 2008 global crisis.

In 2008, in the blink of an eye, the economic crisis and the collapse of the world financial system reverberated around the globe. Ben Bernanke, the head of the US Federal Reserve, succinctly noted that "the financial crisis was the worst in global history, surpassing even the Great Depression."[13] Tim Geithner, the US Treasury Secretary, noted that "the percentage of household wealth lost would be more than five times worse than 1929."[14] Facing a rapidly escalating global and domestic economic meltdown, President-Elect Barack Obama promised to rebuild the US economy and create millions of new jobs by investing in infrastructure and building an information superhighway. In a December speech about his economic recovery plan, Obama, vowing to create prosperity for all, stated, "Here, in the country that invented the internet, every child should have the chance to get online, and they'll get that chance when I'm President—because that's how we'll strengthen America's competitiveness in the world."[15]

This was followed by his visit to Silicon Valley, the epicenter of the new economy, to meet with high tech industry CEOs including Steve Jobs of Apple, Facebook's Mark Zuckerberg, Oracle's Larry Ellison, Google's Eric Schmidt, Yahoo!'s Carol Bartz, Cisco Systems's John Chambers, Twitter's Dick Costolo, and Netflix's Reed Hastings.[16] Obama's visit was not merely to express his gratitude to the tech giants, which were the largest of his presidential campaign contributors, but was also to discuss a "partnership" between the public and private sectors to reboot the process of capital accumulation[17] through the Internet sector in order to shore up the depressed economic system. The search engine industry as a strategic growth industry occupied the center of this broader renewal effort.

Fresh capital was funneled into the Internet sector. As millions of people were losing jobs, homes, pensions, and social welfare rights around the world, the Obama administration, as part of its 2009 stimulus package, injected billions of dollars into incorporating and expanding new Internet-based technologies, with the promise to the American people of economic recovery, prosperity, creation of quality jobs, transparency, and a more democratic society.[18]

With the enhancement of US economic competitiveness, there was a new push for the digitization of the US economy through a series of "public and private" initiatives, interlinking information technologies with strategic sectors. These included a project called Digital Promise backed by the Department of Education, academia, and the tech industry to create "smart demand" in order to move the education system further toward being an appendage of the market;[19] electronic medical records' being mandated by the federal government to open up a new billion-dollar health IT market;[20] promotion of a smart grid by the Department of Energy for trade and investment around the world; the boosting of American economic output by further integrating computer technologies within manufacturing processes; and, all in the name of transparency, the White House's open data policy, which required government agencies to release government data and, in effect, turn over valuable weather, climate, health, and geographic data collected at taxpayer expense to the information market. For decades, the United States has been aggressively reorienting its domestic economy to aid the Internet sector and organizing it into a new economic growth zone.

As the United States continued this effort, the government undertook a new self-serving trade agenda called "digital trade" (commerce conducted over the Internet) and mobilized agencies including the Department of State, the Department of Commerce, and the International Trade Commission in order to remove a range of obstacles so that US digital goods and services could reach global markets over the Internet. The US digital political economic agenda could be seen in the Trans-Pacific Partnership Agreement (TPP), a 2016 trade agreement between the United States and eleven other countries, which was set to be the largest free trade deal in the world and to expand digital trade. It was one of the focal pieces of President Obama's strategic trade policy—a "pivot to Asia"—targeted toward integrating the Asia-Pacific economy while strategically excluding China. The TPP, which was supposed to comprise 40 percent of global trade, included strong digital trade provisions to serve the interests of the US tech sectors. In regard to the TPP, Obama stated, "My top priority as President is making sure more hardworking Americans have a chance to get ahead. That's why we have to make sure the United States—and not countries like China—is the one writing this century's rules for the world's economy."[21] In 2017, however, the Trump administration withdrew from the agreement.

In a January 2017 report published by the President's Council of Advisors on Science and Technology, the Obama administration warned that China was a threat to the US semiconductor industry.[22] In order to curb China's tech power, the council recommended that the US government intervene and protect US tech sectors including the semiconductor industry, increase government spending on research and development, tighten up US protections against intellectual property "theft," and reshape national security to deter the use of Chinese technologies in US government procurement. The members of the council included former Alphabet executive chairman Eric Schmidt and former Microsoft chief research and strategy officer Craig Mundie, and the working group members included former Intel CEO Paul Otellini, Qualcomm executive chairman Paul Jacobs, and Stanford University President Emeritus John Hennessy (now chairman of Alphabet).

Subsequently, the Trump administration's schizophrenic economic, social, and foreign policies seemed to diverge from the Obama administration's policies, as they were sometimes at odds with the interests of the US tech sector. Yet the fundamental principle, that of maintaining US-led global capitalism, was still intact, even if the administration's tactics had shifted from being multilateral to unilateral in orientation. Despite the change in strategy, this was not an exception in the sense that the US government has long been trying to curtail the growing power of the Chinese tech sector as well as the country as a whole. The Obama administration understood the geopolitical and economic changes—that the global order was no longer unipolar with the United States alone at the top—and tried to maintain its power by managing a multipolar global order. According to the US National Intelligence Council's 2012 report,

> By 2030, no country—whether the US, China, or any other large country—will be a hegemonic power. The empowerment of individuals and diffusion of power among states and from states to informal networks will have a dramatic impact, largely reversing the historic rise of the West since 1750, restoring Asia's weight in the global economy, and ushering in a new era of "democratization" at the international and domestic level.[23]

The US-led geopolitical economic order in place since World War II is being reshuffled. As historian Vijay Prashad points out, the United States can't accept this new reality and continues to push for global supremacy through economic coercion backed by its diplomatic and military power.[24] In fact, the Trump administration's unilateral moves unmasked the changing order, because the technology industry is at the center of global power struggles between major political economic rivals (the United States, China, and Europe) in which transnational capital is trying to cope with a new and rapidly shifting geopolitical landscape.

Having a cozy relationship with the US government during the Obama administration, the US Internet sector was able to coordinate with it to maneuver the changing global political landscape. However, the Trump administration's blatant assertion of unilateral power in the global arena, in particular with regard to China, put US tech companies at risk. Testifying before the House Energy and Commerce Subcommittee on Communications and Technology, Samm Sacks, a senior fellow at the Center for Strategic and International Studies, stated, "In confronting China, we must have a clear understanding about the consequences of our actions and where there will be costs to ourselves. . . . The challenge is that the US's and Chinese technology developments, supply chains, commercial markets are tightly intertwined."[25]

In 2018, with the escalating trade war, the US government placed the Chinese tech giant Huawei, the world's biggest telecom provider and second-largest smartphone company, on its blacklist, banning the company from working with US companies and purchasing US-made chips and software. The intent behind this move was to curtail China's technological advances; by dislodging Chinese tech companies, however, it also damaged US tech suppliers by cutting access to the burgeoning Chinese market. Google's cutting off of Huawei cost the company as much as $425 million in annual revenue.[26]

As of now, the US tech sector is still ahead of China's in the areas of Internet services and software where Google, Microsoft, Facebook, Amazon, and Apple operate, and also has the upper hand in the global market in critical technology value chains in semiconductors;[27] however, China is rapidly gaining ground. Huawei is struggling to survive, having lost market share outside China to its Western rivals Ericsson and Nokia after the imposition of US trade sanctions, but the company is still the biggest provider of 5G networking equipment in the world and also is working on next-generation 6G networks. Chinese Internet giants Baidu, Alibaba, and Tencent are competing against the US tech sector in the areas of AI, cloud, autonomous cars, mobile payments, and e-commerce. The current contention between the United States and China has accelerated China's efforts to wean itself from US technology and move up the value chain. China has unveiled an industrial policy, Made in China 2025, with which it aims to manufacture 70 percent of its semiconductors domestically by 2025. In 2020 China announced its fourteenth five-year plan, in which self-reliance in technology was front and center in its economic development.[28]

The US government and tech sectors are extremely uneasy with China's pursuit of tech power that could outpace that of the United States and break its dependence on key US technologies, and they are trying to contain China's technical advances by attacking it for IP theft as well as on the ground of being a national security threat. While the Biden administration touted the differences between its approaches and those of the Trump administration, its China strategy has been consistent with those of its predecessors. As an offensive move, the Biden administration is pushing expansive industrial policy legislation. The US Senate passed a $250 billion spending bill called the US Innovation and Competition Act of 2021.[29] In February 2022, the House approved its own version, originally called the America Competes Act of 2022, with a $350 billion spending plan.[30] Both bills were designed to strengthen America's competitive edge against China by funding US tech sectors and national research and development.

While these two nations are engaged in a tug of war, the European Union is renewing its on-again, off-again efforts to insert its—mostly regulatory—power, both to influence the development and use of digital technologies and, perhaps, to curb US and Chinese dominance in the information sector. According to *Politico*, a leaked document suggested that Europe would take more hardline trade measures against the United States and China and also fund the European tech sector to create European-based digital champions.[31] The document mentioned Google, Facebook, Apple, Amazon, Microsoft, Baidu, Alibaba, and Tencent as firms against which Europe needed to compete. There is no European version of tech giants, so European lawmakers have been using aggressive regulatory devices ranging from privacy and competition law to trade in order to stave off the US and Chinese tech giants' encroachment on EU's nascent tech sector.

The European Union has long been in a battle with Google because that firm has greatly profited from the European market. Since 2017, the European Union's European Commission (EC) has imposed a total of $9.5 billion in fines in its several antitrust cases against Google search. In 2021 the EC launched another investigation of Google over its role in the advertising tech sector. Google thus constitutes one of the flash points of an intensifying global geopolitical struggle over the burgeoning Internet market. This is the political economic and geopolitical context in which search is located.

Political Economy of Search

Behind the seemingly clean and simple interface of the search box is an immense and swiftly changing global political economy of information and communication. To clarify the political economy of search, one must explicate how Google and its competitors operate within this milieu: how they are organized and structured, and under what principles they operate and expand across territories.

This raises several critical questions: How did the search engine, which interacts with and intersects a basic human activity, evolve into a ubiquitous commercial service and a key component of today's dynamic global information business, which is restructuring both the wider information industry and our very social lives? How, for what purposes, and by whom is search technology being designed and used? Who is actually laboring behind this enormously profitable information industry—is it only engineers and computer programmers, or is the "reserve army of labor" needed for search to become larger and more heterogeneous? Given that the search industry operates transnationally, what is the role of geopolitics in shaping this most dynamic sector? By engaging with these questions, this book provides a systematic critical analysis of the political economy of search, within the greater context of the dynamic relation between information and capitalism's overall developmental processes.

To that end, the book draws from the critical tradition of the political economy of communication (PEC) to shed light on the links between information and communication technologies (ICTs) and capitalism today and to uncover important ongoing structural changes within a rapidly evolving system of information provision. The political economy of communication is rooted in radical critiques of the nature of capitalism, which reproduces domination, exploitation, injustice, and inequality.[32] It looks at ICTs as integral parts of the economy and at the relation between ICTs and broader structural changes and evolving global capitalism. In particular, Vincent Mosco's and Andrew Herman's foundational work on critical theory is instructive because they lay out a critical political economic research agenda as an alternative to mainstream theoretical social research.[33] They offer four critical themes in which this book is grounded: a world system theory that addresses the unequal social and economic structures of capitalism as a global system, the role of states in capitalist development, technology and labor processes, and an alienated culture that reproduces capitalist social relations. The political economy of communication has returned to these recurrently, in different guises, and scholars in the field have also enlarged on these themes to foreground the conceptual importance of commodification, commercialization, and the diversification and concentration of the communication and information industry.[34]

In recent years a rich body of scholarly work concerning contemporary capitalism and its relationship with the Internet industry has been published. The political economy's eager embrace of digital technologies is described by many scholars who use terms such as "surveillance capitalism," "cognitive capitalism," "informational capitalism," and "platform capitalism."[35] One of the commonalities between these concepts is the idea that today's capitalism is of a new kind that has broken from industrial capitalism with radical technological changes. This book, however, is located within Dan Schiller's concept of digital capitalism, which emphasizes the continuity from the early history of agricultural and industrial capitalism, because digital capitalism is firmly situated within the compulsions, imperatives, and crisis tendencies of this type of political economy.[36] Schiller echoes historian Ellen Wood, who rejects the conceptualization of today's capitalism as a new kind by emphasizing that capitalism is dynamic by definition and constantly changes with new technologies, business strategies, cyclical crises, and so on. Wood writes that capitalism is "a system in which all major economic actors are dependent on the market for their basic requirements of life . . . only in capitalism is market dependence the fundamental condition of life for everyone."[37] This definition still applies to today's capitalism. The integration of new digital technologies doesn't represent an epochal shift in capitalism; rather, as Wood argues, it attests that capitalism continues and extends the market imperative and affects the "types of work that [were] little touched or untouched before."[38]

The current massive absorption of ICTs across economic sectors should be understood within a context in which capitalism is prone to crises as a result of its imperative of continuing accumulation, which drives periodic overproduction—a condition that occurs when surplus capital reaches market absorption capacity, resulting in a falling rate of profit.[39] Since the 1970s, global capitalism has experienced continuous full-scale crises and what Robert Brenner describes as a long downturn driven by capitalist competition characterized by "persistent stagnation" in the advanced capitalist economies.[40] In order to survive and overcome the crises that result, David Harvey argues, capital has an imperative to develop new markets—what he calls a "spatio-temporal fix," which refers to a temporary fix for capitalist crises. Harvey explains that geographical expansion and spatial restructuring are options for absorbing surplus.[41]

Drawing on Harvey's work, Schiller posits that in response to the economic downturn, the US political economy further pivoted to ICTs as a spatio-temporal fix in order to restructure the economy by creating networked information systems to expand business processes as well as to renew profitable growth.[42]

Within this theoretical framework, this book demonstrates that the Internet is a new site of growth and spatio-temporal fix in which tech companies are driving capitalist restructuring to renew growth through the most dynamic economic sector: the web.

The rise of the Internet giants and their growing power has drawn political economists to the theory of monopoly capital. Robert McChesney and John Bellamy-Foster of the Monthly Review School illustrate how capitalism has shaped the Internet, revealing the long-term dynamics of monopoly capital.[43] The concept of monopoly capital, first articulated in the tradition of Paul Baran and Paul Sweezy in 1966, foregrounds the theory of accumulation and the rise of a few dominant corporate giants in each industrial sector during the twentieth century.[44] These large and concentrated units of capital are typically able to exert control over prices, productive resources, labor processes, and politics. According to one important variant of this theory, as they had done before with steel, rubber, electrical products, and auto manufacturing, giant companies also quickly acquired primacy over the Internet sector, suppressing competition and following the general trend of modern capitalism. The concept of monopoly capital is important for understanding the roles of the tech giants in shaping the Internet.

Yet the theory of monopoly capital often mutes the role of competition, despite the persistence of competition between the major Internet companies with respect to new markets and at the edges of each big company's existing market turf. The search industry constitutes a revealing concentration of capital, but monopoly isn't devoid of competition because the industry operates across sectors and internationally. Challenging the monopoly school, Anwar Shaikh, Howard Botwinick, and others emphasize the intensification of competition in contemporary capitalism.[45] Rhys Jenkins posits that competition is not simply about the number of firms and their market power but relates to the ability to sustain growth and reproduce surplus value.[46] This doesn't mean that scholars like Shaikh and Botwinick, who challenge the theory of monopoly capital, undermine or discount capital's tendency to control and concentrate; rather, monopoly needs to be located within the context of competition. The two are often seen an oppositional; however, market concentration needs to be understood as a form of competition.[47]

Tech companies' attempts to control the Internet and their competitive pressure are expressed in their division of labor and labor control. The current rapid digitization of the global economy, combined with a new wave of automation enabled by network technologies, has renewed debates among scholars and policy makers about technology's impact on labor and the future of work.[48] The search engine industry as a highly automated sector reflects this changing labor process. While there are few studies specifically concerning labor in the search industry per se, there has been a plethora of studies looking to understand seemingly new forms of work that are enabled by and performed over network computer technologies and, in particular, those under the concept of digital labor—a concept that has, thankfully, reignited interest in labor writ large.[49] Particular attention has been paid to workers for tech companies such as Uber, TaskRabbit, Door Dash, and Upwork, whose business models rely on online platforms to supply and organize labor markets. Their precarious, exploitative, and alienating work practices are encapsulated by broad terms such as *gig economy*, *demand economy*, and *sharing economy*. These works provide valuable local insights into issues affecting the Internet industry.

This book, however, breaks from the concept of digital labor by arguing that, in order to understand the place of labor in the Internet industry, a different conceptual starting point is necessary. Instead of artificially abstracting a supposedly separate digital realm demarcated by the experience of working online, the book situates search industry labor within the wage and occupational structure of the overall political economy. This is because ICTs and telecom networks are embedded in virtually every industrial sector and occupation; the implementation of ICTs is not limited to the Internet sector.[50] For instance, in 2018 Walmart was the largest IT spender behind Amazon and Google, at $11.7 billion, followed by JPMorgan Chase at $11 billion.[51] As Ursula Huws, Dan Schiller, and a few other scholars have emphasized, those who labor with computers need to be analyzed by way of comparison and contrast with each other and with other employees.[52]

This view challenges autonomist Marxist scholars such as Maurizio Lazzarato, Michael Hardt, and Antonio Negri, who deploy a concept of immaterial labor, considered one of the characteristics of a post-industrial society and distinguished from "physical" labor that produces material goods.[53] Tiziana Terranova's influential work associates immaterial labor with free labor on the web as a distinctive form of labor in the digital economy that builds websites, produces content, offers feedback, and is appropriated for creating value for capital.[54]

This book argues that if one only focuses on the concept of digital labor, one undermines the complexity and multifaceted range of the actual division of labor that attends the deployment of network technologies—notably in the search industry—and neglects the other kinds of labor that are concurrently involved in constructing it.

In order to move the conversation beyond local conditions of labor in the Internet industry and engage labor under capitalism in general, Harry Braverman's work—which renewed attention to capitalist labor processes—remains relevant, for it discusses the essential characteristics of labor control and the effect of technology on the nature of work in capitalism. As Mosco and Herman explicate, Braverman's seminal work *Labor and Monopoly Capital* challenged post-industrial theorists and refuted the common claim that modern work, owing to the deployment of new science-based technologies and automation, would result in more "white-collar" jobs requiring higher levels of education and training that would involve more intense intellectual work by employees while diminishing low-skilled production jobs.[55] By analyzing occupational structures from the nineteenth century to the twentieth century in the United States, Braverman identified a general trend of growth in the number of low-wage workers in service and retail sectors as new occupations while employment in industrial sectors with above-average wages had actually decreased.[56] With the introduction of advanced technologies and scientific management under capitalism, Braverman argued, even initially highly skilled work such as clerical work had become mechanized, rationalized, and routinized. There was a strong tendency toward mechanization and use of Tayloristic scientific management to bring about a systematic *deskilling* and *degrading* of many working-class—as well as white-collar—jobs by breaking down work into smaller mechanized tasks with the implementation of technologies. Critics such as Michael Burawoy and P. K. Edwards argue that Braverman undermined the class struggle and workers' resistance; however, in reality, his work provides a mechanism for labor to resist control and rationalization.[57]

Historians Lizabeth Cohen, Sanford Jacoby, Stuart Brandes, and others have revealed that within this despotic form of labor control, corporate-sponsored welfare programs such as pensions, healthcare, education, and housing—so-called welfare capitalism—was also deployed by large industrial enterprises such as Ford Motor Company, National Cash Register, and IBM as a management strategy to counter the rise of labor unions in the twentieth century, and they show how it managed to survive over time.[58] There is a striking similarity between these and the contemporary Internet giants, in which corporate welfare programs have been renewed for select skilled workers; the firms provide extensive perks and benefits such as family care, free food, a full year of paid maternity and paternity leave, and paid vacations. While this can be viewed as a new kind of relation between labor and capital, by contextualizing labor control and management within the longer historical trajectory of capitalism, this book shows that industrial labor control techniques are clearly manifested in the contemporary Internet industry.

The search engine industry is expanding outward. Its expansion across national boundaries hinges not only on technical capacity and business strategies but also on geopolitics. In the 1980s, Herbert Schiller illuminated how information technologies had become central in the global political economy, noting that "the information industrial power has become a vital determinant of existing and future power relations within and between nations."[59] Anthony Smith reaffirms the idea that information cannot be separated from other political economic conflicts.[60] While witnessing the movement for a new international information order, Smith warned that new electronics could be a greater threat to the national sovereignty of developing countries than colonialism itself. Geopolitics and global political economy have radically changed since Smith was writing more than forty years ago. Yet geopolitical struggles over global network infrastructure have only been heightened with the new geopolitics coupled with the emergence of the Internet as a site of capitalist development.

In particular, China's reentry into the global capitalist system and the rise of its Internet industry have drawn the attention of many academics, policy makers, and businesses. The mainstream argument is that the People's Republic of China (PRC), an authoritarian regime, is an emerging imperial power striving against Western democracy.[61] Yet scholars of critical political economy such as Yuezhi Zhao, Yu Hong, Min Tang, and Hong Shen argue that this approach pays scant attention to the fact that a multifaceted Chinese Internet is a vector of China's transnationalization and structural integration into US-led digital capitalism.[62] They clarify that this new geopolitical dynamism is reorganizing digital capitalism today.

The common analysis situates ICTs as tools for territorial and political expansion within traditional interstate rivalries in the framework of classical imperialism.[63] This book, however, challenges the idea that territorial expansion is the main axis of geopolitical conflict; rather, it deploys Wood's concept of capitalist imperialism, which brings nation-states under the capitalist economy and is governed by economic imperatives rather than territorial logics.[64] Capitalist imperialism consists of a system of hierarchies and complexities surrounding multiple capitalist states; each state within the system has had to interact with the United States, the current capitalist imperial power, and its allies while also having to respond to its own domestic pressures, and its own capitalist logics, and also having to create and exist within conditions of a global capitalist system.[65] Within this analytical framework, this book looks at the current contention over the Internet, particularly among the major economic power blocs of the United States, China, and the European Union. It scrutinizes the relations and the dynamics between global capital and nation-states within an increasingly transnationalizing capitalist system.

The extraterritorial nature of the Internet is intertwined with the global political economy and has turned into a vital site for profit making and an axis of expansion for capital. Thus, as control over the Internet is crucial for gaining political economic power, the Internet has become a place of battle among states, different units of capital, and various social actors. The world is undergoing a radical transformation of information technologies and international information provision—one that is still taking shape as the Internet has begun to more fully unleash its explosive potential for capital. Facing an economic crisis compounded by the coronavirus pandemic, the global power centers are waging a new political fight over the Internet while the United States is trying to ensure its continuing leadership of the global capitalist system. Search is at the fulcrum of this conflict. With this as background, this book's argument proceeds as follows.

Chapter Outline

This book relies on a new and far-reaching conception of the political economy of the Internet in general and of search in particular. The human activity of information seeking originated eons before our era of capitalist development, and it is not intrinsically commercial. Chapter 1 takes the reader through the history of search engine development and shows that search engine technology itself did not inherently have economic value. Initially, search technology was developed in noncommercial academic spaces, and users and some early search engine firms vehemently opposed the idea of advertising-based search engines, believing that search results should not be influenced by commerce. How, then, has the shift to an ad-based business model occurred? What factors and conditions have driven search engine technologies that were outside the money economy into the marketplace?

To answer these questions, the chapter examines the process of commodification of search and the role of government in creating conditions for capital. It discusses how early search engine firms—in the 1990s, when the Internet was being rapidly commercialized—evolved and experimented with various business models from subscription to licensing to advertising, and under what conditions they finally alighted on the ad-based model and configured the advertising system and its infrastructure beneath the search engine.

Today, the crucial function of search on an Internet served by and for the marketplace seems naturalized and accepted with no alternatives and nary a blink of an eye. By looking at its history, however, the chapter shows that this has been a long march for capital, hand in hand with the US government's policy efforts, to transform information activities into a marketplace.

Chapter 2 situates search within a broader political economy of the Internet. It illustrates how the search engine market is dominated by Google but also how it is under extreme competitive pressures. Within the dynamics governing a monopolistic tendency and competition, the search engine industry is moving beyond simply competing with the major tech companies like Facebook, Apple, Amazon, and Microsoft to also ally and work with those companies across economic sectors. This has driven a new wave of capital accumulation by restructuring the political economy. To maintain their existing profit centers and cultivate new profit opportunities and geographical expansion, the Internet companies are also configuring and reconfiguring global network infrastructures. Google is known for its search engine, which facilitates the effortless user experience that the company claims is rooted in its intricate algorithm; however, underneath Google's myriad services is a colossal physical base that consists of massive numbers of customized servers, mega data centers, fiber optic and submarine cable systems, and terrestrial networks connecting spatially dispersed markets. This chapter reveals how the Internet giants are constructing the global network infrastructure, which is a key site of control and competition.

Driven by competition, control, and expansionary pressure, the search engine industry not only occupies network infrastructure but also impels efforts to establish distinctive labor processes that maximize profitability. Chapter 3 uncovers a wide array of labor organization behind the search engine, all of which underlies and enables the generation of profit, and offers a glimpse of the realities of labor processes within today's capitalism.

This chapter explicates the organization of labor under capitalism and challenges the pervasive myth of the Internet companies as exclusively or generally reliant on young, highly paid and educated workers. Rather, it identifies four interlocking categories of work that support the search engine industry: a reserve army of labor that consists of the unemployed and underemployed and is generated by capitalism's constant restructuring process; a cadre of highly skilled full-time workers; and below that, propping it all up, legions of contract and process workers as well as unpaid consumer and volunteer labor that supports capital accumulation projects. The chapter proceeds in light of historical scholarship and holds that unwaged labor is deeply rooted in capitalism and has been a vital part of capitalist development. By tracing the current labor structures in the search engine industry within historical context, the chapter shows that today's hierarchical and fragmented organization of labor challenges the building of solidarity among workers.

While Chapter 3 examines the division of labor underlying search, Chapter 4 extends the analysis of the labor process to an examination of the methods of labor management and control employed by Google, which sets the trends for the wider industry. Google is known for maintaining a productive workforce through the provision of its unusual working environment, where its highly paid workers are given unprecedented freedom and have a voice in the company, and employee benefits are applied by means of a data-driven labor management strategy. The company is often portrayed in media as genuinely exceptional and is setting new trends in labor management techniques based on data. On the surface, Google seems to defy traditional exploitative capital-labor relations and goes against their capital logic; however, the chapter demonstrates that Google's current labor control techniques and its labor management strategies stem from an earlier era of industrial economy. Here again, the book contributes a historically grounded conception of today's Internet economy.

In particular, this chapter compares Google's labor control processes to those of an earlier industrial era. It looks at such major firms as Ford Motor Company, National Cash Register, Western Union, and AT&T, which were the pioneers of new kinds of labor control including company programs that gave workers a variety of benefits such as pensions and stock shares along with the bureaucratic management of these programs. As part of corporate management strategy, welfare programs were a way to increase productivity, curtail the tensions between labor and capital, and stem the tide of labor unions. This was strikingly different from Taylorist techniques, in which workers were treated as parts of the factory's machinery. Labor historians refer to the more "humane" labor management that emerged in the late nineteenth century as welfare capitalism, or industrial paternalism. By contextualizing Google's current labor control and management practices within the historical continuum of capitalist development, Chapter 4 posits that welfare capitalism and scientific management—the marks of an industrial economy—are reemerging in the era of the information economy.

Finally, Chapter 5 explicates the transnational nature of Internet industries and the role of geopolitics in organizing the search engine industry and in animating the dynamics of transnational capitalism. Specifically, this chapter examines the People's Republic of China and the European Union, where the US-based Internet giants are facing the most serious opposition. China constitutes an especially significant exception to Google's market dominance, not only because it is the world's largest Internet market by number of subscribers and the world's most significant economic growth zone, but also because its reentry into the US-led global capitalist system is changing the geopolitical landscape. Meanwhile, Europe, a longtime US ally, has been attempting to bolster its own information economy, and tension over the control of information has once again been reignited with the emergence of the Internet. Motived by the deep-seated fear over US information dominance in Europe and the ascendance of the Chinese Internet industry, Europe is reasserting its political economic power over the Internet by setting rules and regulations and fostering the European digital economy. By analyzing these two different conflict zones, this chapter illuminates the role of geopolitics in the dynamics of today's transnational capitalism with respect to the Internet industry.

Chapter 1

SEARCHING FOR PROFITS

Today, a noncommercial Internet search service is hard to imagine, given that the search function is one of the most dominant forces in restructuring and driving the political economy of the Internet and shaping the capitalist global marketplace. The origin of search was rooted, however, in the public institutions where many search technologies were experimented with and developed. The Internet was originally funded with federal research grant money and only later turned over to the private sector, yet the wider public little realizes this history.[1] Moreover, the public initially contested the idea of advertising-supported search engines and argued that search results should not be influenced by commercial interests.[2] So, what happened? Why did search not stay within the sphere of public information provision? Under what conditions did our daily information-seeking activities and search technologies move to the market, transformed into an extremely lucrative business, and how was capital able to bring advertising into the equation?

To answer these questions, this chapter draws on the concept of commodification, which is an entry point to understanding the political economy of search. Vincent Mosco defines *commodification* as "the process of transforming use values into exchange values, of transforming products whose value is determined by their ability to meet individual and social needs into products whose value is set by what they can bring in the marketplace."[3] Immanuel Wallerstein remarks that no social and economic activities are intrinsically excluded from commodification, which is the driving force of capitalist expansion.[4] Nonetheless, the extent and the degree of commodification hinge on the role of government, public service provision, and other factors.[5] Commodification is often perceived as a naturally technical progression and promoted as an efficient way for goods and services to be produced, bought, and sold. But as Christoph Hermann notes, commodification is not "a state of affairs" but, rather, something that requires a long process. This process was accelerated with the ascendance of neoliberalism in the 1970s, involving privatization, deregulation, outsourcing of public institutions and resources, and marketization.[6] Information and communication have been among the key sectors where this process has been boosted.[7]

Thus, to explicate the emergence of search as an industry, this chapter begins with the history of the search engine, illuminating the role of public funding in the development of search technology. Second, the chapter highlights the political economic context within which the US government eliminated the possibility of a publicly funded search engine by chronically defunding public information provision and promoting "public-private" research partnerships that facilitated the shift away from publicly funded research on search technologies to the private sector. It shows that the commodification of search was undergirded by the initial reduction and limitation of availability of alternatives, and the political power relations that enabled the process.[8] This process is rooted in the enclosure of public resources by taking them away from people with little to generate more wealth for the rich. David Harvey explains this as "accumulation by dispossession."[9] The chapter shows how the history of search has been presented as if there is no choice for the public other than depending on market solutions for information-seeking activities, all the while opening up the conditions for capital accumulation and for capital to move search technology to the market.

Third, the chapter delineates the organizing principle of search, revealing capital's domination of the process and its persistent attempts to remove technical and political obstacles by investing immense sums of venture capital to mobilize the commercialization of search during the dot-com boom and afterward. In pursuit of profit and new growth sectors, various new technologies and business models were experimented with and introduced. Initially, there was no particular prescribed business model for search, but the process of organizing the search marketplace was far from arbitrary. The creation of search as a marketplace also required technical and business innovations; however, those innovations weren't primarily about designing a superior search technology for retrieving the most relevant information for social needs. Rather, they were about building a technology wrapped in a marketplace concept built for speed to generate profit.

This chapter illustrates that the rise of Google wasn't merely about developing superior search engine technologies. The search engine industry—and Google as the dominant search company—emerged by adopting a century-old advertising practice within a particular political economy during the dot-com boom and bust. This is what Matthew Crain calls the "marketing complex," in which players from various economic sectors pursue mutual interests in search of profit making over the Internet as an ongoing process rather than breaking from the past.[10]

Today, the search engine, commonly described as a "platform," is what the economists Jean-Charles Rochet and Jean Tirole would describe as a two- or multi-sided market bringing together disparate groups and creating value.[11] As Elizabeth Van Couvering rightly points out, while the term *platform* is associated with the digital environment, the multi-sided business model, or multi-sided platform (MSP), is not new; rather, it existed in the predigital era in credit cards, radio, and newspaper publishing.[12] With the implementation of network technology, however, MSPs have emerged as a more prominent business model because they are more able to scale up the market, manage complexity, and extract value.[13] While surveillance, privacy, algorithm use, and the culture of transparency have been the central issues of search, this chapter focuses on the long process of the deliberate commercialization and construction of search within a marketplace, bringing together advertisers, content publishers, and users and underwritten by the state. By looking at the transformation of basic human information-seeking activity into a commodity, the chapter shows how capitalism sustains and renews its accumulation through appropriation of previously nonmarket areas of our social lives.

A Brief History

Although search engine technology on the web emerged in the 1990s, the history of computer-based information retrieval systems (IR) goes back to the 1940s. During World War II, the US government invested massive amounts of capital in scientific research, and it mobilized scientists, the military, and private industries as part of the war effort. This resulted in the generation of a large quantity of scientific and technical documents and academic literature that spurred the advancement of methods of IR.[14] By the 1950s, the basic principles of IR had been established, and during the 1960s and 1970s, scientists and librarians did considerable work on IR development funded by US government agencies and the US military. While current technical configurations of the search engine are quite different from earlier ones, their technical foundation owes much to US government subsidies through the academic-military-industrial complex that gave birth to the Internet.

It is no secret that most early pre-web search engines were created in academic institutions within noncommercial environments.[15] Archie (short for "archives"), developed at McGill University in 1990, indexed files from various FTP servers and is considered the Internet's first search engine. Following Archie, Gopher was developed at the University of Minnesota in 1991. It was both a protocol and an application to transport hierarchically organized text files. Gopher was widely used in universities and libraries, and it led to search software Veronica and Jughead. Veronica came about in 1992 at the University of Nevada, Reno, to index information on gopher servers; Jughead, from the University of Utah in 1993, an alternative to Archie, also searched for files on gopher servers (see table 1.1).

Table 1.1. Search engines/directories developed within academic institutions, 1990–1998

Year	Search Engines/Directories
1990 (Pre-WWW)	Archie, McGill University Gopher, University of Minnesota Open Text, University of Waterloo Veronica, University of Nevada, Reno Jughead, University of Utah
1993	World Wide Web Wanderer, MIT W3Catalog, University of Geneva, Switzerland JumpStation, University of Stirling, Scotland World Wide Web Worm, University of Colorado
1994	Webcrawler, University of Washington Lycos, Carnegie Mellon University MetaCrawler, University of Washington Yahoo!, Stanford University
1995	S.A.P.O., University of Aveiro, Portugal
1996	Inktomi, University of California, Berkeley
1998	Google, Stanford University

Sources: Data extracted from Elizabeth Van Couvering, "Search Engine Bias: The Structuration of Traffic on the World-Wide Web" (PhD diss., London School of Economics, 2010), 96–97; Wikipedia, "Search Engine," last modified February 20, 2022, https://en.wikipedia.org/wiki/Search_engine.

The first web search engine—WWW Wanderer, developed by Matthew Gray at MIT in 1993—was also the first web crawler, designed to measure the growth of the web. One of the first full-text crawler search engines was Webcrawler (1994), created by Brian Pinkerton at the University of Washington, which allowed users to search for words on web pages. Webcrawler was acquired by America Online in 1995 and later sold to Excite. Not all but the majority of the early search engines evolved in academic research institutions, most often with public funding, for example, Lycos from Carnegie Mellon University, Inktomi from the University of California, Berkeley, and Excite, Yahoo!, and Google from Stanford University.[16]

It is widely known that Google's algorithm, called PageRank, has its roots in academia as part of the Stanford Digital Library Project (SDLP), one of the first six awards of the multi-agency Digital Library Initiative, financed by the National Science Foundation (NSF).[17] Google founders Larry Page and Sergey Brin, supported by an NSF Graduate Research Fellowship, developed the initial PageRank algorithm as part of their work on the SDLP project. At that time, the primary goal of the SDLP project was "to develop the enabling technologies for a single, integrated and 'universal' library, prov[id]ing uniform access to the large number of emerging networked information sources and collections."[18] Not coincidentally, this is quite similar to Google's mission: "to organize the world's information and make it universally accessible and useful."

In 1990 there was only one website, but by January 1997, a year before Google released PageRank, the web had grown to 1,117,259 pages, a 334 percent jump.[19] With such rapid growth, search engine technology became an ever more important utility for accessing information on the Internet. Given this necessity and the growing scale, no longer could a few individuals build and manage a search engine; the task soon required a large information infrastructure and capital investment.

Considering that the most significant web-based search technologies were developed mainly in noncommercial academic settings, the function of the search engine as a gateway to information seemed to fall within the domain of public information provision. Libraries, for instance, as existing public information infrastructure, early adopters of computers, and armed with Google's PageRank, could have ensured that the search engine would remain in the public realm and be built and maintained with public funding, creating a public search utility. Why, then, were there few attempts to organize search engines in this way? The answers to this question are multifaceted because political, social, and technical factors are dynamically interlocked in the commodification and commercialization of search technologies. The defining role of the capitalist state, however, was vital in commodification of public resources as the government directly and indirectly subsidized corporate ventures and actively created the conditions for capital accumulation.

The Role of the Capitalist State

The capitalist crisis of the 1970s was brought on by the decline of the postwar reconstruction boom, the ballooning costs of the Vietnam war—which cost $168 billion, or $1 trillion in today's dollars—and the Middle East oil shock, all of which combined to create a pivotal historical moment that shaped today's deeply market-oriented information provision landscape. In response to the global capitalist accumulation crisis, the capitalist class launched what David Harvey described as neoliberalism, a capitalist political project that expanded and accelerated privatization and deregulation to attack labor power as well as public and social sectors that traditionally sit outside or at the periphery of the market. Concomitantly, to seek new sites of capital accumulation, the US political economy further moved toward information and communication technologies as it was being restructured by creating networked information systems to expand business processes as well as to reboot capitalist economic growth. In recent decades, trillions of dollars' worth of information and communication technologies (ICTs) have been invested across all economic sectors for strategic profit, which is the basis of the current political economy—which Dan Schiller describes as digital capitalism.[20] Within this political economic context, public information institutions such as libraries, museums, and archives were and continue to be reorganized and further opened for markets through digitization driven by capital.

Since the late 1970s, public and academic libraries have faced continuously shrinking budgets, which have resulted in less funding for materials, staffs, library services, and service hours. This starvation of public information-providing institutions coincided with the growing demand for information access as well as the expansion of the commercial information technology sector. Libraries, facing a choice between constrained budgets and rapidly growing information needs, embraced more commercial information services, and they have increasingly outsourced information access in response to public demand.[21] In tandem with this, in the 1980s the Reagan administration strongly promoted information policy that would commodify, commercialize, and privatize government information produced at taxpayer expense; thus, libraries had to increasingly rely on licensing commercially produced information products—which put a further squeeze on already shrinking library budgets—to provide access to the public.[22]

The state's direct and indirect intervention at various levels was needed to pry open undertapped public information institutions by capriciously strangling the information and cultural sector through budgetary constraints. By the 1990s, resource-starved public cultural institutions had little capacity and lacked the collective will to build their own free means of public cultural and information provision. Libraries, for instance, began to relinquish their role as custodians of public information and further embraced corporate-driven digitization and outsourcing of their traditional descriptive and collection functions. As libraries increasingly provide digital content in lieu of traditional analogue content, they rely more and more on commercial information providers, and that information is held under license rather than copyright. This effectively bypassed a long-standing legal structure that has a specific fair-use carve-out for libraries which allows them to collect, preserve, and give public access to books, journals, and other materials. When search engine technologies emerged, libraries were the major consumers of commercial information services. However, the library was not the only player in the information provision space. As described above, academic institutions were deeply involved in the development of search engine technologies. So, could academic communities have been custodians for search to serve the public interest?

By the 1990s, universities already were systematically accelerating commercialization of their scientific research output. In the 1970s, in response to the economic slowdown and facing new international competition from Japan and western Europe, the US government pivoted its science research policy and opened the sector to privatization by commercializing publicly funded scientific research and promoting partnerships between universities and industry. During the presidencies of Carter, Reagan, Bush Sr., and Clinton, Congress passed bipartisan legislation—such as the Bayh-Dole Act of 1980, the Stevenson-Wydler Technology Innovation Act of 1980, the Federal Technology Transfer Act of 1986, and the Goals 2000: Educate America Act of 1994—to promote commercialization of scientific research by facilitating commercial spin-offs of federally funded research. The Bayh-Dole Act of 1980, for instance, allowed universities to retain their intellectual property through patents on publicly funded research outcomes so that they could license their intellectual property to corporations and generate revenue. The majority of major universities quickly established offices of technology licensing to speed up the commercialization process and expand their market activities. In the early 1980s, a large number of universities set up technological "incubators" on campus to attract venture capital and spin off private companies, which were often led by their faculty.[23] By the year 2000 the number of patents granted to university researchers had increased more than tenfold, generating more than $1 billion per year in royalties and licensing fees.[24] Funding-strapped universities continue to actively encourage the creation of startup firms by their researchers and students in order to finance themselves. As Clark Kerr has pointed out, "The university and segments of industry are becoming more alike."[25]

When the Internet was handed over to the private sector by the NSF and other federal granting authorities, academic institutions, in collaboration with the tech industry, were leading forces in this commercialization as they became deeply embedded in the first dot-com boom. Many Internet technologies were researched and developed in universities. This became the so-called Silicon Valley Model, adopted in cities around the world, which connected academic institutions, the technology industry, venture capital, and regional labor markets and drove the generation of tech startups.[26] Within this context, social and political forces lacked the coherence to shape new technologies for social good, and there were barriers to ensuring that new technologies would remain in the public domain, while the capitalist state created and fostered the conditions for capital accumulation. Without strong public information provision as an alternative, the vision of the "new economy" was buttressed by the state and technical elites promoting the Internet sector as a "new" kind of capitalism that was supposed to spur a more egalitarian and democratic society. This political economic context opened search to capital as it naturalized the processes of commodification and commercialization. But this didn't mean that there was a clear, preordained business model for search. While the state created the conditions for a marketplace for search, it took a decade for corporate capital to transform search into a business.

Searching for Profits

With the privatization and commercialization of the Internet, the rise of the search engine industry intersected with the first dot-com bubble of the late 1990s and early 2000s, when large sums of venture capital fueled a host of Internet-based software startups as well as telecommunication and networking equipment companies.[27] The Internet bubble emerged after the recession of the early 1990s, following the stock market crash of 1987, as capital was seeking a new site of accumulation to overcome the economic downturn. In order to assist capital and renew capital accumulation, the US government implemented a series of policies and subsidized Internet infrastructure to commercialize the web and further orient its economy toward the information and communication technology sector to cultivate new market growth. In particular, the passing of the watershed 1996 Telecommunications Act accelerated the commercialization of the Internet by restructuring the U.S. telecommunication market, removing regulatory barriers, and opening up the regulated telecom network.[28]

With this as backdrop, massive amounts of financial capital flowed into Internet startups in search of new high-growth sectors, spurring the dot-com bubble. Brent Goldfarb, Michael Pfarrer, and David Kirsch, in their 2005 study, estimated that from 1998 to 2002, fifty thousand new ventures were formed to invest in the newly commercialized Internet.[29] At the peak of the dot-com bubble, venture capital was investing $25 billion per quarter.[30] Yet despite these significant amounts of investment, Internet firms did not have traditional business models, physical assets, or products; rather, they were dealing in "mind share" or "eyeballs" in order to build brand awareness for nascent services and technologies.[31] A host of venture capital–funded startups intended to leverage the "eyeballs" they had collected to expand their consumer base as rapidly as possible, build brand recognition quickly, and bring in advertisers in order to increase their valuation—the idea was to "get big fast."[32] In 1998 Bob Davis, founder and CEO of Lycos, echoing this business model, said, "Our sole focus is audience size. . . . Any place there are consumers, there are advertisers."[33] In the 1990s, betting on this game of attracting views, a slew of major venture capital firms such as Sequoia Capital, Softbank, Kleiner Perkins Caufield & Buyers, Highland Capital Partners, Institutional Venture Partners, and Draper Fisher Jurvetson invested in search engine startups like Yahoo!, Infoseek, Lycos, Excite, AltaVista, Ask Jeeves, and Google. Draper Fisher Jurvetson invested more than

$30 million in search services.[34] Timothy Draper, a managing partner with the venture capital firm, said, "Search is going to be hot as long as people continue to be frustrated."[35] Draper Fisher Jurvetson was also one of the US investors in the Chinese search engine Baidu, which is discussed in a later chapter.

Though it had no clear business model, to build a brand name Yahoo! spent $5 million for the first national-scale ad campaign on television in the run-up to its IPO in 1996.[36] Along with pouring money into on- and offline advertising, Yahoo! early on deployed expensive and expansive public relations strategies. Yahoo!'s PR agency—paid in Yahoo! stock—published hundreds of articles in business and trade journals as well as mainstream publications.[37] From 1995 to 1998, Excite spent more than $65 million in marketing to build its national brand, which was a significant amount of capital for a newly emerged Internet company at that time.[38] Ironically, search engine firms were sellers of online ads while being among the largest advertising spenders as well.

In search of user traffic, search engine firms also pursued a series of partnerships with established Internet companies. With a one-time $5 million fee, Yahoo! allied with Netscape, the most valuable property on the Net at the time, making Yahoo! one of the featured search engines for Netscape's browser users for a few years.[39] Excite, the number two search engine, struck a strategic deal with Netscape, Microsoft, and America Online (AOL) to expand the distribution channel of their search engine services.

The mix of extensive PR, partnerships with other Internet firms, and the rapidly increasing web user population helped leading search engines such as Yahoo!, Lycos, Infoseek, Excite, and AltaVista to draw millions of users by the late 1990s. And they all followed a textbook dot-com path: Once big enough to have "mindshares," companies pursued one of two lucrative exit strategies: (1) file an IPO to raise more funding and to expose its brand, or (2) sell themselves to a bigger company and merge. During this period a variety of search technologies were explored, but these technical innovations were constrained within the market logic of profitmaking. Despite having no defined business model at that time, the possibilities of search technologies had already been limited, and their success was determined solely by the seeking of profit.

By the mid-1990s several search engines companies began to pursue IPOs. After the Canadian company OpenText, which came out of research projects at the University of Waterloo, made its IPO, Yahoo!, Excite, Lycos, and Infoseek—the top four search engines at that time—held IPOs and together raised $162 million.[40] Still, none of them had a concrete working business model. However, announcing an IPO without a specific revenue source was not uncommon for dot-com startups that relied on a strategy of attracting eyeballs. The major search engine firms had millions of users, even if they hadn't yet figured out ways to monetize those views.

In preparation for its IPO, Yahoo! was mulling over three possible revenue sources: licensing its directory, offering fee-based services, and advertising. Unlike other search engines, Yahoo! couldn't license its search engine software because it started with a human-edited directory with every new site reviewed by a hired professional librarian.[41] Yahoo! was licensing its search technology to OpenText at that time. The company was nervous about driving away users by placing ads on the site and was unsure whether the web could ever drive sufficient advertising revenue; even if it did, there was intense competition with hundreds of dot-com sites that were chasing after the same advertising dollars.[42] It also knew that users would not pay for its services when there were already plenty of free services available online. Tim Brady, the firm's marketing director, argued, "No one pays for picking up the Yellow Pages. . . . I don't think it's going to happen online."[43] In the end, the company nonetheless chose the advertising model because there was demand for online ads from dot-com firms that wanted to build their brands quickly. Along with Yahoo!, such first-generation search engines as Excite and Lycos initially pursued advertising solely or in combination with the licensing of their technology.[44]

At first, search engines served banner ads, the main advertising format at that time. Banner ads were popularized by *HotWired*, the first commercial digital magazine on the web and the online version of *Wired* magazine, which first sold pictorial banners at scale in 1994, on a cost per thousand impressions or cost per mille (CPM) basis.[45] This meant that when an "impression" or "hit" occurred, a banner ad would be displayed. Because there was no specific pricing model for online ads, web publishers used the CPM model, borrowing from models used in traditional print publications and other media. With the CPM pricing model, whether or not users saw the ads or interacted with them made no difference as long as the ads were displayed in front of users' eyeballs. This model offered no data on the actual effect of an advertisement, which was far from the one-to-one interactive marketing that the Internet promised.[46] Thus, the major advertisers and marketers were hesitant to shift significant portions of their marketing budgets to a new platform that did not guarantee a return on investment. They were looking for more accountability and metrics from web publishers, but there were no established standards or criteria for measuring web audiences.[47]

In order to draw advertisers and sell search, these search engine companies needed to provide some sort of audience measurement and user information. This was not because this information had inherent commercial value. Rather, as Joseph Turow pointed out, advertisers pressured Web publishers to provide concrete audience measurements so that they could see if ads were actually working and compare those measurements with the effects of traditional media programs.[48] This market dynamic drove the search companies to come up with more sophisticated tracking mechanisms to exploit user information as time went on.

In 1996 Proctor & Gamble (P&G), one of the world's biggest advertisers, made the first move. Leveraging its market power, P&G demanded more accountability from Yahoo! and pushed a deal with the search engine to pay for advertisements on a cost per click (CPC) basis rather than CPM. This meant that P&G paid only when a searcher actually clicked on an ad. Yahoo!, followed by search engine site LinkStar Communication, also began offering a CPC option. This stirred fear among major publishers, which were reluctant to adopt the CPC model lest they see a decline in revenue.[49] The largest Internet service provider at that time, AOL, knew that the CPC model could reduce its revenue. It spurned the P&G deal and touted its ability to deliver user traffic in the millions.[50] Along with AOL, other web publishers balked at the CPC model.[51] In the end, P&G settled on a hybrid impressions-and-clicks model, which continues to be the dominant model today. Yet tensions between marketers and publishers persisted, with major marketers claiming that they would only invest limited capital in experimentation on the web because there was no reliable standard of measurement to see what worked and what didn't.[52] In 1998 a survey conducted by the Association of National Advertisers revealed that advertisers were reluctant to buy online ads because of the lack of a tracking mechanism for return on investment.[53] From the advertisers' point of view, web advertising based on the CPM model did not offer any palpable advantage over traditional commercial media.

For these reasons, the search engine was once considered almost a failed business idea because it was only a conduit to other pages. Shortly after major search engines had IPOs in 1996, *Fortune* ran an article saying that search companies were losing money and that search was an "illusive business" with little interest from advertisers.[54] In the article, Jeff Bezos, CEO of Amazon, expressed his doubts about online advertising and said that while Amazon advertised on all four search sites, he considered print ads in such major publications as the *Wall Street Journal* to be more effective at delivering business to Amazon.

In response to this skepticism, search engines struggling to generate ad revenue scrambled to try new business strategies. They shifted to being portals to the web and offered various new services to attract and retain more users in an effort to create "stickiness." Yahoo!, Excite, Infoseek, and other major engines provided a variety of other services such as website hosting, news, email, and chat rooms. By the late 1990s, Yahoo!, MSN, AOL, Lycos, Excite, and other web portals were growing rapidly as primary entries to the Internet. Van Couvering observed that they rushed to acquire other companies or were acquired by traditional media and telecom conglomerates such as Disney and AT&T, which were looking to exploit the commercializing Internet.[55] Yet even the portal model did not last long.

In 2000 the dot-com bubble burst and Internet stocks lost $1.755 trillion from their fifty-two-week high.[56] Between 2000 and 2002, $5 trillion in market value was wiped out, which meant that people's pensions, retirement savings, and mutual funds simply disappeared. The political economist and historian Robert Brenner describes this as "stock-market Keynesianism," [57] which was the result of state regulations that encouraged a speculative bubble by permitting retirement, pension, and mutual funds to invest in risky assets as a form of venture capital and offering an extremely low interest rate which helped dot-com startups to easily raise capital to commercialize the Internet.

During the peak in online advertising spending in 2000, dot-com firms were buying 77 percent of advertising on the web.[58] As this spending dried up, the dominant form of advertising—banner ads—collapsed, making it more difficult for search engine firms to generate revenue through advertising. Advertisers were moving away from banner ads and questioning the brand-building capabilities of online advertising in general. This resulted in surplus ads space, shifting the market to the advantage of advertisers.

Selling Search

After the dot-com bubble burst, the *Wall Street Journal*, reporting on a study by Harris Interactive, Inc., and Jupiter Media Metrix, Inc., noted that "the very nature of the web may be incompatible with effective advertising. Users simply have too much ability to ignore or click off what they don't want to see."[59] Advertisers and marketers reduced their budgets for online ads, forcing web publishers to find new sources of revenue. Major search engines realized that banner ads could not generate enough revenue to make them profitable.[60] Thus, they tried to reduce their dependence on online ads and shifted their business model to fee-based services. In fact, Yahoo! was adding new fee-based services in the late 1990s to see if users would be willing to pay for content or services.[61] Given this, how did the current advertising-sponsored model of the search engine become the norm?

Google is the best-known search engine today, but capital's attempts to sell search have a longer history. In 1996 the search engine OpenText first offered "preferred listing" services, selling special placement in search results. The service allowed publishers to pay for higher-ranking search results without requiring them to buy more expensive banner advertising. The company received scathing criticism for adopting paid search, however, and ultimately had to abandon the practice. Within some early search engine companies, there were questions about paid search as a viable business model. In response to OpenText, Bob Davis, CEO of Lycos at the time, said, "With the Yellow Pages, listings are delivered alphabetically. There's no illusion there. . . . To me, this damages the integrity of the search service. This is like librarians putting books on the end [of a bookshelf] if you pay [them] some extra money. We would not do it with Lycos."[62] Abe Kleinfield, a vice president at OpenText, said, "People thought it was immoral."[63] In an interview with Danny Sullivan, editor of *Search Engine Watch*, Brett Bullington, executive vice president of strategic and business development at Excite, expressed it thus: "My feeling is that the consumer wants something more [*sic*] cleaner than commercialism."[64] And Lycos search manager Rajive Mathur said, "I'm not sure it's really providing value to the user in the long term. I think they want some independent sorting."[65]

In the midst of the depressed ad market that resulted from the dot-com crash, GoTo.com (which was founded in 1998, later became Overture, and then was incorporated into Yahoo! Search Marketing in 2002) was attracting advertisers as it resurrected the OpenText business model of selling search results.[66] GoTo.com was having advertisers bid for preferred placement in search results for specific keywords.[67] This was called "paid search," in which advertisers paid for preferred placement in search results. Advertisers and marketers were drawn to the new yet familiar GoTo.com business model because it had several features that enticed them—and that were later adopted and adapted by Google—that set it apart from the other search engines.[68]

First, GoTo.com offered the performance-based CPC pricing model, which was preferred by advertisers and marketers because they would only pay when a visitor actively clicked on their ad and landed on their site. Second, keywords were sold in an automated auction in which marketers bid for placement and the highest bidder was placed at the top of the search results. This guaranteed the targeted placement of advertisers' sites. Third, after the bid, human editors reviewed each submitted link to ensure that the site and keywords were relevant, so the search engine displayed only relevant ads to users.[69] This increased the possibility of searchers' clicking on advertisers' ads. This concept of relevance, discussed later in this chapter, became a core principle of Google's advertising system. Fourth, it deployed a self-service advertising platform with no minimum spend, which removed the barrier between salespeople and ad inventories and bypassed the paper contract, cut overhead costs, and allowed companies to scale up their serving of ads.[70] With this potent combination of CPC pricing, ad relevance, and self-service, GoTo.com attracted both small businesses and large corporations. The search engine began its service with fifteen advertisers, and by the end of 1999 it had thousands.[71]

Unlike Google, with its high volume of traffic, the problem for GoTo.com was on the user side, because the company didn't have enough user traffic to monetize. When GoTo.com entered the search market, there were plenty of better-known search engines, so it was not easy to draw traffic. Thus, GoTo.com had to turn to sites that already had heavy user traffic such as Yahoo!, MSN, AOL, and Netscape, and it decided to syndicate its service. Despite its early success, GoTo.com still faced a dilemma because it had to rely on larger search engines or portals to serve the traffic it needed. This put the firm in a vulnerable position because user traffic is the precondition for search. The company had to pay a hefty traffic acquisition cost by placing ads for GoTo on other high-traffic websites.

GoTo.com and Google entered the search business at a similar time. Unlike GoTo.com, Google had plenty of traffic, but it had no working backend advertising system. In PageRank, Google had a powerful and technically superior ranking algorithm. Yet simply having the algorithm alone wasn't adequate for Google to create a marketplace to generate profit. When Google was looking for revenue sources, the ad-based business model was not its first choice. In fact, Brin and Page were opposed to ad-supported search services because Brin believed that "advertising-funded search engines would be inherently biased toward the advertisers and away from the needs of consumers."[72] At first, the firm considered licensing its PageRank search technology to other search engines. Because a search engine was an expensive and capital-intensive business, most portals—including Netscape, AOL, and even Yahoo!—later outsourced search to Google. But Google still had to compete with incumbents such as AltaVista and Inktomi, both of which concentrated on the development of search technologies rather than moving to a portal model.[73] In particular, AltaVista, with its so-called super spider, was one of the most widely used search engines before Google gained popularity. It was created by Digital Equipment Corp to test one of its supercomputers. AltaVista, at that time known for having high-end processors, was using a centralized index to answer queries from users, which made it difficult to deal with the large and ever-growing amount of web content.[74] Google, meanwhile, chose to adopt a distributed crawling architecture in which the task of URL crawling and indexing was distributed among multiple machines, making it markedly faster and more scalable.[75]

Google quickly gained a large number of users and built a national brand as a search engine, but its business options—licensing of its technology, subscription, and advertising—were limited. At that time, there were not enough enterprises to which to sell search services and generate enough revenue,[76] and Google wasn't able to generate subscription fees as AOL did or ad revenue as Yahoo! and the other portal sites did, given that Google didn't have content on which to display banner ads.[77] Before Google figured out a way to monetize its traffic, the dot-com bubble burst, and advertisers began to withdraw from online ads, questioning the effectiveness of the new medium.

Nick Srnicek has noted that the bursting of the dot-com bubble pressured startups to lean toward the advertising model.[78] Google was running out of cash, and with few options for generating revenue, the company decided to explore the ad model because it depended on the financial markets, which demanded return on investment.

Google remained hesitant to run banner ads, however. Brin said, "We are about money and profit. . . . Banners are not working and click-throughs are failing. I think highly focused ads are the answer."[79] This illustrates that Google's initial position regarding search ads had shifted, and its hesitancy to run ads was no longer about serving the information-seeking public; rather, it was about its profit imperative. As an alternative to banner ads, Google was planning to run small, targeted text ads. It was unsure whether such ads would be attractive to advertisers because text ads had never been used for brand building. Google had a backup strategy of using DoubleClick, which it eventually acquired in 2008. John Battelle recounts that Brin and Page said, "If we start to see that we're running out of money, well then we'll just turn on a deal with DoubleClick and we will be fine because we have a lot of traffic."[80] Given that DoubleClick was the leading banner ad operator at the time—and the leader in behavioral advertising, which exploited cookies[81]—Google was planning to outsource its ad business to DoubleClick in case its own ad system failed.

It is noteworthy that by the late 1990s ad-serving Internet companies such as DoubleClick were already using cookies to track user data. In 1994 Netscape engineer Lou Montulli had developed this still-dominant user tracking technology, the cookie, which is a piece of code that contains a unique identifier allowing a site to recognize and distinguish a user whenever the user visits the site. When Netscape implemented cookies, they were accepted by default in browsers, and users were unaware of their existence. Soon, however, there were growing privacy concerns about cookies. The Internet Engineering Taskforce (IETF), a volunteer Internet standards body, led the development of cookie specifications. Montulli and Lucent Technologies's David Kristol, both members of the IETF working group, and other members recognized the invasive nature of cookies; while they were not against using cookies for web advertising, they were concerned about user tracking mechanisms without explicit opt-in consent.[82] Crain noted that there was a range of debates within the IETF among different players—including Web publishers and third-party ad networks like DoubleClick—from user privacy over third-party cookies to questioning the organization's involvement in the issue itself.[83] Crain (*Profit over Privacy*) and Turow (*Daily You*) recount that online advertisers vehemently objected to the proposals that restricted third-party cookies because they recognized that limiting cookie usage was a threat to their business model.[84]

In the end, the IETF adopted the third-party default cookie specifications, favoring corporate rather than public interests. In the mid-1990s the US Federal Trade Commission (FTC) held workshops and two hearings on the privacy issues surrounding cookies and released a report supporting the industry's "self-regulation."[85] The result of this was to create the conditions for the proliferation of today's surveillance-based business model. When Google launched its advertising business, the use of cookies had already become a normalized practice in the Internet industry.

In October 2000 Google introduced its AdWords advertising system on a flat CPM pricing model.[86] It was self-service and was restricted to relevant text ads. Google limited ad titles to twenty-five characters and one link and displayed no more than eight small ads on the results page of any search. The results looked like part of the search results. Google had a few tactical reasons for choosing small and targeted texts ads: not only to offer an alternative to banner ads but also to try and ease some immediate technical and social obstacles.

Adding to their ineffectiveness, banner ads often took too long to load and slowed down the system. In early 2000 most users were still connected via dial-up Internet connections with 56k modems. By mandating its twenty-five-character text ads as the standard, Google was able to speed up the ad serving process, which allowed for users to conduct more searches and the company to serve more ads at any given time. Early on, speed was a vital element for Google's search business. This compelled it to build a massive private network infrastructure to expand its market (this will be explored more in Chapter 2). With its text ads, Google improved efficiency and speed, which became major factors in the firm's profitability. Further, such ads gave users the illusion that the ads were part of the results, blurring the line between search and ads results by treating them in a similar way. "If you treat advertisements as a great search result, they will work as a great search result," said Omid Kordestain, vice president of business development and sales at Google.[87] This helped deflect users' resistance to paid search and ensured that the users' side of the market remained intact.

Yet AdWords didn't immediately take off because it didn't really solve the advertisers' side of the market. As Ken Auletta notes, Google's CPM-based ad model—the same as the traditional network ads exposed to an audience of millions—didn't quite appeal to advertisers, and major advertisers weren't willing to bet on unfamiliar keyword search ads.[88] According to Jeff Levick, who worked on the Google ad team at that time, "For the first two years of Google we were cold-calling people, trying to get them to buy keywords."[89] Google still had to build an advertising system that could remove advertiser uncertainty about online advertising.

Making a Perfect Search Engine

Less than two years after launching the first iteration of AdWords, the company overhauled its ad system. In the second iteration of its system, Google deployed a CPC pricing model. It was more attractive to advertisers because it imposed less risk to them; they did not need to pay for impressions that were not clicked on. At the same time, Google had to ensure that users clicked their ads as often as possible; thus, the company had to design a "perfect search" in which an ad system hit the trifecta: It needed to maximize its profit and concomitantly draw both users and advertisers into the marketplace, all the while persistently projecting a public image that was "all about the users."

Google distinguished its system from rival GoTo.com's generalized first price auction system, in which the first position was given to the highest bidder. Google employed a generalized second price auction to reduce the volatility in pricing and inefficiency in investment that tended to occur in generalized first price auctions.[90] In second price auctions, the price that the advertiser paid was not its maximum bid, helping assuage advertisers' fears of overbidding or overpaying for ad services.

In addition to the generalized second price system, Google incorporated a user feedback loop into the system. To place more "relevant" ads, it included the click through rate (CTR) as a way to measure audience engagement so as to determine ad ranking for each query in real time. This system, called Ad-Rank, determined the order of ads in response to a user's query. Despite being a controversial web metric standard, CTR was one of the accepted measurements among both advertisers and publishers, who associated CTR with user interest and intent. Google's incorporation of CTR into its ad algorithm was merely the beginning of its systematic attempts to generate more "relevant" and targeted ads. Google quickly introduced the "Quality Score," which included the relevance of each keyword to its ad group, landing page quality and relevance, the relevance of ad text, and historical AdWords account performance, among many other undisclosed proprietary ingredients of relevancy factors.[91]

The principle of relevance seems like an obvious factor in designing a traditional information retrieval system; however, for a money-making advertising system, it seemed paradoxical on its face. One would think that if Google relied on the highest bidder, as did GoTo.com, it would receive more in return, yet Google's seeming unselfishness toward users in relying on relevance proved to be the core driver of its profit making: It resulted in the building of an ad system in which the house always won at that time. Eric Schmidt affirmed this, saying, "Improving ad quality improves Google's revenue. . . . If we target the right ad to the right person at the right time and they click it, we win."[92] The proprietary search engine was built on bias—a bias toward profit making.

For decades, Google has been insisting that its ad algorithm is scientific, objective, and purely data-driven and vowed that its complex proprietary ad system was primarily for users and user experience. Yet Google's concern about its users' or advertisers' experience per se hinges on its calculation of capital logic: maximizing its profit. Google organized its ad system to generate more profit by putting its version of relevant ads higher on the list, where they would have a greater chance to be seen and clicked on by more users.[93] In fact, Google's emphasis on relevance led it to eclipse the other search engines. The most relevant ad has the most profitable auction price point.[94] Omid Kordestani, Google's twelfth employee, described Google's ad system in an interview with John Battelle:

> We applied auction theory to maximize value—it was the best way to reach the right pricing, both for advertisers and for Google. And then we innovated by introducing the rate at which users actually click on the ads as a factor in placement on the page, and that was very, very useful in relevance.[95]

Jason Spero, the head of global mobile sales and strategy at Google at the time, called AdWords the "nuclear power plant at the core" of the company.[96] As Google was rapidly taking off, Yahoo! began to strengthen its own search service by acquiring Inktomi, as well as AltaVista and AlltheWeb, via its acquisition of Overture (nee GoTo.com) in 2003. Soon after this, Yahoo! stopped licensing Google's search technology and began to use its own in-house search engine. In 2006 Microsoft also joined the sponsored search auction business. By 2007, Yahoo! had added its own quality-based bidding to its sponsored auction ad system to combat Google. Despite all this, Yahoo! was never able to build an advertising system on a par with Google's.

In addition to its AdWords system, which was built on top of search, Google also launched its AdSense program to place ads beyond its search site and other web properties by embedding them on websites willing to be part of Google's content network in exchange for a share in advertising revenues. Google acquired the technology behind AdSense from Applied Semantics in 2003 for $102 million.[97] AdSense enticed online publishers by giving access to the massive network of advertisers from AdWords to any web publishers who signed up with its program. With a few lines of JavaScript code inserted into a web page, AdSense would search for and embed relevant ads from its ad network using Google's search algorithm. The AdSense program was a way to commercialize the entire web on a large scale and also externalize the labor to the publishers' side.

While Google was able to craft a proprietary ad system to control and compete in the market, its corporate profit making again relied on the government. Three years after launching its AdSense program, Google strengthened it by acquiring the online display advertising firm DoubleClick for $3.1 billion, outbidding Microsoft. The acquisition of DoubleClick was one of Google's biggest deals, and the Federal Trade Commission allowed the merger despite serious concerns about Google's market dominance as well as about consumer privacy given the two companies' extensive data-collection capacity. The FTC dismissed its critics and gave the green light to Google to acquire DoubleClick, stating, "The Commission wrote in its majority statement that 'after carefully reviewing the evidence, we have concluded that Google's proposed acquisition of DoubleClick is unlikely to substantially lessen competition.'"[98] In 2007 European Union regulators—who are now pursuing several antitrust cases against Google—also ruled that Google's acquisition of DoubleClick didn't violate anti-monopoly rules. Indeed, DoubleClick strengthened Google's ad business via DoubleClick cookies because it was then able to analyze users' browsing history. The combination of Google search and DoubleClick gave Google enormous leverage to control the online advertising market. Thus, Google's current dominance didn't come simply from technical innovations and corporate power; it was again assisted by the state.

Numerous other acquisitions and the always-improving Google ad platform boosted Google's ad business; however, there was also a less well-known yet vital ingredient in Google's advertising system. In 2005 Google acquired the San Diego web analytics firm Urchin Software Corporation. Google rebranded its service as Google Analytics and began to offer free web analytics services to AdWords customers. Google Analytics was advantageous for three reasons.

First, it generates detailed statistics on web traffic, traffic sources, page visits, views, time spent on a specific page, and conversion rate (the rate at which a visit would translate into a purchase). It provides customers with quantitative data that tracks user behavior in real time, as well as the performance of their ads. It can also follow users as they travel from website to website, feeding data back to Google.

Second, by giving away Google Analytics, Google was able to appeal to marketers who were hesitant to adopt online advertising. If it could attract more advertisers by providing a feedback loop for measuring the effectiveness of their advertising, the company calculated, it could be more profitable.[99] Web analytics was still evolving in the early 2000s; more than 80 percent of advertisers on the web were not using analytics at that time.[100] Other firms were charging fees for analytics, and Yahoo! and Microsoft did not have a sufficiently powerful analytics tool for their advertisers, who were clamoring for more data about the effectiveness of their ads. If Google Analytics could be adopted widely, the thinking went, then it could become the de facto web analytics standard.[101] By offering quantifiable return on investment, Google provided a tool for justifying ad spending on search engines.

The third leg of the Google Analytics stool was the data themselves. Google Analytics users must insert Google-provided JavaScript into every web page they serve, and all their site statistics end up on Google's servers. This is a way for Google to acquire massive amounts of two-way web traffic data in exchange for its free tool. All of these data are then fed into its advertising system. In 2014, Google acquired the marketing analytics firm Adometry to fortify its analytics. Adometry specialized in online and offline advertising attribution, which measures the actions of individual users online in the period leading up to purchase. Google integrated Adometry into its Attribution 360 tool, which is now a key component of the Google Analytics 360 suite. Today, Google Analytics has become the definitive web analytics service, reaching 70 percent of the market.[102]

Google Analytics ensured a stream of data. At the same time, Google enticed advertisers and began to normalize surveillance as everyone from small mom-and-pop stores to conglomerates participated in mining and managing user data. Collecting a large quantity of personal data is not a new practice. Traditional media such as television and radio have been collecting data for decades. Nielsen ratings, for instance, which provide audience measurement, go back to the 1930s for radio ratings.[103] Thus, Google's resorting to the surveillance-for-profit model of today is not a new business model or a new form of capitalism; rather, it is the scale and the extent of data collection that have greatly intensified in this multisided marketplace, in which market logics reach more deeply into every aspect of our lives. The mere collection of data didn't automatically generate profit, however; the company also needed to deploy mass production of advertising and mechanization to reduce labor costs.

Mass Production of Advertising

Google built and assembled its universal tracking tools and ad auction system to generate profit, but there is still another question to explore: How was it able to scale up its ad business and run it around the clock as the web grew exponentially? The journalist Steven Levy describes Google's AdWords as "the world's biggest, fastest auction, a never ending, automated, self-service version of Tokyo's boisterous Tsukiji fish market."[104] The famed tuna auction in the Tsukiji fish market is run by skilled auctioneers from 5 a.m. to 7 a.m., but Google has built an automated system that runs 24/7 with an auction-based online marketplace on a massive scale. This is what enabled the company to scale up its ad business without hiring huge numbers of sales personnel to sell billions of ads per day. The world is Google's Tsukiji.

Traditional advertising production is labor- and time-intensive. It requires staff to customize ad designs, campaigns, schedules, and placement, and these in turn may require meetings, phone calls, and production schedules. Even in the early days of the Internet, the process of buying, selling, and serving ads depended on manual recording, ad scheduling, and tracking of numbers of visits or impressions. Ads were also bought and sold via individual contracts negotiated on a case-by-case basis, and advertising sales were oriented toward the larger advertisers.[105]

This rapidly changed in the mid-1990s dot-com era, when a range of new advertising technologies was developed including online ad networks, data-profiling technologies, web metrics, and ad-serving and management technologies. Advertising processes were further automated and mechanized. By the mid-to-late 1990s a host of technology firms including Focal Link, MatchLogic, Flycast, DoubleClick, NetGravity, AdForce, SoftBank, and CMGI had developed capabilities for ad sales, targeting, serving, and tracking using central integrated systems. For instance, in 1996 Yahoo! used NetGravity's AdServer to schedule, place, target, track, measure, and manage banner ads and to further automate and speed up ad management. In particular, DoubleClick first deployed its ad network model in its centralized online ad serving system, which built a foundation for large-scale online advertising.[106] As mentioned above, DoubleClick, as the largest ad broker, was considered the Google of its time, used by many major advertisers and publishers. In 1997 DoubleClick's network of servers delivered more than five hundred million ad impressions a month, and by 1999 it was delivering five hundred million *per day*.[107] Nonetheless, DoubleClick adhered to the idea of the Web as a publishing platform and still limited itself to large advertisers, which required formal sales contracts with those sites.[108] The company was known for having one of the largest sales forces on the Internet, and roughly five hundred of its fourteen hundred employees were working in its sales unit.[109] The coming years would see the search engine industry figure out ways to exponentially scale up their ads businesses through automation.

Emulating GoTo.com, Google launched its self-service platform instead of having thousands of sales representatives to pitch ads directly to every individual advertiser or publisher. Although it still sold premium ads in person, it automated most of the management of ad buying, selling, and serving processes. By instituting this model, with no minimum purchase for CPC bids, Google was able to quickly expand its ad business on a mass scale. Using the Internet as a business platform, the self-service model shifted labor costs to advertisers, marketers, and publishers by giving them the tools to work on buying, targeting, and tracking ads themselves. For search firms to generate profits, a large portion of ad sales had to come from such scalable self-service platforms. In 2007 Google CEO Eric Schmidt described the company as an operating system for advertising,[110] and Google continues to this day to hone this system to serve as many ads as possible—a modern-day advertising factory.

Fueling Ads

On top of its ad system, Google has a seductively simple search box offering free search, a process that fuels its ad business by attracting users and generating massive amounts of user traffic. Google's back-end advertising system alone doesn't make a "perfect" search engine, therefore, because search is needed to ensure ongoing user traffic, creating a user-side market. Every time someone searches on Google, simultaneous auctions take place on Google's back end to determine which ads will show up and in what order. Thus, Google has an economic incentive to perfect its search engine so as to expose as many ads as possible and draw in users by providing "relevant" search results. Google co-founder Larry Page described the perfect search engine as a machine that "understands exactly what you mean and gives you back exactly what you want."[111] As Michael Zimmer posits, a perfect search is a perfect recall, which requires that the system identify the desires, intents, and wants of a searcher as well as meet Google's business motivation.[112] To deliver perfect recall, Google needs vast numbers of searchers whose activities can be digitized, extracted, indexed, computed, and contextualized to feed into its ad systems. In order to perfect its search engine, the company changes its algorithm thousands of times every year and deploys two hundred major ranking signals with up to ten thousand variations.[113] Google persistently presents the compatibility between profit-making and serving public goods by arguing that its paid and organic searches are separate systems; however, the interplay of those two systems is what makes Google's search engine "perfect."

Google systematically configured the combination of the free search and back-end ad system that would become the company's secret weapon, contributing to generating billions of dollars in profits every quarter. The public's free search gave Google the foundation for its technical infrastructure and the leverage to expand its business beyond search. It has immense data reservoirs that are constantly being filled and refilled by searchers' everyday information-seeking activities across Google's search and other Web properties. One former employee described the firm as "a living laboratory processing data that reveals what is effective and what is not."[114] Yet this laboratory is a closed vault door because the company defends its search algorithm as a trade secret, what Frank Pasquale calls part of the "black box society."[115] Still, although the details are hidden behind the search box, the fact that the black box is built for profit-making is clear. The recent lawsuit filed by several US states reaffirmed this. Under Project Bernanke, it was alleged, Google was manipulating both publishers and advertisers by letting them think they were participating in what was supposed to be a fair and data-driven auction system; meanwhile, as the suit showed, Google had developed its own black box—an algorithm for profit.[116]

Today, Google is not the only company that operates an algorithms-and-data business model. Our social, political, and economic lives are increasingly being shifted over to a privatized Internet, and are increasingly digitized and commodified and turned into new sites of capital accumulation. The intense competition as well as collaboration among Internet companies has driven them to embed the data-driven business model into their profit-making sites. Thus, Internet firms such as Google, Facebook, Amazon, Apple, and Microsoft, whose business models rely on data and computing power, continue to try to figure out ways to exploit data and aggressively lobby governments to preemptively shape privacy laws in their own interests.[117]

Their expansion is not, however, without obstacles. With increasing backlash around the world from lawmakers and the public against digital surveillance, the Internet companies have been forced to respond to the pressure out of self-interest. Google claims to be building "a privacy-first future for web advertising" by phasing out third-party cookies, on which online advertising has depended for decades, from Chrome by the end of 2023. This move is in response to Apple, which had already positioned itself as a "privacy friendly" company, stating that "transparency is the best policy." Google publicized its new alternative to third-party cookies, called Federated Learning of Cohorts (FLoC), which groups people with similar characteristics and targets ads to those cohorts rather tracking individuals. Yet it was soon pressured to abandon the program because of pushback from privacy advocates and its competitors, who argued that FLoC exacerbates behavior-based targeting of ads. The program is not new; rather, it has long been a common marketing method, but the tech giant is now competing to sell its "privacy as a business feature" and to set new privacy rules. Google, Facebook, and other large marketers, even without third-party cookies, are still able to collect data from their own sites and fill data gaps by purchasing consumer data from data brokers.[118]

Responding to mounting pressure from regulators, civil society organizations, and consumers, privacy-focused search companies such as Startpage, Swisscows, Qwant, Brave, DuckDuckGo, Ecosia, and Neeva are getting traction from venture capital. Privacy-focused technology has become an increasingly lucrative business. Google is now being pressured to respond in order for the company to maintain and continue to expand its market power. The question is, what adjustments could Google pursue without hurting its bottom line?

So far, Google has been able to sustain and grow its ad business; however, the online advertising environment is constantly and rapidly changing due to global economic crises, competition, regulation, ad tracking technologies, and increasing consumer use of a range of new Internet-connected devices such as smartphones, tablets, and smart TVs. Google needs to counter this volatile digital environment and understand that it is not enough to maintain control over its ad business; thus, it is now radically diversifying its data streams and revenue sources in ever-widening social and economic sectors.

Conclusion

Search has become naturalized in the marketplace. Still, the process of search's commodification tells a different story from the mainstream idea of its inevitable technological progression. The process was far from imperative; rather, it involved the depletion of public resources and capitalist state intervention, providing the preconditions for accumulation processes and removing technical and political obstacles.

As Tony Smith observes, capital-intensive basic units of technical innovation don't just happen in a corporate lab; in fact, a large proportion of the costs were socialized.[119] The initial research and development of search technologies, which required significant capital, were primarily funded by the government. The US government also facilitated the transfer of technologies to the private sector by promoting the commercialization of the Internet, implementing self-regulation of privacy law, strengthening IP laws, and removing the possibility of the public provision of public information by search engines. Within these conditions, capital was mobilized to remove social and technical barriers and invest in search technologies, which subsumed the technology into capital and converted search into a marketplace. This process demonstrates that the surveillance business model of search was far from preordained, nor was it novel; rather, it was developed and cultivated within a market dynamic whereby maximizing profit and capital accumulation trumps social and public logics and needs.[120] The Internet-enabled search marketplace has integrated capitalist social relations even into our curiosity.

The commodification and commercialization of search could be seen as inexorably technology-driven, but it was, in reality, driven by the market imperatives of the capitalist system. The search engine is no longer merely an information retrieval system but instead has become an expansive and extremely lucrative business. When technology is turned into business, there's an imperative to find new markets and redefine them into spaces where that business can expand.[121]

Chapter 2 explores how the search giant Google controls the Internet in response to competition and pressure to expand into geographies and sectors beyond search and within emerging and existing Internet industries. It highlights the scale of the search industry and the behemoth physical network infrastructures that underpin the global search business.

Chapter 2

SITUATING SEARCH

Early on, the popular notion was that the Internet embodies a decentralized mode of provision; thus, no one entity could control it. In his widely cited book *The Wealth of Networks* Yochai Benkler celebrated the decentralized technical architecture of the Internet, posited how the networked information economy was different from the industrial economy of the pre-Internet era, and promoted a new mode of production outside the market economy.[1] Yet, contrary to Benkler's and others' early optimism—Robert McChesney refers to them as "Internet celebrants"[2]—capital has a firm grip on the Internet while democratic information-providing activities are, for the most part, marginalized. McChesney, Nikos Smyrnaio, Nick Srnicek, and others write that capitalism is the underlying principle in shaping the Internet, which is controlled by monopoly capital: A small number of large corporations controls the economy and sets prices through oligopolistic markets.[3] The large corporations sustain their monopoly power and profit in the long run by creating and maintaining various barriers to entry such as economy of scale, mergers and acquisitions, intellectual property, and availability of financing.[4] This monopoly capital approach captures the emergence of the tech giants and their increasing power over the Internet.

This chapter demonstrates, however, that Google's dominance of search doesn't mean that there is an absence of competition. The search engine industry competes not only in the United States but also on the regional and global levels in tandem with increasingly blurred sectoral boundaries that intensify intra-sector and inter-sector competition. In fact, Google's and other US tech companies' global expansion has ignited current geopolitical conflicts attesting to the mesh between inter-state and inter-capitalist competition. Thus, the thesis of monopoly power alone is insufficient to explain the characteristics of the dynamics of the search engine industry. One must also address the underlying role of competition, which drives accumulation, expansion, and control of labor.

Anwar Shaikh argues that "the intensity of the competitive struggle does not depend on the number of firms, their scale, or the industry concentration ratio. Price-setting, cost-cutting, and technology variations are viewed as intrinsic to competition."[5] The competition of capital compels firms to do anything to cut costs and wages and drives new technical innovation in order to gain more market share and maximize profit.[6] Richard Bryan notes, "Monopoly is the expression of a competitive process, not its negation."[7] Monopolistic tendencies and competition are linked dialectically in capitalism[8] because they are exhibited in aggressive corporate strategies in what Kim Moody describes as "competitive war for profits."[9] The search industry, which is interwoven into and across economic sectors, needs to be situated within the dynamic between competition, ever-changing alliances, and the tendency toward concentration, rather than as a static condition.

With this as framework, this chapter first shows the scope of the search business which is expanding because search engine firms, in particular Google, are no longer merely trying to control this one domain. The most dynamic Internet sectors—search, social media, e-commerce, mobile, cloud—appear on the surface to be separate information spheres. Yet the major tech firms are all moving into each other's territories to compete, defend their existing profit centers, and carve out new profit sectors. In particular, the chapter shows how Google and its competitors are fiercely striving for mobile and cloud space. Furthermore, Google is engaged not only in the Internet sectors but also in the military, automobile, pharmaceutical, agricultural, education, and healthcare sectors and beyond. The Internet companies' dynamics delineate their compulsion to capture at any cost any sectors they can wire and push to restructure into their profit domains with support from the capitalist state.

Second, this chapter illuminates the dynamics of the competition and expansion that are expressed in the infrastructure of control. It demonstrates how Google and its competitors Amazon, Facebook, Apple, and Microsoft are reconstituting domestic and transnational network infrastructures. As David Harvey points out, network infrastructure is a solution to the tension between fixed infrastructure and mobility of capital, data, goods, services, and labor to construct geographically dispersed markets. This is necessary in order to remove physical and spatial barriers to circulating capital.[10] With regard to sectoral competition and geographical expansion, the tech firms contest as well as ally among each other and draw on regional capital to construct transnational network infrastructures. Specifically, the chapter discusses these firms' major private infrastructure nodes—data centers, territorial fiber, and submarine cables—, which are supported by governments, directly and indirectly. Google is the nexus of these colossal global network infrastructures.

Dwayne Winseck argues that the US-based Internet giants don't control the myriad of layers of the Internet and its technical standards because the regional players from the EU and BRICS countries are increasingly playing a role in structuring global network infrastructure.[11] This is true; however, the chapter focuses on the US Internet giants' network infrastructures as part of their competitive and expansionary strategies as they try to outbid and outspend each other, investing massive amounts of capital in building private global networks to extend their Internet businesses and consume and control untapped or undertapped geographically dispersed parts of the world into their profit territories. The ascendance of the US-based Internet giants in network building is creating the geopolitical counterpressures from rivals that are discussed later, but this chapter expounds on the infrastructures that support ever-expanding Internet businesses and shows how they drive a new cycle of accumulation processes and open new "territories of profit," to use Gary Fields's term.[12]

Defending Search

By situating itself between users and the Internet, the search engine industry established a critical point of control over information access. Tim Wu describes Google as controlling the "master switch" on the web in the way telephone operators at switchboards in the past made connections between parties, using the switch that can determine whom and what to connect.[13] This rise of the search engines as an access point to the Internet has shifted the dynamics of and destabilized the information and communication sectors. The entire gamut of traditional media industries now has to rely on the search engine to reach potential audiences on the web. Google's ongoing disputes with publishers, newspapers, and the music and film industries over copyright issues and privacy, with the computer and mobile industries over patents and antitrust cases, and with the telecommunication industry over "net neutrality" around the world are demonstrating the battles between different units of capital as the information and communication sectors are being restructured. Drawn from the work of the economist Joseph Schumpeter, this is often described as creative destruction by technical innovation and creative entrepreneurship;[14] however, this explanation overlooks the role of capital. In capitalist markets, entrepreneurs seek technical innovations not because they are entrepreneurial but because they have an imperative to maintain their market share to survive as capitalists.[15] This involves the destruction of existing industries and the creation of new ones and the restructuring of old ones to renew capitalist accumulation.

In 2010 Google touted its success, saying that it "may be the only company in the world whose stated goal is to have users leave its website as quickly as possible."[16] Its chief executive at the time, Eric Schmidt, reiterated this point, once stating that Google would not be involved in the content business but, rather, would maintain itself as a "neutral platform for content and applications."[17] That perspective didn't last long, because the company soon pivoted. Google and other search engine firms are no longer merely pointing to information; rather, they own, manage, host, store, digitize, and duplicate information to extend their marketplaces and to pre-empt potential high-profit functions and services. Their businesses have been woven through the entire Internet value chain so as to control and extend profit territories encompassing the Internet backbone, hardware, software, content, services, and applications.

According to its 2021 annual report, Google's business is made up of two segments: services and cloud. Google Services is the largest division of its parent company Alphabet's business, which includes search and display advertising, the Android operating system platform, YouTube, consumer content delivered through Google Play, Enterprise, and Commerce, and hardware products.[18] One of the company's major business focuses is still "access and technology to everyone." Thus, to maintain its position of control as the main gateway to the Internet, Google has to compete with and block any companies that offer an access point to the Internet. In other words, the fight over search is not among horizontal search companies Microsoft Bing, Yahoo!, Yandex, and Baidu; rather, it is about control over the entire Internet value chain. Given that most of Google's revenue still comes from advertising, Google can't stay in its dominant position by merely being a superior search engine. If it is to secure its core territory of profit from advertising, Google has to control or at least have a hand in any route to the Internet by any means, including paying very large sums to its competitors. The company's attempts to prevent its rivals from accessing Internet entry points can be seen in the 2020 Department of Justice antitrust lawsuit against Google.[19]

The department's filing reveals that the main charge against Google was its control over "search access points." The investigation showed that Google paid billions of dollars to device manufacturers Apple, LG, Motorola, and Samsung, to major US wireless carriers AT&T, T-Mobile, and Verizon, and to the Mozilla, Opera, and UCWeb browser developers to make Google their default search engine and restrict these companies from working with Google's competitors.[20] In order to secure its position, Google has locked in its search distribution channels and paid between $8 billion and $12 billion per year to Apple alone, which is between 14 percent and 20 percent of Apple's annual profit and a third of Google's annual profit.[21] The filing also reported that Google colluded with its major rival Facebook by manipulating its online advertising auction as a way to rein in its competitors. Besides forging a relationship with its competitors by leveraging its power, Google acquired hundreds of companies and filed for tens of thousands of patents. The largest number of patents in a single year that Google filed was 3,483 patents in 2012 to control the market and block future competition.[22]

On the one hand, Google's use of these control strategies, from locking up its competitors to alliances with its rivals to patents, is an exercise of its monopolistic search power, but on the other hand it is also a response to competition and to capitalism's imperative for expansion. As Rhys Jenkins writes, competition is a consequence of the self-expansion of capital.[23] While Google's US search competitors Microsoft Bing and Yahoo! have made only little dents in the company's search market share, there is intense competition over hundreds of billions of dollars in the digital advertising market among other Internet companies and traditional media companies.

Facebook and Amazon are trailing closely behind Google's core business. In particular, the social media giant Facebook has been directly going after Google's main ad revenue sources. Facebook has been drawing on its massive user base and hoarding individual "intent data," which is at the core of the search engine industry. It is challenging Google's most lucrative business as it offers information through Facebook, Instagram, WhatsApp, and Messenger, all of which bypass and outflank Google. In response, Google launched its own—failed—social media platform, Google Plus (Google+). Despite facing uproar from both the public and lawmakers over its privacy practices, political ads, and cyber-currency business, Facebook still holds the second most visited website in the world after Google. The company generated $84.2 billion in ad revenues and drew more than ten million active advertisers across its services in 2020.[24]

Amazon, once Google's biggest advertiser, now threatens Google's advertising business. In 2021 Amazon generated $31.2 billion dollars in ad revenue,[25] a distant third place behind Google and Facebook but surpassing 11 percent of the US digital ad business. Over the years, Amazon has become the primary search engine for e-commerce, which also cuts into Google's core function and pulls searchers away from Google's web properties. Ninety percent of Amazon's ad revenue came from sponsored products and brands on its e-commerce platform.[26] If Google has built its advertising business by transforming the Internet into an ad platform, Amazon, the modern-day Sears catalog, has built its business by organizing the Internet as a vehicle for retail business. Since Google sells ads and Amazon sells products, they would seem to be in two different business sectors. Yet because the same companies that buy ads on Google are the companies the sell products on Amazon, if searchers go directly to Amazon and bypass Google to find products to purchase, then those companies pull or reduce ad spending on Google. For a decade Google made attempts to compete directly against Amazon by introducing the same-day delivery service Google Express, but these efforts haven't borne fruit. However, once again the company is trying to reboot its e-commerce to protect Google's core business as well as grab a controlling share of the almost $5 trillion e-commerce market by leveraging search, enticing sellers, and partnering with PayPal and Shopify.[27]

The real threat to Google's advertising business is coming from Amazon's accumulated data on over two hundred million active customers. They are not merely clickstream data, but detailed data on what people searched for, actually purchased, and paid for those purchases. This is still an undertapped gold mine for marketers. In his *Cnet* interview Jeff Lanctot, the chief media officer for Razorfish, the Seattle-based digital marketing agency, said, "Amazon understands better than anyone else what consumers want" because advertisers were eager to get their hands on Amazon's data.[28] Some major marketing companies such as WPP PLC and Omnicom Group. Inc. have already begun to shift some of their advertising budgets from Google to Amazon.[29] In 2019, according to the *Wall Street Journal*, WPP PLC, the world's largest ad buyer, spent $300 million on Amazon search ads in 2018, and its 75 percent share of Amazon's ad search spending was drawn from its Google search budget.[30] In 2020 the car insurance company Geico was the largest buyer of Amazon ads, at, $11 million, followed by Comcast, P&G, Acura, and American Express.[31] These increased revenues from ad sales mitigate Amazon's high capital costs and strategy of having a thin retail profit margin. Amazon's advertising has turned into a third major revenue source for the company after its e-commerce and cloud businesses.

From a different direction, the telecom giants pulled together to take on both Google and Facebook, both of whose ad businesses are built over the telecoms' network infrastructures. The telecom companies controlled the pipes, but they still needed wider distribution channels, content, and ad technologies to challenge the Silicon Valley ad giants. Thus, there was a flurry of mergers and acquisitions of media companies by traditional telecom companies to allow them to move into online advertising.

Verizon bought AOL in 2015 and followed that up with the acquisition of the search engine Yahoo! in 2017, spending close to $10 billion, and created Verizon Media (formerly Oath, Inc.), a division of its media and online business, which integrated AOL and Yahoo!. Verizon Media made a multiyear deal with Google competitor Microsoft, as Microsoft's Bing Ads exclusively served search advertising platforms for Verizon Media properties including Aol.com, Yahoo.com, AOL Mail, Yahoo! Mail, Huffington Post, and TechCrunch. But the company struggled to draw advertisers and sold 90 percent of Verizon Media to the private equity firm Apollo Global Management for $5 billion because the company faced fierce competition against AT&T and T-Mobile concerning the 5G network. Soon Softbank scooped up Yahoo! Japan, paying for the perpetual rights to the brand and related technologies. Yahoo! Japan is still one of the most popular websites in Japan with more than 20 percent of the search market share in that country. Verizon has retreated from its online ad business for now.

Verizon rival AT&T also bulked up its advertising business. In 2018, AT&T acquired a Google competitor, the ad technology platform *AppNexus*, integrating its advertising and analytics businesses to make its television spots more enticing to advertisers. This was after AT&T's $85 billion acquisition of Time Warner, forming WarnerMedia, which includes CNN, HBO, TBS, TNT, Turner Classic Movies, Cartoon Network, and more. But AT&T didn't take over Time Warner merely to compete with its main rivals Comcast and Verizon; rather, it was to compete with Internet firms like Google, Facebook, Netflix, Amazon, and Apple. In 2015 AT&T had also bought satellite television provider DirecTV for $67 billion. This buying spree put AT&T seriously into debt, and the company's big bet on digital advertising didn't pay off quickly enough.[32] A short three years later, in 2022, AT&T sold off Warner Media to Discovery, creating a new company called Warner Bros. Discovery, which is the second-largest standalone streaming behemoth, competing against Disney Plus, Netflix, Amazon Prime, and Google's YouTube. The competition over the capital-intensive streaming business is cutting into ad revenue as well. Meanwhile, the cable giant Comcast, which owns NBCUniversal, launched an ad-supported streaming service called Peacock to grow its targeted ad business. As the company continues to lose television subscribers, Comcast is bolstering its ad-supported Internet business.

Despite facing competition on multiple fronts, Google still reigns over its core advertising business so far. Yet its dominance in advertising is far from secure. In order to preemptively fend off its rivals and continue to grow, the company had to get a grip on mobile devices, on which a growing majority of people access the Internet today. The combination of mobility and Internet connectivity opened up new dimensions of commodification and commercialization for capital. This allowed capital to overcome physical obstacles to reach consumers 24/7 and to expand in space and time for capitalist production in previously untapped markets.

Going Mobile

In 2014 Google's chief business officer, Nikesh Arora stated, "The fundamental tenet is not to speak about mobile, mobile, mobile. It's really about living with users."[33] That is, the tenet of capital is not simply maintaining dominance over one's own domain; rather, the imperative is to expand by organizing and reorganizing every inch of peoples' social lives into the profit domain. Given this expansionist compulsion, mobile Internet is a vital platform for capital, with the goal being to actually live with users and their always-on mobile devices, tied to an individual identification that can be tracked, and monitored, and commodified.

After acquiring the mobile-phone software start-up Android in 2008, Google launched its Android OS, followed closely by Apple's first mobile OS, in order to expand its ad business into the mobile marketplace, where Google competes with Apple. These firms took different routes in their accumulation and control strategies—Android was an open-source operating system while Apple was a closed system, a walled garden. Google's approach of allowing Android OS to be installed on as many phone models as possible meant that Samsung, LG, HTC, Sony, and Motorola all built Android-driven phones. Google CEO Eric Schmidt declared, "Android is by far the primary vehicle by which people are going to see smartphones. . . . Our goal is to reach everybody."[34] As the Department of Justice's filing in its antitrust suit reported, Google uses a version of open-source software but deploys various measures including anti-forking, preinstall, and revenue-sharing agreements to maintain control. It's "open source" but with rules by Google.

To compete against Google in the mobile space and diversify its revenue sources, Apple launched *iAds*, its mobile ad platform, in 2010, integrating advertisements into applications sold only in its iOS App Store. Apple tried hard to chip away at Google AdMob's lead in mobile advertising. Yet iAds failed and was discontinued. In particular, by exclusively serving iOS devices, Apple wasn't able to reach lucrative emerging markets where Android was dominant. While the company continues to seek alternative revenue sources such as subscription fees from Apple Music streaming, Apple Pay, and licensing—and while it faces a slowdown in device sales, a whopping 80 percent of its revenue—Apple hasn't fully abandoned its advertising business. It expanded its ad business via its app store. Armed with the knowledge that 70 percent of Apple store users use search to find apps, Apple moved into Google and Facebook territory and launched its mobile app search ads in 2016. In 2020 the *Financial Times* reported that Apple was developing its in-house search engine for displaying its own search results on iOS 14.[35] And Apple's Siri already competes against Google Assistant, Amazon's Alexa, and Microsoft's Cortana. The development of its own general search engine and voice search is a direct attack on Google's core business, but it also gives Apple an alternative if regulators break up the lucrative agreement with Google.[36]

As mentioned in Chapter 1, Apple has increasingly positioned itself publicly as the vanguard of privacy, pushing privacy and security as a corporate strategy and a brand feature of its devices. If Google's accumulation strategy is surveillance, Apple's is exploiting privacy to curb its competition and regulatory pressure from the state. By deploying its new privacy policy, App Tracking Transparency, in April 2021 Apple asserted its privacy enforcement in its app store, forcing third-party app developers to ask users for permission to collect a unique identifier used by advertisers.[37] App Tracking Transparency could negatively affect Google, Facebook, and in particular third-party ads companies that have less capital and infrastructure to cope with changes. Pushing privacy is a positive development, but Apple's move was far from altruistic. After it implemented App Tracking Transparency the company's ad revenues rose, and its own targeted search ads in the App Store increased.[38]

In the mobile advertising domain, one of Google's biggest competitors has been Facebook. Facebook released its own in-app advertising network, called Facebook Audience Network, in 2014, putting it into competition with Google's AdMob for mobile advertising. Facebook draws major advertisers such as Disney, Procter & Gamble, Walmart, and the *New York Times* with its billions of users.[39] As of 2022 it is the second-largest player in the mobile space and has reached nearly 25 percent of mobile ad market share. In 2019 mobile ads accounted for 93 percent of Facebook's total ad revenue.[40] The site's increasing power over the mobile space was threatening Google. To deflect competition and stymie Facebook's infringement on its core ads business, Google was willing to collude with Facebook and offer it preferential treatment in bidding for ad placement.[41] A Texas-led antitrust case against Google revealed that the deal between the two companies concerned "header bidding," which enabled online publishers to bypass Google's ad auction.[42] Ad tech companies such as AppNexus, OpenX, MediaMath, and Pubmatic all built header bidding technologies to compete against Google's ad platform. By 2016 more than 70 percent of publishers used header bidding in an attempt to avoid Google. Google was worried that Facebook's ad service would adopt header bidding, which would significantly damage Google's ad revenue. In 2017 Facebook announced that it was working with ad tech companies and experimenting with the technology. However, the company soon changed its position and backed Google's ad platform after the secret deal with Google.

Google's competition in the mobile space does not come only from US companies. It also comes from its main Android manufacturers, Samsung and Huawei. Google's original strategy for its open-source OS was to rely on a number of different hardware companies to distribute Android and avoid letting one company get too big. But that strategy has faltered because Samsung has become a major seller of Android phones. Because of this development, Google could simply lose control over the mobile market if Samsung decides to use its own OS and leverage its market power against Google. Samsung once introduced its own mobile OS, Tizen, but failed to fully develop it. So far, Google has been able to maintain its control over device manufacturers by closely controlling its closed-source Google apps platform.[43]

The intensification of the geopolitical rivalry between the United States and China has also exposed Google's vulnerability. Amid the tensions between the two nations over trade and national security, the US government blacklisted Huawei on its Entity List,[44] forcing Google to reluctantly revoke Huawei's Android license. This meant that Huawei was no longer able to access various Google services such as Gmail, YouTube, Google Maps, or the Google App store. As of now, Google has the upper hand and can exercise its power over the mobile market, while Huawei suffers without Google's apps. In the long run, however, Google could lose its grip on the mobile market given that Huawei was one of Google's major app distributors, selling more than two hundred million smartphones in 2018. Moreover, Huawei had a sizeable market outside the United States and had sufficient financial and technical capacity to build its own mobile OS system to move away from its reliance on Android.

Early on, Google and Huawei had preemptively pursued an alliance despite pressure from the Trump administration to reconsider the partnership on the basis of claims of a national security risk to the United States.[45] This was not the first time Google had worked with Huawei, which was an important ally not only for Google's mobile business but also for its access to the unreached and potentially huge Chinese market. Even after Google was forced to pull Huawei's Android license, Google continued to try to persuade the US government that banning Huawei was bad for national security, arguing that it would be better for Huawei to be dependent on Google's Android OS than for there to be a Huawei-modified version of Android with a greater likelihood of being hacked.[46] This is exactly what happened, as Huawei soon released its own OS, an open source–based fork of Android called Harmony OS. While it is still an open question whether Huawei will be able to bear the brunt of Google's ire without the support of Android in the global market, Google also clearly knows the risks and the strategic importance of mobile manufacturers for its business.

Google knew there was vulnerability in not being able to control the entire production process from design to manufacturing of its devices because the company sought full vertical integration. Google's acquisition in 2012 of Motorola Mobility, which made Android-based smartphones and tablets, for $12.5 billion was a way to prevent hardware manufacturers like Samsung from having too much control over Android.[47] The acquisition did not turn out as Google had expected, and it sold Motorola Mobility to the Chinese firm Lenovo less than a year later—with Google keeping the majority of Motorola's patents. Google hasn't given up on manufacturing its own devices, however. It acquired HTC's smartphone design division, including "acqhiring" its two thousand engineers, for $1.1 billion and plans to control the entire design and manufacturing process, emulating Apple.[48] The vertically integrated Google mobile phone Pixel launched in 2016. By manufacturing its own phone, Google can also mitigate the potential regulatory issues that could impact usage of its own services.

Google's phone gained less than 2 percent of the global market share, but it was part of a broader defensive and offensive accumulation and competition strategy. While Google tried to assert its power in the mobile space by managing to control the entire software and hardware production chain to secure its core business, the company needed to diversify its profit sources and bring its adjacent markets into the core. Cloud computing—on-demand availability of computer system resources, especially data storage and computing power, without direct active management by the user—was first brought into Google's profit orbit because it was capable of mass data processing, storage, and distribution. Vincent Mosco underscores the point that the evolution of cloud computing goes back to the 1950s and 1960s, when the concept of computer utility and information as a resource like water and electricity was first discussed; however, today it is driven by the goals of profit maximization and control, completely erasing the idea of computing as a public utility.[49]

The Cloud

The "cloud" was popularized after Google competitor Amazon created its first cloud service, called the Elastic Compute Cloud, in 2006; however, after the 2008 Great Recession, cloud computing was heavily promoted across the information industry as an efficiency and cost-cutting measure aided by the US government, which tried to boost the IT sectors in response to the crisis by spurring a new round of digitization of the economy. Corporate PR machines relentlessly promoted the message of cloud computing's prowess, brushing off labor, environmental, security, and privacy issues.[50] By 2019 global IT spending had reached $3.76 trillion, with one of the key drivers of IT spending being the shift to the cloud across enterprises.[51]

For Google, cloud computing was not new territory per se. Google's most popular products, such as search, Gmail, Google Docs, Google Maps, Google Calendar, Google Now, and Google Drive, all run on Google's cloud infrastructure, where products are developed and data about users' information-seeking activity are stored and managed. All along Google was running the biggest cloud-computing operation in the world—just with a different purpose. The company leverages its internal physical infrastructure to build out its cloud business, but Google's internal platform isn't easily configured for enterprise services as the company needed to bring the biggest spenders on IT—oil and gas companies, banks, governments, telecommunications firms, and healthcare companies—onto their cloud.

To entice corporate enterprises, Google tried to differentiate itself by bundling AI and machine-learning capabilities with its own Tenor Processing Unit chip for speed, along with developer tools. The company has also allied with Elon Musk's SpaceX, in which Google invested $900 million to install the space company's satellite Internet service, Starlink terminal, at Google's data centers around the world.[52] Major corporations like Deutsche Bank, Ford Motor Company, the Mayo Clinic, and Univision have signed with Google cloud, but Google, with its mighty technical capacity, is still struggling to attract more large enterprises that are substantial revenue sources.

Microsoft and Amazon understand well the enterprise side of the cloud business; many enterprises have experimented with or are running apps on Amazon Web Services (AWS). While Google has wedged itself into the enterprise cloud market, Amazon has been working to cement its dominant position.

Despite Google's massive investment in cloud infrastructure, Amazon and Microsoft still lead the cloud market with over 50 percent market share combined.[53] In 2006 Amazon launched its cloud computing platform AWS as a side project for its e-commerce, but AWS quickly turned into a major profit source, while its e-commerce business was in the red until 2017. Amazon sells its data storage and processing power to companies around the world. Fortune 500 companies including Apple, GE, Shell, Adobe, BMW, Netflix, and Pfizer avail themselves of AWS.

Microsoft's Azure cloud platform trails closely behind Amazon since the company transformed its Windows and PC business into one of the leading enterprise cloud providers in the world. As the global PC market waned, Microsoft quickly positioned itself as a cloud service provider. Leveraging its existing enterprise business, Microsoft made cloud its most important piece. The company supplies a range of services, including Microsoft 365 as apps, development platforms, and hybrid cloud services, which means consumers can combine cloud services and software.

The most lucrative market, the US government, is still up for grabs, however. Government patronage is vital to controlling the market. In 2021 the federal government spent a total of $8.2 billion by contracting out to private cloud services, an almost 20 percent increase over the previous year.[54] All of the cloud giants have taken aim at the state, the largest organization in the enterprise market.

The US government was the main cheerleader in stimulating cloud computing and generating demand when corporations were hesitant to move their IT operations to the cloud. It has been facilitating the expansion of cloud computing by mandating the implementation of cloud computing for federal agencies. The Obama administration launched its "Cloud First Policy" to shift federal IT infrastructure into cloud computing under the premise of efficiency, flexibility and cost cutting.[55] With its policy of IT modernization, the Trump administration continued to support the migration of federal government IT infrastructure to the cloud. In particular, the Department of Defense (DoD) and Central Intelligence Agency (CIA) made strides toward enterprise cloud service as they increasingly deploy cloud computing on the battlefield and for cybersecurity. Under the umbrella of the Commercial Cloud Enterprise program the CIA also expanded its use of cloud services to power technologies for US intelligence. The result is what Mosco describes as the construction of the global surveillance state.[56]

In 2017 Google was awarded a DoD contract for Project Maven, which deployed AI on the battlefield.[57] Google's work with DoD had received little attention until *The Intercept* and *Gizmodo* revealed the company's involvement in the military project.[58] The revelation mobilized Google employees to protest against the military contract. This forced Google to drop the bid and pull out of Project Maven. For the moment, Google had withdrawn from its defense contract, but the question remained whether the company could afford to *not* work with DoD because its competitors were swiftly lining up for billions of dollars in government business.

After not renewing its contract with DoD, in 2018 Google CEO Sundar Pichai stated in a blog post, "We will continue our work with governments and the military in many other areas. . . . These collaborations are important, and we'll actively look for more ways to augment the critical work of these organizations and keep service members and civilians safe."[59] This statement suggested that future work with DoD hadn't been foreclosed after all. In 2020 Google's cloud division was awarded a new contract by DoD's Defense Innovation Unit to work on cybersecurity. The unit is the Pentagon's Silicon Valley outpost, established in 2015 to strengthen the existing ties between DoD and Silicon Valley. By working with the Defense Innovation Unit, Google signaled that the company had reinserted itself into the military-industrial complex. The United States spent $714 billion on defense in 2020; Google couldn't afford to lose this very lucrative market because Amazon and Microsoft have both become deeply involved in the business of war. In 2022 Google established a new division—Google Public Sector—aiming to bid on Pentagon and other government cloud contracts.

Amazon has already taken a significant share of the government cloud infrastructure market. The company has opened two dedicated secret cloud regions for the US government. In 2013 Amazon won a ten-year, $600 million contract with the CIA, unseating IBM, a long-time federal contractor. Unlike other contracts, which provide that its cloud resides inside Amazon's data center, the CIA contract required that cloud services be held within the CIA's data center—a completely separate, private cloud.[60] This contract opened the door for Amazon to garner other major government contracts including one with US Immigration and Customs Enforcement. In 2014 Amazon pocketed about $200 million from the federal government, but by late 2019 the company had pulled in $2 billion from the CIA and other intelligence- and military-related agencies.[61] Amazon is poised to be the leading federal government cloud contactor, but Microsoft is nipping at Amazon's heels.

Microsoft's winning the $10 billion, ten-year Joint Enterprise Defense Infrastructure (JEDI) cloud contract in 2019 promised to further pave the way for Microsoft to be the forerunner in the military-information-industrial complex.[62] But Amazon filed a lawsuit challenging the DoD's decision, arguing that JEDI's awarding process involved "clear deficiencies, errors, and unmistakable bias."[63]

Amazon referred to former president Donald Trump's feud with Amazon CEO Jeff Bezos and the *Washington Post* (which is owned by Amazon) over the *Post*'s critical coverage of the president. The president denounced the *Post* and Bezos and had considered intervening in the JEDI contract;[64] Amazon argued that his bias had influenced DoD's decision. In 2021, under the Biden administration, DoD annulled the disputed contract with Microsoft and announced that a new multibillion-dollar program called Joint Warfighter Cloud Capability would replace JEDI. Defense stated that multiple vendors including Amazon, Microsoft, Google, Oracle, and IBM would be involved in the new project.[65] This signals that DoD will prop up and stimulate the growth of the US cloud industry by enlisting the major tech companies and broadening the US military-industrial complex.

The JEDI contract was not Microsoft's only military contract; the company had long sought out lucrative military procurements. In 2019 the company won a five-year, $1.7 billion contract with seventeen intelligence agencies including DoD, CIA, the NSA, and the FBI.[66] Microsoft was also awarded a $479 million contract with the US Army to provide HoloLens augmented reality headsets, which were intended for military training and combat.[67] This brought a protest from Microsoft workers, who demanded that the company terminate the contract. The company defied the workers' protests, stating, "We believe in the strong defense of the United States, and we want the people who defend it to have access to the nation's best technology, including from Microsoft."[68] The cloud war between Google, Amazon, and Microsoft is thus heating up, but they are certainly not the only players. Salesforce, IBM, Oracle, Rackspace, Virtustream, GoGrid, and Softlayer all have thrown their hats into the cloud ring.[69]

For years Google did not consider cloud computing part of its core business, but now the company is looking to this space as a major source of profit. Urs Hölzle, a senior vice president of technical infrastructure at Google, in a 2014 interview with *Wired* magazine, said that the revenue from the cloud could exceed the revenue that the company generates from online advertising.[70] Google cloud hasn't exceeded ad revenue yet, but in order to seize the cloud market, the company seeks to "industrialize" the burgeoning multi-billion-dollar cybersecurity industry, which is predicated on network connectivity. The resulting battle between tech firms over the cloud is set to be huge and protracted and will give rise to conflict over controlling the Internet's infrastructure itself.

Infrastructure of Control

This battle to compete and control the Internet is manifested in the physical infrastructures of the Internet firms. Because Internet services hinge on networks, Google and its usual competitors have overseen a massive build-out of their global Internet infrastructures, ownership of which is strategically important to controlling traffic and speed and is the enabling condition for global expansion.

According to Google, from 2016 to 2018 the company spent $47 billion on capital expenditures.[71] The majority of its capital investments went towards data centers, networking, and properties around the world, as Google operates in more than two hundred countries. In 2018 Google's capital expenditures reached $25.46 billion, almost double those of the previous year.[72] The *Wall Street Journal* reported in 2022 that Google, Amazon, Microsoft, and Facebook together have spent $90 billion on capital investments.[73] US Internet companies are building out global Internet infrastructure because they have become its major investors, outpacing Internet backbone providers such as AT&T and Verizon in recent years. Although this infrastructure is invisible, Internet services rely on it to compute and transfer massive amounts of data back and forth. Led by Google, the Internet companies are racing to build major global network infrastructure nodes from data centers through the "middle mile" (territorial fiber and submarine cables that connect data centers) and the "last mile" connecting consumers and business users to this huge infrastructure of control.

Data Centers

Large-scale data centers, sometimes called "server farms" in an oddly quaint allusion to pre-industrial agrarian society, are centralized facilities that primarily contain large numbers of servers and computer equipment used for large quantities of data storage, processing, and high-speed telecommunications. For production of material goods, access to cheap labor has been one of the major criteria for companies in selecting their places of production, but data centers require only a small number of employees. The common characteristics of data center sites have so far been good fiber-optic infrastructure, cheap and reliable power sources for cooling and running servers, geographical diversity for redundancy, cheap land, locations close to markets, and government subsidies.[74] The Internet giants are increasingly reshaping not only cyberspace but also the landscape as their hyper-mega data centers are increasingly occupying areas with some combinations of these components.

The tech journalist Steven Levy, describing Google's haphazard infrastructure, documented that initially Google rented only one collocation facility in Santa Clara, California, to house about three hundred servers.[75] Soon, however, the company was purchasing entire buildings that were available at low cost (collocation sites) due to overexpansion during the dot-com era. Google began to design and build its own data centers, containing thousands of custom-built servers, and expanded its services and global market in response to competitive pressures. At first the company was highly secretive about the locations of its data centers and related technologies; a former employee called this Google's "Manhattan project."[76] Google eventually came clean to the public about them. This may seem as if the company had a change of heart and wanted to be more transparent about the data centers, but in reality it was more about Google's self-serving public relations onslaught. It wanted to show how its cloud infrastructure was superior to that of its competitors to secure future cloud clients.[77] Now Google is building out its data centers around the globe to augment both its myriad services and its cloud business.

As of 2022, according to Google, the company has data centers in twenty-three locations around the globe—fifteen in the Americas (only one in South America), two in Asia, and six in Europe with hundreds of leased collocated data centers worldwide.[78] Google's own data centers are still highly concentrated in the United States, where it receives 47 percent of its revenue;[79] however, it has expanded in terms of scale and computational capacities domestically and internationally. Google currently has a data center in Singapore and in Taiwan and is adding a second one in Douliu, Taiwan, where multiple sea cables pass between the United States and Asia. The company also has one in Chile, and along with its centers in the Netherlands, Finland, Ireland, Denmark, and Sweden, it has acquired a site in Luxembourg and invested further in its existing Belgian site.

Google has also set its sights on the gulf region, a quickly emerging digital market. American corporations are not unfamiliar with doing business with Saudi Arabia, to which the United States sells billions in military arms every year. Silicon Valley firms have joined defense contractors in looking for potential business opportunities in this longtime US ally. In 2018 Google and Saudi Arabia's state-owned oil company, Aramco, discussed a partnership to build data centers.[80] In the same year, the Saudi crown prince, Mohammed bin Salman, toured Silicon Valley and met with tech executives including Google CEO Sundar Pichai, Google co-founder Sergey Brin, Google VP of technical infrastructure Urs Hölzle, and Apple CEO Tim Cook.[81]

Amazon has also been in discussions with the Saudi government to offer its cloud service, but Amazon's expansion into Saudi Arabia was temporarily put on hold after Jamal Ahmad Khashoggi, a *Washington Post* journalist and critic of the Saudi government, was brutally killed by Saudi operatives inside the Saudi consulate in Istanbul in October 2018. Meanwhile, thirty-eight human rights groups demanded morality over profit and urged Google to withdraw from its Saudi cloud service contract because of the country's targeting of political dissidents.[82] As of this writing Google has shown no signs of halting its plans to build the data centers, and its competitors are also expanding their cloud footprint in that region.

Google's search and cloud competitor Microsoft is also ramping up its computing power as the software giant accelerates its cloud business. In 2007 Microsoft built its first in-house data center in Quincy, Washington, which had a dependable and inexpensive supply of hydro-generated power available from the Columbia River. Since then, the company has invested more than $15 billion on infrastructure[83] and currently spends about $1 billion per month on enterprise cloud computing infrastructure.[84] Taking aim at the multi-billion-dollar government market, Microsoft built two data centers in undisclosed locations near Washington, DC, to exclusively host the government's classified data. Microsoft's cloud service is used across the federal government. Globally, Microsoft's network is composed of more than one hundred of its own and colocated data centers in places such as Abu Dhabi and Dubai, where Google, Amazon, and the Chinese e-commerce giant Alibaba already operate cloud services.[85] In particular, Microsoft made an early move among US tech firms on the African continent, a key strategic growth region. There had been little hyper-scale data center presence in Africa due to the need for large-scale capital investment and lack of power supply; thus, the vast majority of African Internet content is stored outside the continent. In 2019 Microsoft opened a data center in Cape Town and one in Johannesburg for its Azure cloud service, beating out Amazon, which opened an AWS data center region in Cape Town in 2020 targeting African government agencies and enterprises.

Amazon, which generates more profit from its cloud business than from e-commerce, set up its first data center in 2006 in fiber-optic-rich Northern

Virginia—where the US government in the late 1960s experimented with fiber optic networking—and has added eleven more data centers in Virginia since then.[86] The exact number and location of the firm's data centers had never been revealed until 2018, when WikiLeaks published an internal Amazon document listing them.[87] According to WikiLeaks, the document described as the *Amazon Atlas* indicated that the company has more than one hundred data centers, including colocations in fifteen cities across nine countries. Since then, Amazon has added at least three data centers in Bahrain, aiming for the Middle East region.[88] According to the company, Amazon is offering its AWS cloud service across twenty-six regions, within which there are eighty-four separate locations that it refers to as "availability zones." Each region is supposed to have between two and five availability zones, and each zone has one to eight data centers. Its cloud business has grown so fast that Amazon is now the fifth-largest software provider in the world, trailing just behind software companies Microsoft, IBM, Oracle, and SAP.[89]

Meanwhile, Facebook's capital expenditures continue to soar although the company has faced several legal issues over data privacy both in the United States and in Europe. So far, this hasn't slowed down Facebook's infrastructure expansion. The company opened its first server farm in Prineville, Oregon, in 2011, and since then has built eighteen data centers worldwide.[90] This includes Facebook's first Asian data center in Singapore, an eleven-story, 1.8 million-square-foot building that is one of the largest data centers ever constructed. Singapore, also home to Google, Microsoft, and Amazon data centers, is a global financial hub situated in a prime geographical location as an entry into the Southeast Asian region.

Even Apple, which had relied on third-party cloud service providers such as Amazon, Microsoft, and Google, has now begun investing in its own data center infrastructure as it tries to reduce its reliance on the Internet cloud giants that are its competitors. Apple operates seven data centers in the United States including those in North Carolina, Oregon, Arizona, and Iowa.[91] Outside the country, Apple opened its first data center in Guizhou, in southwest China, in 2021 to comply with data regulations instituted in the Chinese government's 2016 cybersecurity law,[92] which require that Chinese consumer data be stored within the country. Its second Chinese data center is located in Ulanqab City, in northern China's Inner Mongolia Autonomous Region, where data centers for

China's domestic Internet giants Huawei and Alibaba also reside. For Apple, China—the world largest smartphone market—is one of its most strategically important markets.

These hyper data centers are all built with custom-designed software, servers, and chips as the companies try to better control critical computing power, as well as to reduce costs and reliance on middlemen. Google was the first company to design and make its own microchips; however, most of the major Internet firms including Amazon, Apple, Facebook, Baidu, Alibaba, and Tencent have now followed Google's lead and are designing their own chips. This has become even more important as companies invest and compete in the burgeoning field of AI, which requires speed and massive computing power. These firms' involvement in chip and hardware making undercuts such traditional chip makers as Cisco, Intel, HP, Qualcom, and Nvidia, threatening the existence of major networking equipment vendors.[93] Given the scale of the hardware required for data centers, Internet firms have turned into big hardware manufacturing companies in their own right, independent of traditional chip industry and able to control their own supply chains.

Fiber

Data centers built with customized software and hardware do not stand alone. Geographically dispersed data centers are interconnected through the "middle mile," which connects Internet providers via several means, for example, telephone lines, fiber optics, submarine cable systems, microwave, and radio spectrum. Google, Amazon, Microsoft, and Facebook have all invested billions of dollars in middle-mile infrastructure to connect their data centers to circumvent the telecom companies, which own many of the Internet's pipes. Google is leading the pack. Google's Urs Hölzle asserted that "Google, for one, needs to double its transmission capacity every year to sustain the seamless appearance of its 'Cloud 3.0' computing."[94] Only a few companies have the financial resources, technological capability, and labor to build private network infrastructure; at the same time, there is a clear reason for wanting to control networks: the tech companies are competing over milliseconds of Internet traffic speed. Google calls this its "Gospel of Speed," a rule that it requires all Google engineers and product managers to follow: "Don't launch features that slow us down."[95] According to Hölzle, a 400-millisecond delay would lead to a 0.44 percent drop in search volume,[96] while Amazon found that 100 milliseconds in latency would cost 1 percent of its sales.[97]

Early on, Google understood that network infrastructure was critical for it to process the yottabytes of data that the company handles on a daily basis. Since 2005 it has been aggressively acquiring "dark fiber," the unused underground cable left dormant by the dot-com crash of the late 1990s and early 2000s, or constructing private fiber-optic cables exclusively for its data center connectivity on land. In 2013 the *Wall Street Journal* reported that Google owned or controlled more than one hundred thousand miles of fiber-optic cable globally—compare that to Sprint, one of the largest global network operators, which controlled less than forty thousand miles at that time.[98] Google's private backbone network has thousands of miles of fiber-optic cables that connect its data centers. Hölzle has said that Google built the world's largest network, delivering 25 percent to 30 percent of all Internet traffic.[99] Facebook, Microsoft, and Amazon have also laid cables or bought dark fiber in addition to leasing network capacity. In 2018 Facebook revealed that it had deployed a new high-capacity underground cable in its Los Lunas, New Mexico, data center to diversify its flow of data routes.[100] In fact, Facebook created a subsidiary called Middle Mile Infrastructure to sell its unused network capacity to local and regional telecoms, moving into the wholesale fiber market as it invested in fiber-optic routes with direct connectivity between its data centers in Ohio, Virginia, and North Carolina.[101] In Indiana, the company has run fiber optic cables across the entire state and reaches to the border of Ohio.

Terrestrial fiber-optic cables are not sufficient to cover the global market, given that oceans cover 70 percent of the planet. The tech giants, therefore, have to go under water, resorting to a nineteenth-century technology—submarine cables—to reach and connect global markets. Submarine cables carry 99 percent of international Internet traffic and are the main conduits for intercontinental information flow including financial data. Submarine cables function as global economic nerve systems, illustrating the expansionary dynamism of digital capitalism. The Brussels-based Society for Worldwide Interbank Financial Telecommunication transmits forty-one million financial messages per day to more than eighty-three hundred banking and security institutions and corporate customers in more than 208 countries via submarine cables.[102] Ten trillion dollars' worth of global financial transactions go through the cables daily.[103] The global economy thus hinges on the undersea network infrastructure that was initially developed and constructed by various colonial powers to connect and control their territories.[104] Submarine cables are concentrated in the Atlantic Ocean, but there has been a rise in new submarine cable routes to Asia, Africa, and Latin America as Internet traffic rapidly expands in those regions. Over the period 2017–2022, the Asian Pacific and North American regions together were expected to account for about 70 percent of all traffic.[105] The Middle East and Africa are closing this gap. They account for only 10 percent of total traffic, but they are the fastest-growing regions with a growth rate of 41 percent per year.[106] In response to a compounded annual growth rate of 26 percent of global IP traffic overall from 2017 to 2022, new submarine cables were rapidly deployed to facilitate planetary digital capitalism.[107]

Google, Amazon, Microsoft, and Facebook have emerged as major new players in the construction of submarine cables. This is hardly a surprise considering that these four companies consume more than half of submarine cable capacity.[108] Less than a decade ago Internet firms used less than 10 percent of cable capacity; in 2020, they used 66 percent.[109] The Internet giants have built out private submarine cables to better control their own traffic in terms of speed and have determined locations and routes to connect because they require expansive network capacity to coordinate data flows between their geographically dispersed global network of data centers.

By their very nature, submarine cables are capital-intensive infrastructure projects; thus, many companies have joined consortia comprised of groups of private firms to build cables and share network capacity. Roughly 90 percent of submarine cables are funded privately. [110] Today's major involvement of private capital in the construction of submarine cables rather than state telecom carriers is the result of the deregulation that accompanied the ascendance of neoliberal telecommunication and Internet policy in the 1990s. After passing the Telecommunications Act of 1996 at home, the United States had spearheaded the effort to open telecom markets across the globe and pushed through the World Trade Organization's basic telecommunication agreement in 1997, which liberalized the global telecom industry.[111] In addition to private capital, multilateral development banks such as the World Bank have also financed submarine cable projects, but this represents only 5 percent of submarine cable investment.

Recent years have seen a new trend in the undersea cable sector in which exclusive privately financed cables are on the rise, as content providers are increasingly participating in building out their own private cable networks. As of 2020 Google owned or had a stake in nineteen intercontinental submarine cables, six of them exclusively owned by Google, reaching from the United States to Europe, Latin America, Asia, and Africa, connecting to their data centers around the globe (see table 2.1).[112]

In 2018 Google began to lay out a trans-Atlantic cable connecting the United States and France. This was the first trans-Atlantic submarine cable to be built by a non-telecom company.[113] The Dunant cable launched from Virginia Beach and landed at Saint-Hilaire-de-Riez. On the US side, it is close to northern Virginia in an area called "data center alley"—the world's densest intersection of fiber networks—where 70 percent of Internet traffic is routed.[114] On the other side of the Atlantic Ocean, the cable is close to Google's Belgian cloud region, where one of its hyper data centers resides. To cover the northern part of the Atlantic route, Google and Facebook, along with Irish firm Aqua Comms and the Norwegian firm Bulk Infrastructure, agreed to build the Havfrue cable between the United States and Scandinavia.[115] The Havfrue cable, completed in 2020, connects New Jersey to the Jutland Peninsula of Denmark with branches to Ireland and Norway. It was the first submarine cable serving the United States and northern Europe to be built in the past twenty years.[116] And the Havfrue extension, named AEC2, links New York and Dublin with routes to England and Denmark.[117] In 2019 Amazon signed an agreement with Bulk Infrastructure for the use of Bulk's stake in the Havfrue trans-Atlantic cable.

Google's presence in the routes to Asia is undeniable, with eight cables—SJC, Unity, Faster, Pacific Light Cable Network (PLCN), Japan-Guam-Australia (JGA), Indigo, and Echo—covering most of the strategic hubs and key markets in Japan, Hong Kong, Taiwan, Sydney, Singapore, Indonesia, and the Philippines. These trans-Pacific cables were built by consortia among regional and national telecom carriers including China Mobile. As the media scholar Nicole Starosielski has documented, the private consortium model doesn't necessarily transcend nation-states, because sources of investment and landing stations still need to be negotiated between nation-states.[118] The state plays a vital role in controlling the data flow, so alliances between transnational capital and national interests are still required. These alliances, however, are not permanent. Thus, submarine cables as critical network infrastructure are geopolitical conflict points when

Table 2.1. Google submarine cable holdings

Cable	Ownership	Landing Country Stations	Ready-for-Service Date
Unity	Part	JP, US	2010
SJC	Part	BN, CH, JP, PH, SG	2013
Faster	Part	JP, TW, US	2016
Monet	Part	BR, US	2017
Junior	Sole	BR	2018
Tannat	Part	AR, BR, UY	2018
Indigo-West	Part	AU, ID, SG	2019
Curie	Sole	CL, PA, US	2020
JGA-S	Part	AU, GU	2020
Havfrue*	Part	DK, IE, NO, US	2020
Dunant	Sole	FR, US	2021
PLCN*	Part	PH, TA, US	2022
Equiano	Sole	NA, NG, PT, SH-TA, SA, TG	2022
Grace Hopper	Sole	ES, UK, US	2022
Echo*	Part	GU, IN, PW, SG, US	2023
Firmina	Sole	AR, BR, US, UY	2023
Topaz	Sole	CA, JP	2023
Blue	Part	CY, FR, GR, IL, IT, JO	2024
Apricot*	Part	GU, ID, JP, PH, SG, TW	2024

*Facebook is a part owner of the cable.
Sources: Drawn from Alan Maudlin, "A Complete List of Content Providers' Submarine Cable Holdings," *TeleGeography*, November 9, 2017, https://blog.telegeography.com/telegeographys-content-providers-submarine-cable-holdings-list; "Submarine Cable Map," *TeleGeography*, https://www.submarinecablemap.com/.

transnational capital and national interests collide. Pacific Light Cable Network is a case in point.

Amid the tension between the United States and China, the PLCN cable—a 2016 joint venture with Google and Facebook, each having 20 percent ownership and the Chinese company China Soft Power Technology Holdings, a subsidiary of Pacific Light Data Communication, owning 60 percent—was put on hold.[119] The PLCN was to be the first undersea cable with a direct connection between Hong Kong and Los Angeles, anticipating the growth of the region by further connecting Asia with its data centers in the United States. Hong Kong is the regional financial hub that links the Philippines, Malaysia, and Indonesia as well as mainland China. The US Justice and Defense Departments opposed the construction of the cable for "national security" reasons in 2020, however, and asked the Federal Communications Commission to defer permission to land the cable in the United States.[120] Google therefore had to revise its request to operate part of the PLCN cable. Its new plan would route data through Taiwan, where Google also has a data center. The FCC approved Google's revised request to operate a portion of the eight-thousand-mile PLCN, leaving the line between Hong Kong and mainland China as yet unbuilt.[121] Due to this pressure from the US government, Google and Facebook have both withdrawn the cable line between Hong Kong and China for now.

In Latin America, Google has aggressively asserted its power, along with regional players such as Telefonica América Móvil and Telxius, linking together the region where the United States and its allies have suffocated the Bolivarian Revolution and brought in the International Monetary Fund to further push neoliberal policies in order to pry open the region for transnational capital.[122] The neoliberal comeback drew billions of dollars into the burgeoning tech sectors in Latin America and, in particular, Brazil and Chile. In 2018, Google, Facebook, Telefónica Open Innovation, Qualcomm Ventures, and Telefónica OpenFuture formed the Latin American Tech Growth Coalition to attract private capital investment to the Latin American tech sector. Although it is a small amount compared to funds spent in Asia, North America, and Europe, capital investments in tech startups in Latin America grew more than fourfold, from $500 million in 2016 to a record high $2.6 billion in 2019.[123]

Google is seizing opportunities in this burgeoning market. The company has laid out four new cables—Monet, Tannat, Junior, and Curie—connecting the United States to Latin America and Africa. For Monet, Google was the main investor, teaming up with the Brazilian telecom giant Algar Telecom, the African telecommunications operator Angola Cable, and Uruguay's government-owned telecom company Antel to build a link between the United States and Brazil. The cable stretches from Boca Raton, Florida, to Fortaleza and Santos in Brazil This cable connects the growing markets of Latin America and Africa, so it is more of a long-term accumulation strategy for Google. Meanwhile, Google's first private cable, nicknamed Curie, connects the Equinix LA4 International Business Exchange data center in El Segundo, California, and the Valparaiso region of Chile, where Google's only data center in Latin America resides. This is the first submarine cable landing in Chile in two decades, and the cable has the capacity to branch out to Panama in the future.[124]

In search of every inch of land to absorb into its market as it races to new territories of profit, Google has reached to Cuba, the country that has been defying US capitalist imperialism and fighting for decades against US economic sanctions and embargoes.[125] In 2014, with the goal of promoting a "free and open Internet," Google chairman Eric Schmidt visited Cuba after touring North Korea and Myanmar with his delegation of top Google executives. Google intended to open up Cuba for transnational capital by facilitating the free flow of capital and the marketplace over the Internet. This didn't come out of a vacuum. Internet access was one of the central policies of the Obama administration in normalizing relations with Cuba. Soon after Schmidt's visit, Google was able to put its servers in the territory of Cuba to host content. The servers were part of Google's Global Cache service, which caches YouTube videos and other Google content to deliver them to local users faster. Cuba only connects to the global Internet through a cable called ALBA-1, short for Latin American Bolivarian Alliance for the Peoples of Our America, running between Venezuela and Cuba. It was built in 2010 to bypass US-owned cables.

In March 2019 Google signed a memorandum of understanding with the Cuban telecom ETECSA for a peering agreement connecting their Internet networks. This deal will require an actual cable connection in the near future.[126] It seemed to contradict the Trump administration policy that imposed a new round of sanctions against Cuba, strangling the country's economy and hurting ordinary Cuban people's lives. Google's venture in Cuba, however, was consistent with the goals of US policy: integration of the socialist economy into the global capitalist system through digital commerce. According to a 2019 report by the US State Department's Cuba Internet Task Force, it was recommended that Cuba's Internet infrastructure be improved by building a direct submarine cable between the United States and Cuba to promote unfettered Internet access.[127] Google has been backed by over seventy-five years of US government "free flow of information" policy, which was also used against the New World Information and Communication Order movement in the 1970s as a weapon to force Cuba into the global capitalist economy.[128]

Another land mass at which Google has taken aim is Africa. Often seen as a little-connected continent, Africa is increasingly turning into a new battlefield among global Internet companies. Given that fewer than half of Africans are online, the continent is the region with the highest growth potential for Internet use in the world, and Internet firms see it as a land of opportunity and a massive potential market. Google's third private submarine cable, Equiano, is on its way, linking Portugal to South Africa with branches to St. Helena, Togo,

Namibia, and Nigeria, the first African country where Google rolled out WiFi hotspots.[129] This is Google's first cable to stretch from Europe to Africa, opening up the spigot of capital flow into Africa.

Facebook is not far behind Google. The company is part of a consortium composed of units of China Mobile Ltd., MTN Group Ltd. (South Africa), Orange SA (France), Saudi Telecom Co., Telecom Egypt, Vodafone Group PLC (United Kingdom), and WIOCC, which is owned by fourteen African telecom carriers. The consortium is constructing a megacable, 2Africa, originally called Simba, which stretches twenty-three thousand miles to cover the entire continent, with routes to Europe and the Middle East.[130] According to a 2019 Telegeography report, Facebook was part of ten submarine cable projects in Asia, Europe, and Latin America.[131] In Latin America, Facebook funded a twenty-five-hundred-kilometer submarine cable called Malbec connecting Buenos Aires, Argentina, with São Paulo and Rio de Janeiro, Brazil, and stretching to the Brazilian city

Table 2.2. Facebook submarine cable holdings

Cable	Ownership	Landing Country Stations	Ready-for-Service Date
APG	Part	CN, JP, KR, MY, SG, TW, TH, VT	2016
Marea*	Part	ES, US	2018
Jupiter**	Part	JP, PH, US	2020
Havfrue	Part	DK, IE, NO, US	2020
Malbec	Part	AR, BR	2021
SJC 2	Part	CH, JP, KH, KR, SG, TH, TW, VT	2022
Amitie*	Part	FR, UK, US	2022
CAP-1**	Part	PH, US	2022
PLCN	Part	PH, TA, US	2022
Echo	Part	GU, IN, PW, SG, US	2023
2Africa	Part	AO, BH, CD, CG, CI, DJ, EG, ES, FR, GA, GH, GR, IN, IQ, IT, KE, KM, KW, MG, MZ, NG, OM, PK, PT, QA, SA, SN, SC, SD, SO, TZ, ZA	2023
Apricot	Part	GU, ID, JP, PH, SG, TW	2024
Bifrost	Part	GU, ID, PH, SG, US	2024
BtoBE	Part	CN, MY, SG, US	withdrawn
HKA	Part	CN, TW, US	withdrawn

*Microsoft is part owner of Marea and Amitie.

**Amazon is part owner of Jupiter and CAP-1.

Sources: Drawn from Alan Maudlin, "A Complete List of Content Providers' Submarine Cable Holdings," *TeleGeography*, November 9, 2017, https://blog.telegeography.com/telegeographys-content-providers-submarine-cable-holdings-list; "Submarine Cable Map," *TeleGeography*, https://www.submarinecablemap.com/.

of Porto Alegre.[132] The cable was built in partnership with a private company called GlobeNet, which is part of the Brazilian finance company BTG Pactual.

To cover the Atlantic Ocean, Facebook joined Microsoft and Telefonica's Telxius to build the MAREA cable, with termini at Virginia Beach, Virginia, and Bilbao, Spain. Both Facebook and Microsoft have cloud data centers located in Virginia, and these centers link to Bilbao, which is on a strategic path to network hubs in Africa and the Middle East. In Asia, Facebook is racing against Google, with five cables in the region: the Asia Pacific Gateway (APG), Bay to Bay Express (BtoBE), Southeast Asia-Japan Cable 2 (SJC2), Jupiter, and Hong Kong-Americans (HKA). Eventually, BtoBE and HKA were canceled due to US government pressure. These cables connect to Japan, Taiwan, the Philippines, Singapore, Thailand, and Malaysia, circling East and Southeast Asia. Amazon is also part of the BtoBE and Jupiter Cable System consortia, but separately Amazon invested in the consortium that built the Hawaiki Submarine Cable, which links Oregon, Hawaii, Australia, New Zealand, and American Samoa. The state of Oregon has a heavy concentration of submarine cable landing stations because of its geographical proximity to both Silicon Valley and Los Angeles and to the Pacific rim.[133]

These newly emerging submarine cables built by the large Internet firms are strategically laid around the major global nodes, linking data centers to data centers to entwine the global market. The size and capacity of these networks is almost compatible with tier one Internet backbone companies, so they are even able to exchange traffic without extra cost and more quickly deliver traffic close to their users. These companies' hyper data centers and massive private backbones of terrestrial and submarine cables combine to form these firms' cloud networks, which consist of points of presence (POP), edge nodes, content delivery network locations, and dedicated Internet locations.

According to Google, the company has over ninety Internet exchange points where Google's backbone connects with other network operators via peering.[134] The company has more than seventy-five hundred edge nodes around the globe where Google caches its content on its servers, hosted in local ISPs, to speed up delivery of content and services.[135] This is possible because Google has a backbone infrastructure large enough to allow network traffic exchange with other tier one network providers[136] as well as the ability to leverage its heavy traffic with local ISPs where Google can cache its content in order to realize efficiencies of localized data in its network and servers. Google operates its Cloud Content Delivery Network, which has more than one hundred cache sites across major metropolitan areas to serve out services and applications more quickly and reduce costs.[137] Amazon and Microsoft have organized themselves similarly. Amazon's infrastructure is made up of different geographical regions divided into availability zones. Amazon has a network of 190 points of presence and 179 edge locations in 72 cities across 33 countries,[138] and Microsoft has 54 regions in 140 countries.[139] These Internet companies not only own their backbone infrastructure but also operate and control the largest agglomeration of smaller infrastructures. They are building the privatized Internet.

Last Mile

Although building out their own network infrastructures for internal operations and data center connectivity is vital, it is also important for Internet firms to connect to end users for the consumer side of their business. Completing the last mile is the precondition for any consumer Internet business. Thus, Internet firms have been advocating for ultrafast fiber-optic networks to speed up the last mile using such PR façades as the "digital divide," "equal access," and the "digital revolution." This seems outwardly to be an extremely thoughtful gesture, but these companies are actually motivated by corporate self-interest. The more access to high-speed Internet is available, the more Google is queried, the more YouTube videos are viewed, the more apps are used, the more Amazon orders are placed, and the more Facebook images are liked—all of which mean more revenue for these companies.

In 2010 Google ambitiously launched its Google Fiber project with the promise of providing free Internet access to consumers up to five Mbps, and one gigabit per second for $70 per month, which was one hundred times faster than the average US broadband service.[140] Google first rolled out the service in Kansas City, Kansas, and Austin, Texas (heavily subsidized by the municipalities themselves, it must be noted) and subsequently in six other US cities.[141] One of the reasons behind Google's venture was to spur the telecom and cable industries to improve their broadband offerings and enhance broadband speeds and penetration. All of this is necessary for Google to expand its wide-ranging services, which require fast and widespread broadband infrastructure to incentivize their adoption and use.

Seven years later Google abandoned the project because it realized that laying out actual pipes consumes enormous amounts of capital and has a slow rate of return. As the legal scholar Susan Crawford pointed out, last-mile access was a capital-intensive project requiring a long-term investment, but Google's shareholders weren't willing to wait; they wanted to see a return on investment sooner.[142] Google fiber was also often delayed, since the company needed permission to access local utility poles that were already being used by incumbent telecom companies such as AT&T and Comcast. The former sued the city of Louisville for allowing Google to install its wires and temporarily move existing AT&T wires without prior consent to create space for new ones.[143] This legal process was used by telecom companies to slow down the Google Fiber project. In August 2018 the FCC approved a rule known as One Touch Make Ready, allowing Google Fiber and other ISPs to install their wires on utility poles without waiting for incumbent telecom companies to move their wires. This was too late for Google because the company had already begun phasing out the project.

Google's entry into the realm of the telecom industry nonetheless fueled the broadband war. Google Fiber had been a direct challenge to such telecom giants as AT&T, Verizon, and Comcast, who had long battled over Internet services to generate more profit from their infrastructures. To a certain extent, Google's initial goal had been achieved because it pressured the incumbent telecom behemoths to invest more in their infrastructures to support high-speed Internet.[144] Meanwhile, Google's retreat from its fiber project didn't mean that the last mile was no longer in the company's interest. Google was and is searching for alternative technologies for its last-mile connections and has pivoted its strategy to wireless broadband. In 2015 Google acquired Webpass (now called Google Fiber Webpass), a wireless home broadband company offering wireless Internet services in several metro areas. Google also experimented with millimeter wave technology, which uses the radio spectrum between 30 GHz and 300 GHz for 5G wireless Internet access.

Google continues on its quest for alternative last-mile technologies that don't require laying down capital-, labor-, and time-intensive fiber-optic cables. Meanwhile, instead of building its own network, Google decided to piggyback on unused networks of other mobile carriers such as like Sprint, and T-Mobile. Google operates its own mobile virtual network operator called Google Fi (nee

Project Fi). Google Fi automatically configures and switches to the strongest mobile network and provides a low-cost wireless service while also avoiding competition with traditional phone companies.

Google's pursuit of last-mile connectivity goes well beyond the United States since the company is eager to capture the entire global population. In order to reach "the last billion,"[145] Google has experimented with a range of Internet technologies in remote areas of the world where little affordable network infrastructure is available. In 2013 Google embarked on its Loon project, which worked on last-mile solutions to rural and remote areas of the world including Kenya, Peru, and Puerto Rico. The idea was to use high-altitude balloons to beam Internet signals into such regions. Google also signed a commercial deal with Telkom Kenya and established several ground stations in Nairobi and Nakuru. However, after almost ten years Google walked away from the project, not because there were no longer social needs but because it was "commercially not viable." Although Google withdrew from Loon, its wholesale broadband infrastructure project, the Csquared urban network project is still operating in Uganda, Ghana, and Liberia with funding from ICT investment companies Convergence Partners, Mitsui, and the International Finance Corporation, which is part of the World Bank Group.

Meanwhile, Facebook raised its flag of "universal Internet access." Facebook's stated plan is to wire the world, as the company is betting on bringing fiber-optic cables to Africa to connect more than one billion people to the Internet. The company, along with the Indian telecom giant Airtel and African carrier/operator BCS, laid five hundred miles of terrestrial fiber across the East African country of Uganda.[146] Also, aiming at the end users of the global South, Facebook pushed out Free Basics, previously called Internet.org, to provide limited Internet access to selected sites including Facebook, news, weather, employment, health, local government information, and education for free through local telecom operators. This program was quickly and roundly criticized, however, for feeding corporate content focused on the West and violating net neutrality.[147] In India, the program was banned by the Telecom Regulatory Authority in response to pressure from net neutrality advocates and other civic groups. This didn't hinder Facebook and in 2016 the company launched Express Wi-Fi for low-cost Internet access, partnering with local ISPs to offer hotspots in India, Indonesia, Kenya, Nigeria, and Tanzania.

Google and Facebook have received much attention for their global ambitions, but Microsoft is also quietly investing in various last-mile technologies in the United States and the global South. Microsoft has deployed its well-known liberal capitalist philanthropy, which is designed to favor capital by committing to market-based social investments.[148] As part of its Affordable Access Initiative, Microsoft has given out grants and free software to businesses that work on last-mile access technologies. It is also pursuing the white space on the television spectrum to connect rural parts of the United States, utilizing unused television airwaves in the 600 MHz frequency. Microsoft demanded that the FCC relinquish the unlicensed spectrum for free.[149] This has become known as the Rural Airband initiative, currently operating in several states. Google's fiber venture faced opposition from telecom companies; Microsoft's use of the television spectrum for broadband has drawn opposition from the National Association of Broadcasters. Outside the United States, Microsoft teamed up with local ISPs across Latin America and Sub-Saharan Africa to launch its Airband initiative, pushing to open up white spaces on the television spectrum in those countries as well and asserting that it planned to connect forty million people to the Internet by 2022.[150]

This quest by Internet firms to bring the next billion Internet users online has been enshrined in public relations language as improving people's livelihoods and providing technological opportunities. But in actuality, they are building infrastructures of control by paving, mapping, and interconnecting territories of profit where people's economic, social, cultural, and political lives depend on private network infrastructure and marketplaces.

By way of illustration, in 2015 Google was restructured as Alphabet. In his Alphabet announcement letter, Google co-founder Larry Page stated:

> What is Alphabet? Alphabet is mostly a collection of companies. The largest of which, of course, is Google. This newer Google is a bit slimmed down, with the companies that are pretty far afield of our main Internet products contained in Alphabet instead. What do we mean by far afield? Good examples are our health efforts: Life Sciences (that works on the glucose-sensing contact lens), and Calico (focused on longevity).[151]

In Google's 2021 annual report, "Other Bets" was once described as "Far Afield"—the rest of Alphabet apart from Google—on which Alphabet spends hundreds of millions of dollars outside the traditional information sectors.[152] Other bets span Google's venture arm GV, its self-driving car Waymo, and its life science subsidiary Verily. These "other bets" often started off as Google's

"Moonshots" or Google X projects. In 2019 Google's other bets caused a $1.3 billion operating loss, and Google's investors wanted to see a quicker return on investment. But the company has sufficient financial and infrastructural backing to take a short-term loss in the interest of its potential long-term profit-making. Google's other bets illustrate a new wave of global capitalist restructuring as it enters a broad range of major industrial and service sectors including automobiles, agriculture, health, life science, and education by further incorporating digital technologies and morphing them into their profit sites.

As capitalism continues to incorporate digital technology, driving a new cycle of accumulation, Internet companies are not vying over the tech sector only. Google's competitors are no longer Microsoft, Apple, Amazon, Facebook, AT&T, Verizon, and Netflix; it is now competing or allying with Ford, GM, Monsanto, and Pfizer. With their industrial-sized network infrastructures, the Internet firms are leading capitalist development by accelerating the digitization of the economy, and they have driven the creation of new geopolitical and economic flash points across the globe.

Conclusion

This chapter shows that the dynamics of the Internet sector can't be sufficiently explained by monopoly capital. While Google dominates search by employing the tactics outlined above, it faces intense intercapitalist competition both domestically and around the globe. Google's control of access to the Internet through search does not guarantee its continued growth or dominance over the Internet. Thus, in addition to pursuing their own areas of focus, the Internet giants are opening new sites for accumulation beyond the traditional Internet sectors and driving the digitization of the wider economy. Google must leverage its search power, competing with others and weaving itself throughout the Internet value chain from distribution to content, hardware, software, and infrastructure, and opening new profit domains, both geographically and within and across sectors, from mobile to cloud to military and beyond the traditional tech sectors.

To facilitate their inter- and intrasectoral and geographic competition, control, and growth, the Internet companies are building out their massive physical infrastructures, reconstituting domestic and global networks. Led by Google, the US Internet companies are not only strengthening existing network infrastructure but also extending new network nodes that previously were barely connected or were completely unwired territories. In particular, the international excursions by Google, Facebook, Amazon, and Microsoft, executed alone or by the forging of relationships between them as well as with local and regional telecom companies, are building out private Internet infrastructure. Outpacing traditional telecommunication companies, the tech giants are investing a great deal of capital in building submarine cables to manage and control intercontinental Internet data flow. They are paving the way for and interconnecting territories of profit—though not without complexity and contention. The dominance of the US-based multinational tech companies of the entry point of the Internet and of infrastructure have regalvanized geopolitical and economic conflicts between the United States, the European Union, and China. The geopolitical situation is further discussed in Chapter 5.

Google's power and its pervasive competition with other capital has not only expressed itself in aggression between firms and expansion of the global network infrastructure of control but also has manifested in labor structures in the search industry. Chapter 3 will illustrate how Google as a representative of search and of the Internet sector more broadly is organizing and reorganizing labor to support the major network infrastructures, competition, market control, and continuation of growth that drive automation, fragmentation, and intensification of work and decrease real wages around the globe.

Chapter 3

LABORING BEHIND SEARCH

According to one IT industry expert, the search engine is twenty-first-century infrastructure, and "building and maintaining a search engine is so expensive and labor-intensive that it requires the same kind of planning and upkeep that, say, the Golden Gate Bridge does."[1] This statement defies the popular perception of the digital economy as knowledge-based, immaterial, and weightless,[2] and, unlike the industrial capitalist economy, needs very little in the way of human labor and low-wage workers, if the industry's mythology is to be believed.

In reality, digital activities facilitated over network technology as a social process embody human labor, and the search engine is no exception; every link on the web and each keystroke on a computer, tablet, or smartphone contains human labor. Search engine technology is so seamlessly embedded in our daily lives, however, that it masks a cut-throat competition to maximize profit that manifests itself in a whole series of complex labor processes and divisions of labor that enable and animate it. This chapter uncovers the occupational structure of the search engine industry to clarify both the social relations between capital and labor and the search industry's profitable expansion.

What are the distinctive modes and forms of labor processes and organization that assist in the search engine industry's profitable accumulation? Who is actually laboring to deliver information instantaneously and in a seemingly highly automated way in response to humans' never-ending search queries?

To answer these questions, this chapter draws on Harry Braverman's theory of labor, in which the labor process is increasingly mechanized and Taylorized as labor is broken up into ever-smaller, simpler, and more discrete tasks to speed workers up and disassociate them from the entire labor process in order to increase productivity and reduce labor costs.[3] Though new industries and new technologies require new kinds of occupations and skills, under capitalism, that does not negate the impact of the division of labor, mechanization, and rationalization that constitute the degradation of working conditions and deskilling of labor affecting all levels of workers. Braverman's concept of the degradation of labor refers not only to precarious working conditions with routinized and repetitive tasks but also to alienation from the workplace and social structure.[4] This process also involves structural displacement of labor as labor-saving technologies replace workers and create structural unemployment, which he describes as systematic surplus labor, or the "reserve army of labor" (RAL). Drawing from Karl Marx, Braverman writes that RAL is a necessity of working for the capitalist mode of production; it controls labor by increasing or absorbing the entire workforce depending on the economic cycles of expansion and contraction.[5]

The political economy and technology have changed since Braverman originally wrote in the 1970s, but this chapter demonstrates that the central features of work within capitalism that Braverman observed persist in the digital age. The chapter argues that with increasing competition and the introduction of digital technologies, labor degradation and deskilling have intensified as capital mechanizes, rationalizes, and innovates in the division of labor to increase profit. Thus, his critique of the capitalist mode of production is still pertinent because capital has continually deployed networked information technologies across economic sectors by attacking labor processes as they exist, with the aim of altering and even reconstituting everything from the sequencing of specific tasks to the technical division of labor within companies and industries to the location of production processes. By applying Braverman's work, this chapter underscores the broad occupational division of labor and the nature of work that enables capital accumulation and expansion in the search engine industry, centering on Google as a representative of the sector and the wider Internet sector in general.

The chapter begins with the changing technology sector within the broader political economy within which search is located. It shows that there is a pool of RAL in the tech industry that is the result of ongoing restructuring, technical innovation, and periodic capitalist crises and their impact on paid labor. Second, it discusses three broad categories of work in Google that not only represent the search engine industry but reflect wider trends in labor structures today. The chapter discusses Google's hierarchical occupational structure—specifically, skilled labor, low-wage processing workers, and unpaid labor. These categories seem overly simplistic, but the purpose is not to identify a comprehensive and detailed division of labor; rather, it is to draw attention to the broader characteristics of today's labor organization in the Internet industry. These divisions illustrate that, despite the industry's creating a new segment of highly skilled occupations, it also generates an extremely large segment of low-wage processing and appropriates unpaid user/consumer labor. Rather than looking at this feature as a distinctive phenomenon, this chapter locates it within the longer development of capitalism. By demonstrating how the highly automated and science- and technology-based search industry generates and relies on masses of precarious processing workers and unpaid labor for its capital accumulation, the chapter offers an unmatched window into the labor organization of the most dynamic economic sector in contemporary capitalism.

Surplus Labor

Braverman explains that the RAL, or body of surplus labor, consists of various forms—people are unemployed, underemployed, and precariously employed with extremely low wages. The reserve army of labor is a structure of capitalism that shouldn't be separated from employment given that the RAL dynamically affects the precariousness of the working class.[6] As Fred Magdoff and Harry Magdoff put it, "One of the central features of capitalism is the oversupply of labor, a large mass of people that enter and leave the labor force according to the needs of capital."[7] Capital's continuing introduction of labor-saving technologies with crises-prone capitalism expand the RAL, which has become the instrument for capital to control workers, keep wages down, and maintain profits. Looking at the pool of surplus labor is helpful as a starting point in discussing labor in the search engine industry within the broader political economy.

Five years after the great recession, which wiped out 8.4 million jobs between 2008 and 2009 (6.1 percent of all payroll employment),[8] former US president Barack Obama celebrated the nation's US economic progress and declared, "We have got back off [*sic*] our feet, we have dusted ourselves off. . . . Construction is up. Manufacturing is back. Our energy, our technology, our auto industries, they're all booming."[9] He reminded the public that the unemployment rate was at its lowest point since September 2008 and that the economy was improving. In fact, in 2019 the Department of Labor reported the unemployment rate as 3.6 percent, down from its official recession peak of almost 10 percent.[10] Carrying on Obama's economic optimism, the Trump administration boasted that this was the lowest unemployment rate since the 1960s and that the economy was booming.

Although the official unemployment rate is typically used as an indicator of the health of the economy, it doesn't offer a full picture. The official statistics conceal real counts of unemployment. The number does not account for missing workers who are neither employed nor actively looking for jobs because they are discouraged by job prospects and have given up searching for a job. If missing workers were added to the official count, the unemployment rate in June 2019 would have been 7.2 percent.[11] This was at a time when unemployment was at a record low. Moreover, there is a significant number of workers who are chronically underemployed, which is the case when workers want to work full-time but are forced to work part-time (involuntary part-time) due to economic conditions or work at jobs for which they are overqualified. These members of the RAL are often muted from the US government's official unemployment rate and the media. Thus, even before the current economic crisis was compounded by the coronavirus, the "booming economy" had never quite resonated to the millions of poor working people who were struggling to survive and being left behind.

The RAL is a constant threat to currently employed workers. Their need to compete with the unemployed keeps wages down[12] in addition to serving an ideological function for the Internet industry to serve its interests. The industry promises over and over that it will create a large quantity of good, high-paying jobs as such tech firms as Google, Facebook, Amazon, Apple, and Twitter are increasingly occupying cities and suburbs around the world with their mega data centers and shiny new campuses complete with associated amenities. Political elites and their allies offer massive government subsidies to tech firms to bring these Internet giants to their towns and cities with a promise to their citizens of economic prosperity. Meanwhile, the existing tech industry is being restructured to renew its profits as the industry faces new competition.

The Internet sector has spoken ad nauseum of its ability to create more good jobs and boost economies; meanwhile, traditional tech firms such as IBM, Cisco, Hewlett-Packard (HP), Intel, AT&T, and Microsoft, faced with competition from the emerging Internet services sector and a rapidly changing IT market, have been showing a lot of volatility in their labor forces and laying off record numbers of workers as they constantly restructure and automate their businesses. Cisco slashed 5,000 workers in 2012 and has shown only modest workforce gains since 2018 despite the rapid implementation of 5G networks.[13] Since 2011 HP, whose garage in Palo Alto is the mythical birthplace of Silicon Valley, has eliminated 300,000 jobs, almost equivalent to the populations of two Mountain Views and two Palo Altos combined.[14] Hewlett-Packard's workforce contracted from over 340,000 workers in 2011 to 51,000 in 2021.[15] Between 2013 and 2022 IBM cut its workforce from 466,000 to 345,000.[16]

As it reoriented its business toward cloud computing, Microsoft cut 14 percent of its workforce in 2014—as many as 18,000 people—mostly from Nokia, the mobile business it had acquired that year. According to the company, this was the largest layoff in its history.[17] In response, Chinese workers at Microsoft's Nokia factory at Yizhuang Industrial Park took to the streets to protest. In his public memo to Microsoft employees, CEO Satya Nadella said that this drastic change was necessary for the company to become "more agile and move faster."[18] After 2016, Microsoft gradually expanded its workforce because it had succeeded in shifting its business to the cloud.[19] While the Internet companies earned record-breaking profits during the COVID-19 pandemic, AT&T cut almost 9,000 jobs between June and September 2020.[20] In fact, AT&T, the world's largest telecommunication company, currently has 78,000 fewer workers than it had in 2015.[21] This continuing trend across the tech sector was succinctly described by Kay Roger: "Layoff is a permanent feature in the tech sector."[22]

On the surface, these frequent layoffs seemed contradictory, given that tech is the most dynamic economic sector. Yet this was indicative of an IT sector that was demonstrably undergoing a wide-ranging reorganization with the rise of new Internet businesses but was also highly uneven and volatile in terms of workforce restructuring. Also, it exhibited disparate and even contradictory trends that were deeply marked across the length and breadth of the information workforce. This permanent layoff/hire cycle constantly replenished the RAL while weakening labor power and depressing wages.

Labor as incarnated in the search engine industry needs to be situated and understood within this vortex. I now turn to an examination of some characteristic trends of the high-pay, high-status segment of the occupational structure that receives the most media adulation in the information industry in general and the search industry in particular.

Top of the Pyramid

As the Internet sector expands, it restructures existing tech sectors and generates new kinds of occupations, labor demands, and workplace structures. One of the characteristics of the labor structure within Internet industries such as search is a concentration of disproportionately well-paid and highly skilled workers at the top. As the search industry extends its profit territory to include mobile, the cloud, app development, autonomous vehicles, and artificial intelligence, workers categorized as high-skilled by the industry are computer and data scientists, software engineers, computer programmers, product managers, quality assurance engineers, machine learning engineers, and those doing similar jobs.[23] These IT workers are often said to be akin to well-paid young "Googlers" who have four-year or advanced degrees in computer science, engineering, and business, and the nature of their work has to do with computer systems design, scientific research and development, or management and business. Initially, many of them came from elite institutions such as Stanford University, University of California, Berkeley, MIT, Carnegie Mellon, and UCLA, the historic hubs of the Academic-Military-Industrial Complex. This was not surprising given that the origins of the search engine industry are within this complex, where engineers have historically had access to both technical training as well as government and private capital. Engineers, working hand in hand with venture capitalists and guided by capital expansion, have transformed search into one of the most powerful sectors of the information industry.

Google described itself as an engineering company. The long-time Silicon Valley journalist Ken Auletta has stated that Google is run by engineers: "Google's leaders are not cold businessmen; they are cold engineers."[24] These engineers, under the guidance of corporate goals, design and build search technologies to be productive and profitable. Tech firms typically do not reveal the number of engineers they have, but Google reported having 27,169 employees in "Research and Development" in 2016.[25] Although not all workers in R&D are engineers, this number indicates the scale of the company's research unit. In 2018, when Google acquired the design unit of the Taiwanese smartphone company HTC, the major part of the deal was the assimilation of more than 2,000 HTC engineers into Google—thus the portmanteau "acqhiring," a combination of "acquisition" and "hiring." To give some perspective, the total number of tenured and tenure-track engineering faculty members from across twenty-three engineering disciplines in the United States was 28,521 in 2017.[26]

This engineer-driven Internet sector has taken in highly skilled IT workers for quite a while. After the 2008 economic downturn, the worst since the Great Depression, when other established IT companies such as IBM, Cisco, and HP were shedding workers in a rapidly restructuring market, Google announced that it added more than 4,500 workers in 2010 in engineering and sales and recruited more than 6,200 workers in 2011.[27] In that year, when other tech firms were still trying to recover from the recession, Google's workforce increased by 33 percent, or more than 8,000 employees.[28] Facebook, Apple, and other Silicon Valley companies also were on a hiring spree, and by 2016, the number of tech jobs in the San Francisco bay area surpassed the peak of the dotcom era.[29] Clearly, there was a surge in technology jobs in Silicon Valley and beyond driven by Internet firms.

This demand for highly skilled labor by the Internet companies resulted in pushing up wages for this class of young IT workers with an average age of less than thirty-five—the average age of workers at Google was thirty, at Facebook twenty-eight, and at Apple thirty-one in 2017.[30] Google's median pay package was $246,804 in 2018, followed by Facebook with a median pay of $228,651.[31] The median salary at Google, Facebook, Netflix, and Twitter surpassed that of Exxon, Chevron, Goldman Sachs, and Verizon.[32] By comparison, in the United States the average starting salary of a public school teacher was $38,617 and the average teacher's salary was $58,950 for 2016–2017.[33] Worse, when adjusted for inflation, the average teacher's salary was down by 5 percent, and in some states down by as much as 15 percent, since the Great Recession of 2008.[34]

This tells us that new Internet companies indeed create well-paid jobs; however, what is concealed is that they tend to nourish and enrich only a small cadre of very highly skilled workers by generating a relatively narrow array of jobs that require considerable education and expertise. For instance, according to the 2019 Science and Engineering Indicators, the STEM workforce consisted of approximately thirty-six million persons, representing 23 percent of the total US workforce.[35] This number includes technical jobs that do not require a bachelor's degree. The majority of highly skilled STEM jobs require at least a bachelor's degree, but less than half of the STEM workforce has a college degree. Even if all STEM workers with a college degree worked in highly paid occupations, they would make up only 10 percent of the overall workforce.

In reality, then, new Internet companies need only a relatively small number of highly skilled, well-paid workers. Compared to traditional IT companies, Google, Facebook, and Twitter didn't require many workers to design their algorithms or service-based products until they expanded beyond their core business domains.[36] In 2012, seven years after its founding, the social news site Reddit had only eleven employees servicing a site handling over four hundred million unique visitors;[37] the photo-sharing social network company Instagram, with a $1 billion valuation before it was acquired by Facebook, had a team of only sixteen to support thirty million users.[38] Thus, the perception that the tech industry creates a large number of high-level jobs does not comport with reality. In actuality, the search engine industry operates with only a small cadre of very high-skilled workers at the top. This labor structure is reflected across Silicon Valley, where Google, Facebook, and many of the Internet companies reside.

According to the 2020 Silicon Valley Index, which tracks the economic trends in the region, since 2010, although there is a slight uptick in highly skilled, high-wage occupations in the Valley, the greatest job growth was in the low-wage service and infrastructure sector, with a shrinking number of middle-income jobs.[39] The region has turned into one of the most economically unequal areas in the world. In 2021 the average annual income in the Valley was $170,000 but the average income for service workers was $31,000.[40] This disparity is not limited to the Valley; rather, the growth of the Internet industry is polarizing the entire US workforce.[41]

Moreover, even this small class of highly skilled workers is no longer insulated from capital's competition-driven efforts to cut labor costs and increase profits, with a vast global reserve army of labor resulting in a new division of labor deployed by multinational corporations and enabled by network technologies. Today, higher-skilled tech jobs such as engineering and computer programming are being automated or are outsourced to places such as India, where there is an increasingly abundant supply of lower-cost, highly educated IT workers. Tech companies are rallying together to further open and reach the global skilled labor market.

Companies in Silicon Valley have long been the most outspoken protestors against US caps on visas for highly skilled foreign workers—though they were silent while the Obama administration deported more than two million working-class immigrants.[42] Google, Microsoft, Apple, Facebook, and other major IT companies are at the forefront of lobbying Congress to reform immigration laws to increase the number of H-1B visa holders so that they can bring more highly skilled workers from other countries, if not completely remove the barriers to bringing in an infinite number of foreign IT workers.

Since the 1990s the US Department of Labor has issued 85,000 H-1B visas per year to allow foreign-born workers with specialized skills to work in the United States on a temporary basis.[43] More than half of these H-1B visas have been issued for technology-related positions. Software and systems engineers, financial analysts, computer systems analysts, and marketing specialists—which make up a large segment of H-1B applicants—are the most commonly sought after by Google, Amazon, Apple, Facebook, Microsoft, IBM, and other tech companies.[44]

In 2019, the top H-1B visa holders were multinational information technology consulting and outsourcing firms such as Deloitte Consulting LLP, Tata Consultant, Cognizant, and Infosys, as well as Internet companies such Google, Amazon, Microsoft, Apple, Qualcomm, Salesforce, and Uber.[45] Google was the fifth-largest H-1B employer in 2019, holding 9,085 H-1B positions certified by the Department of Labor. Apple and other Silicon Valley firms desperately want more access to the global pool of highly skilled workers because those companies seek cheaper and more easily disposed-of, docile workers. Tech companies have long lobbied the US government to enlarge this segment of the workforce.

In 2007 the vice president of Google's People Operations, Laszlo Bock, testified before the US House Judiciary Subcommittee on Immigration and urged Congress "to significantly increase the annual cap of 65,000 H-1B visas, to a figure more reflective of the growth rate of our technology-driven economy."[46] In 2012 Brad Smith, Microsoft's general counsel and executive vice president, said that tech companies were facing a workforce crisis because of the lack of qualified job applicants.[47] He noted the shortage of labor, pointing out that Microsoft had thirty-four hundred open positions for researchers, developers, and, engineers—an increase of 34 percent from 2011—and that the skills gap was one of the biggest problems for the company.[48] Microsoft founder Bill Gates testified before the US House Committee on Science and Technology, stating that US companies were facing a severe shortage of scientists and engineers with the skills necessary to develop future innovative information technologies. Gates asked that Congress reform US immigration policy to increase the numbers of highly skilled foreign workers to work for US companies.[49]

In 2013, publicly warning of a skills gap, Facebook CEO Mark Zuckerberg, supported by Bill Gates and Google CEO Eric Schmidt, formed the political lobbying group FWD.us to focus specifically on immigration reform and rally around bills that would serve the group's business interests. The IT sector also banded together to back immigration bills such as the Science, Technology, Engineering, and Mathematics (STEM) Jobs Act, the Startup Act 2.0, the Brains Act, and the Immigration Innovation Act. Put succinctly, the industry continues to demand that the US government intervene to enlarge its skilled labor force because the barrier to transnational mobility of IT workers can only be resolved by regulation on the part of nation-states.

But the Trump administration's draconian immigration policy complicated the US tech sector's efforts to secure and enlarge its flexible pool of labor. It suspended access to new H-1B visas and H-4 visas awarded to the spouses of H-1B holders through 2020. In response, more than fifty tech companies including Google, Facebook, Amazon, and Microsoft filed a brief backing a lawsuit challenging the ban on entry of foreign workers. During the Trump administration, there was a rise in the rejection rate for H-1B visa applicants. The multinational outsourcing firms that received the majority of new H-1B visas suffered from the declining approval rate.[50] This was one of the reasons why Silicon Valley tech companies joined the rising social movement against

Trump's immigration policy.[51] While Internet firms were willing to fight against immigration policy as it related to H-1B visas, they saw no contradiction in working with the US Immigration and Customs Enforcement Agency to supply technology to facilitate the arrest and deportation of immigrants from Central America. Shortly after the Biden administration took over in January 2021, the Trump-era rule on the restriction of H-1B visa applications was rescinded. According to *Axios*, which obtained a confidential document,[52] a group of tech industry CEOs led by Eric Schmidt and Jared Cohen (CEO of Jigsaw and former adviser to Condoleezza Rice and Hillary Clinton) made several policy recommendations to the Biden administration under the premise of competing against China. They included an immigration policy that encouraged the United States to retain and expand the number of highly skilled workers in the fields of science and engineering.[53] As of this writing, the Biden administration was seeking to allow more foreign skilled workers in the United States.

The industry has warned of catastrophic labor shortages in an attempt to increase the mobility of highly skilled labor and justify the reform of immigration laws in order to have access to foreign labor. Although firms are required to pay foreign workers comparably to American workers, in 2008 there was a significant difference in the salaries of foreign workers holding H-1B work visas and their American counterparts in computer-related occupations.[54] A 2020 study by Costa and Hira of the Economic Policy Institute revealed that all major US Internet companies, including Amazon, Microsoft, Google, Apple, and Facebook, exploit the H-1B visa program and pay their foreign workers a salary that is below the local median wage.[55]

With the increase in demand for tech workers in the growth segments of the sector, the tech industry continues to seek foreign workers to enlarge its labor supply for its accumulation projects because this global labor pool gives capital greater power to hold down salaries and also the flexibility to hire and fire employees depending on market dynamics. In addition, to expand their labor supply, corporations also exploit government subsidies as they use institutions of higher education as their training grounds for both foreign and domestic workers. Workers constantly have to adjust their skills in response to market needs rather than pursuing meaningful work that fulfills their aspirations.

As the competition between and among global Internet companies has intensified, the industry has made a concerted effort to further open global markets for highly skilled labor and reorganize not only low-wage workers but, increasingly, highly skilled workers to create a large and more casualized labor pool for its rapidly changing sector. As Biao Xiang points out, since the high tech industry was financialized in the 1990s, its value has been tightly linked to fluctuations in the stock market, making way for large-scale hirings and firings.[56] The logic of capital here is to have not only a sufficient supply of skilled labor but also a mobile workforce that can quickly "respond to market fluctuations with minimum time lag."[57] This signifies extreme volatility in the tech labor market, and there is no job security even if one is highly skilled in the information-based economy.

Does this mean that the search engine industry depends only on a small number of highly skilled workers? The answer is no.

I turn now to show some characteristic features of the information industry at the other end of the pay scale. As I will demonstrate, Google is able to depend on a small number of skilled workers not only because it is a highly automated industry but also because it has appropriated a massive pool of invisible low-wage and unpaid workers to prop it up.

Precariousness as a Permanent Feature

Braverman captured the essence of labor processes under capitalism, explaining:

> Every step in the labor process is divorced, so far as possible, from special knowledge and training, and reduced to simple labor. Meanwhile, the relatively few persons for whom special knowledge and training are reserved are freed so far as possible from the obligation of simple labor. In this way, a structure is given to all labor processes that at its extreme polarizes those whose time is infinitely valuable and those whose time is worth almost nothing.[58]

Braverman's description sheds light on the highly polarized and mechanized labor process of the 1970s, which resembles the broader organization of labor in today's Internet sector.

Until Google workers exposed the issue to the media, the company barely mentioned an entirely different category of workers toiling at the Googleplex: temporary workers, vendors, and contract workers, known colloquially as TVCs. Google hires a wide range of TVCs, of whom there were 121,000 as of 2018, outnumbering the company's full-time employees.[59] The TVCs are hired by third-party staffing firms such Adecco, Cognizant, and Zenith Talent. The common perception of TVCs is that they are part-time workers, but many actually work full-time. Using TVCs, Google is able to save labor costs such as employee health and pension plans while hiring more workers in more in-demand fields such as AI, cloud computing, and data mining. More important, given that the industry is so fast-changing and competitive, it also wants to have a flexible workforce so that it can easily hire and dispose of workers as needed. Because the pandemic and the chronic economic crises reloaded the reserve army of labor as described above, TVCs have long been disposable workers living in fear that their jobs would no longer be needed soon. In the midst of the global pandemic, for instance, Google revoked job offers to more than two thousand temporary and contract workers globally.[60]

Google's contract workers are far from a homogenous group. They perform a wide range of tasks, including working as software engineers, data analysts, user experience researchers, project managers, linguists, recruiters, lawyers, and content moderators, not to mention nontechnical workers such as bus drivers and cafeteria workers. They are dispersed around the world. Their hourly pay varies from minimum wage to $125 per hour.[61] This illustrates that not only low-wage labor is outsourced. Among this contingent and "flexible" workforce, however, is a large swath of entry-level workers who are paid minimum wage, often isolated from their co-workers or working exclusively online. This groups' much-needed work in the development of the industry is largely obfuscated by seemingly magical technology.

For years, Google has attributed the supremacy of its search results to its automatically configured algorithm. But Yahoo!, one of the leading early search engines, employed human indexers—trained librarians—to collect and organize the information on the web. Human labor was the foundation of its search business, and this distinguished Yahoo! from other early search companies. There are no longer human indexers and librarians per se because automated search engine technology has become the norm, but their work has not been entirely eliminated; rather, this automation has led to the emergence of a new class of low-wage workers who are practically interchangeable and invisible. As David Harvey puts it, "What is on capital's agenda is not the eradication of skills per se but the abolition of monopolizable skills."[62]

Some of these low-wage process workers are called human evaluators, often referred to as "quality raters" or "search engine evaluators," whose task it is to determine the relevance of search engine results before the company releases an alteration to its algorithm. The head of web spam at Google, Matt Cutt, once explained the role of quality raters in responding to the search engine optimization community, which had expressed concern that raters were affecting search results. In 2012 Cutt defended the objectivity of Google's search results and said that human raters were working under Google's Search Quality Evaluation Team only for initial testing phases for proposed search algorithm changes.[63]

Google started to advertise for quality rater positions in late 2004 and at first hired them directly, but today it uses outsourcing companies specializing in supplying a global labor pool to large multinational corporations.

With titles such as Multimedia Judge, Internet Search Administrator, Web Content Assessor, Query Understanding Judge, Ad Assessor, Internet Crowd Worker, Web Content Assessor, Internet Assessor, and Social Media Internet Assessor, these positions are advertised as flexible, telecommuting, temporary work from ten to thirty hours per week. Since the positions are often advertised as work-at-home jobs, they may target stay-at-home mothers on websites like workathomemom.com, telecommutingmommies.com, and baycenter.com. These workers make up Google's search quality evaluation team, but their salaries and working conditions are far from the idyllic conditions on the Google campus that the media touts. They are required to pay their own expenses for high-speed Internet connections and to have a smartphone and tablet and ever-changing computer technologies for their tasks. The average salary for these permanent temporary quality raters is between $12 and $16 per hour with neither benefits nor job security. The positions often require employees to have a bachelor's degree or four years relevant work experience; however, quality raters do not enjoy the prospect of moving up to a full time career at Google or other Internet companies. While their work is tightly connected to the engineers who design Google's algorithm, quality raters do not have any direct interaction with engineers or other workers at the company because they are managed remotely.

The major tasks of quality raters are to evaluate search and/or advertising "relevancy," label spam, and flag problem pages as engineers constantly tweak the algorithm. According to *Search Engine Watch*, whereas the nature of the job for quality raters is presented as flexible and self-directed, it is routinized, mechanized, and tightly managed. The raters perform their tasks according to a manual of specific strict guidelines more than 170 pages long provided by the company.[64] Google points out that the work of quality raters is far from simple because they deal with many complex cases.[65]

According to a Google rater in her 2012 interview with *Search Engine Land*, raters had to meet their productivity goals to stay on the job. She described the nature of the work and said that there was a certain number of tasks that they had to complete every minute.[66] If they fell behind in terms of productivity, they could be put on probation and could not work during that period.[67] The quality of raters' work was tracked based on staying within the time period for rating tasks and the number of tasks that had to be returned.[68] If raters' quality was not up to the company's standard, they were terminated. She offered that "it's a very controlled work environment." Given a large pool of RAL who are always waiting to be pulled into the workforce, Google can easily dispose of them as needed.

Quality raters for searches and ads are not exclusive to Google or to search engine companies; rather, they are a standard workforce in many Internet companies, including Facebook, which rely on search as a basic function in terms of access and revenue generation.[69] It is no longer a hidden fact that there are tens of thousands of quality raters around the world working for the Internet industry.[70] It is important to note that search quality raters are merely a small segment of the substrate of increasingly low-wage processing workers in the industry. Other low-wage workers include content moderators, image viewers and taggers, data labelers for AI, and speech transcribers for voice search. Mary Gray and Siddharth Suri call online process staff "ghost workers," and these are the ones who empower search engines, mobile apps, social media, and e-commerce.[71] Tarleton Gillespie calls them "custodians of the Internet" who labor behind platforms.[72] Ursula Huws intervenes and notes that this kind of work is often characterized as a typical and new kind of labor practice opposed to full-time permanent positions with benefits, but she rightly points out that their work can't be fully explained without looking at the broader changes in the labor market over the decades and separating them from the rest of the workforce.[73]

In the late 1970s, with the dawn of the neoliberal era—which Harvey posited was a project of the corporate capitalist class seeking to curb the power of labor[74]—deregulation of industries, privatization of the public sector, attacks on trade unions, and weakened labor laws began to restructure the existing working class.[75] Facing a crisis of falling profits and heightened international competitive pressure, companies embraced new electronic technologies to increase productivity and reorganize labor to ensure continuing accumulation. Companies adopted so-called flexible organization along with "lean" production to quickly respond to rapidly changing market conditions and international competition. The flexible organization combined with new technologies enabled companies to automate, standardize, and mechanize by breaking down and compartmentalizing much of the labor process. The lean or "just-in-time" production model, with extended supply chains supported by network technologies, segmented various labor forces to increase efficiency and control.[76] These factors have resulted in the growth of the flexible and contingent labor sector—temporary staff, on-call workers, independent contractors, and the like—in the production of goods and services. Contingent work is labor's version of the just-in-time inventory system for lean production: a just-in-time workforce.[77] With weakened labor power and constant restructuring of work processes with new labor-saving technologies, the postwar employment model of full-time permanent jobs with benefits has precipitously diminished; the majority of jobs being generated today are low-wage positions with few fringe benefits. This trend was reaffirmed during the 2008 Great Recession and onward.

In the "recovery" from the 2008 recession, the main employment gains were concentrated in lower-wage occupations.[78] According to a 2021 Brookings Institute report, 44 percent of all US workers aged eighteen to sixty-four have low hourly wages of $10.22 and annual earnings of $17,950 on average, nearly one-third live below 150 percent of the federal poverty line, and females make up 54 percent of low-wage workers, representing a higher percentage than the 48 percent of females in the overall workforce.[79]

Advanced networked technologies are no longer simply applied to routine tasks; rather, they are being extended across occupations such as service, media, transportation, manufacturing, retail, healthcare, and education. Networked digital tools have been deployed to further atomize tasks, aggregate individuals who connect through the network, and control them remotely across national boundaries. Huws describes them as the "automatized workforce" in which workers are made easily interchangeable and exchangeable by stripping the collective power of labor.[80] Today's Internet platforms, built by tech companies such as Uber and TaskRabbit to organize the labor market, are extensions of this trend as they intensify work and give more power to capital to control and monitor workers. The deskilling and degradation of work that Braverman noted decades ago persist today throughout the production of goods and services. A new wave of digitization, automation, and standardization is once again repositioning and restructuring labor.

By locating Google's low-wage processing work within this broader changing labor market, one can see a commonality in labor organization. Despite the seemingly different nature of their businesses, tech companies such as Amazon and Uber have a similar labor structure. Like Google's, Amazon's engineers are paid between $125,000 and $270,000, with equity ranging from $25,000 to $150,000 or more;[81] however, the companies rely on a massive number of low-wage workers whose work depends heavily on and is controlled by intricate supply chains enabled by network technologies. Amazon, trailing only Walmart, is the second-largest private employer in the United States with more than one and a half million workers, among them warehouse staff and delivery drivers. In 2021 Amazon hired 33 percent of all warehouse workers in the United States.[82] It breaks down its individual pieces of the global supply chain to speed up the delivery process, and the workers are pressured to adapt to this supply chain. The difference between Google and companies such as Amazon is that Google's low-wage processing workers are less visible because their work is dispersed over networks and their tasks are separate from the production process. Meanwhile, workers in Amazon's highly automated fulfillment centers and Uber drivers have been more visible recently because of their efforts to organize in response to exposure to extremely grueling working conditions.[83] The commonality between them illustrates the deteriorating working conditions of the working class.

This shows that the search industry's occupation structure is far from an exception or limited to the tech sector. Rather, the model is prevalent across corporate America and even public institutions, reflecting the broader labor structure in today's capitalism. The majority of tech firms have used contract workers for 40 percent to 50 percent or more of their workforce.[84] Similarly, McDonalds, Nike, and the federal government all rely on a form of precarious labor. In the federal government, the largest employer in the nation, more than 40 percent of the workforce consists of contract workers.[85] Today more than one-half of faculty positions in higher education are for part-time adjunct instructors,[86] and between 20 percent and 22 percent of workers in the National Public Radio newsroom are classified as temps.[87] As Jamil Jonna and John Bellamy Foster posit, precariousness is not new; rather, it is "a defining element in working-class existence and struggle" and at "the fulcrum of the general law of capitalist accumulation."[88]

Why, then, was Google's reliance on a large number of contract workers so surprising at first to the public and the media in the United States? This was the success of the ideological work done by capital, the capitalist state, and post-industrialists to privilege the information sector as a site of capital accumulation. They have persistently crafted a message that the new economy, built on information, is a path to prosperity for all and different from industrial capitalism, which historically profited from exploitative labor practices. Yet Google exemplifies a new information industry with the same old industrial capitalist practices.

Unpaid Labor as a Business Imperative

If the "automatized workforce" represented by Google's quality raters is at the bottom of the paid labor supporting the Internet industry, there is another category at the bottom of the bottom: a great mass of unpaid user and consumer labor. Braverman didn't explicitly address the relation between capital and consumers; however, his conceptualization of the deskilling process inscribes consumers' unpaid labor, which is enabled and expanded by automation and standardization. Anyone, including the platform's users, can perform tasks.

Internet user and consumer labor as a form of unpaid work has been the subject of numerous debates among scholars.[89] The notion of user activities on the Internet as a form of free labor reignited the interest in the theory of labor value. Christian Fuchs draws from Dallas Smythe's concept of audience commodity and argues that users as prosumers are being exploited in order to generate surplus value for the Internet and social media platforms.[90] Challenging Fuchs, Arvidsson and Colleoni posit that capital accumulation and realization of value in social media are not due to the exploitation of user labor, rather, they come from rents in a reputation-based financial market.[91] The debate revolves around the kinds of commodities and values that ad-sponsored Internet companies are producing. Despite disagreement among scholars, however, there is little question that unpaid labor rightly offered critiques of and intervention in the initial celebratory techno-utopian optimism of the Internet industry, and the debate draws attention to the role of unpaid labor in Internet companies' profit making. There is a long history of appropriation of unpaid labor by capital. Thus, it is helpful to examine unpaid labor within the historical development of capitalism and question the role of unpaid labor generally and in relation to paid labor.

Ursula Huws points out that there are various forms of unpaid labor in capitalism including domestic labor, consumption labor, unpaid artistic work for self-expression, trade, and volunteer labor.[92] It is a challenge to discern specifically how Internet users' labor is deployed in the Internet sector considering its complexity and scale. Yet Huw's concept of consumption work or consumer labor is instructive as a starting point, for it describes how formerly paid work is replaced by unpaid labor that takes place both online and offline today and directly contributes to capital accumulation.[93]

One of the most prominent examples of capital's appropriation of unwaged consumer labor is taken from the history of self-service, an increasingly common business model today. It illustrates how portions of the work processes in diverse industries have been transferred to unpaid consumers to increase profit and productivity. Widespread today, this business model goes back to the early twentieth century in the retail industry and the late nineteenth century in the fast-food restaurant sector.[94] With the expansion of mass production of food manufacturing, this business model can be seen in the early self-service chain grocery store Piggly Wiggly, established in 1916 by Clarence Saunders in Memphis, Tennessee.

Saunders at first modeled his grocery store on that of Albert Gerrard, who owned a small grocery store in California; but Saunders popularized self-service, adopting a cafeteria-style restaurant and grocery model where consumers served themselves. Saunders franchised Piggly Wiggly across the United States using his patented interior store design with its highly standardized floor plan and fixtures.[95] Tracy Deutsch's study revealed that the first principle of Piggly Wiggly was uniformity. One chain manager noted, "Every store must do everything in exactly the same manner . . . this is one of the greatest advantages of our system. Clerks, goods, fixtures are interchangeable."[96] This self-service mode was increasingly adopted in other retail stores during World War I with its labor shortages and rising labor costs, and it accelerated with intense competition between chain stores and independent grocers in the late 1930s.[97]

This adoption of a self-service model was not exclusive to the retail food industry. The Bell Telephone Company, for example, started to automate its local phone service after World War I. Michael Palm's study demonstrates that by 1930, after a long labor struggle, nearly one-third of all telephones in the United States were rotary phones that automatically connected local calls, replacing many telephone operators,[98] though the full brunt of the evil combination of automation and self-service in US telephony was only felt beginning in the 1950s and 1960s.[99] Today, the self-service principle has been diffused and normalized throughout many other retail and service industries such as home improvement, do-it-yourself furniture, banking and online banking, pharmacies, airports, online ticketing, automated phone systems, print-on-demand publishing, and post offices.

The logic of self-service in capitalism is to transfer tasks from paid workers to the unpaid consumer, allowing firms to cut labor costs. Thus, many service industries in which consumers and firms interact at the stage of production continue to make an all-out effort to incorporate unpaid consumer labor as a means of improving productivity and lowering labor costs.[100] In the 1970s service sectors in the economy were on the rise and service businesses were increasingly rationalized and standardized, mirroring the model of the mechanized manufacturing industry. The concept of the "production line approach to service" or "industrialization of service," introduced by the Harvard economist Theodore Levitt (no relation to William Levitt, whose assembly line produced the Levittown suburban housing developments) applied manufacturing logic to service industries in which processes were simplified, standardized, and routinized.[101] The adoption of this concept created the conditions to further incorporate consumer labor into the production of goods and services.

The question for capital had been how much value could be extracted from unpaid consumer labor, taking into consideration the cost of incorporating and managing that labor. Although the methods and levels of utilization of consumers' unpaid time in capital's profit-making ventures today vary depending on the business, from simply contributing comments about a service or a product to improve quality and quantity for production to completing tasks on behalf of and replacing employees, the use of unpaid consumer labor is radically increasing with the introduction of new information technologies that offer newly direct interactive links between consumers and producers. Capital continues to innovate mechanisms and territories where consumers can be plugged into the labor process. It is constantly reinventing and reconfiguring labor processes via new technologies, management skills, and business models.

What is distinctive about today's unpaid consumer labor, which is integrated into everyday activities, is that it involves the appropriation of various forms of involuntary as well as freely donated labor: usability tests, software bug reports and fixes, comment and content generation and moderation, spam monitoring, map building, translation, service rating, and providing all manner of feedback. While these tasks are not productive labor in the sense of paid labor, they contribute directly to capital accumulation by the performance of various concrete tasks alongside paid labor or in displacement of it. The search engine industry came to rely on unpaid labor as a business strategy.

Unpaid Labor in Search

As the search engine industry became automated and industrialized, the initial need for and use of human labor did not disappear; rather, it intensified and changed form, as large-scale commercial search engines predicated their business models on relying on unwaged labor as well. In the process of its expansion, the search industry has not only created low-wage labor as described above but also externalized many of its labor processes by incorporating a global pool of paid labor. Although user labor is not paid, it is visible and highly valued; in this respect, it contrasts with unpaid domestic labor, which has long been invisible despite its value to capitalists in allowing them to set below-subsistence wages.[102] Given the significant role of unpaid labor in capital accumulation, it is insufficient to understand the labor process of the search engine industry only through the analysis of paid labor. The analysis needs to be extended by relating the search engine industry's incorporation of unwaged labor and its relationship to waged labor within the longer historical process by which capital has continually sought to reorganize labor and lower its costs, among other ways by making greater use of unpaid consumer labor.

Debate about the role of unpaid labor in corporate capital's profit making has been reignited as Internet technologies have provided a ubiquitous platform on which to easily aggregate and manage the entire process for a globally dispersed unpaid user workforce. From its early stages the search engine industry viewed unpaid labor as a valuable resource and competitive advantage. As the industry developed, a range of work including content creation, usability testing, translation, map making, and data correction was performed by unpaid people that could be done by paid workers. It's not easy, however, to extract the precise part of work that is performed by volunteer unpaid labor and that performed in exchange for services given the complexity of the kinds of work involved in the search industry. Thus, the focus here is simply to highlight some of the work that is performed by unpaid labor.

In the 1990s Yahoo! was the leading search engine in the market with its web directory indexed by *paid* workers. NewHoo was launched to compete with it. NewHoo's founders, four Sun Microsystems engineers, noticed that Yahoo! was struggling to keep up with the speed of web growth and maintain fresh content to draw user traffic.[103] They recognized that building a directory was extremely labor- and capital-intensive and decided to apply the open source idea to building a web directory by recruiting volunteer workers as their main source of labor to speed things up.[104] As capitalists provided tools for their waged workers, NewHoo provided tools to their unpaid workers, who, in exchange, selected, described, and organized websites and added to the directory. By the time NewHoo was acquired by Netscape in 1998, the search engine had compiled one hundred thousand websites with the effort of more than forty-seven hundred volunteer editors, compared to Yahoo!'s seventy paid editors.[105] NewHoo sold its directory for $1 million to Netscape, which promptly renamed it the Open Directory Project (ODP). At that time, ODP already had 1.6 million entries, surpassing Yahoo! to become the largest human-edited directory on the web.[106] The major search engine companies, including Lycos, HotBot, Ask Jeeves, and Google, incorporated ODP to augment their search databases and to get fresh content, which allowed them to level the content playing field. When Netscape was acquired by AOL in 1999, the ODP was one of the key assets included in the acquisition.

Ironically, the ODP was often held up as one of the best examples of the new mode of production occurring outside the capitalist market. Yet the ODP was initially built by appropriating unpaid labor specifically to contribute to a profit-making investment rather than to challenge capitalist social relations. The ODP was firmly rooted in a capitalist market in which unpaid labor was integrated into and subordinated to a capitalist accumulation project. NewHoo was not the first or only Internet company to deploy volunteer labor to supplement paid workers. In 1994 a start-up called GeoCities was built with a business model based on "community." GeoCities founders David Bohnett and John Rezner needed a large amount of content and traffic but had very limited capital with which to build their site. Instead of hiring paid workers, Bohnett and Rezner utilized this community-based business model as a way to extract labor power from its users. GeoCities provided free web hosting, suites of utilities, and other "Geotools" to its members, who were called "homesteaders." In exchange, unpaid users created content by building websites focusing on their interests and organizing collections of member web pages by theme and subject for GeoCities, which then used members' websites for advertising to generate revenue. Contributing to the firm's success was its cost-efficient editorial structure: the most labor-intensive part of the work was performed by volunteers.[107] Bohnett touted the fact that GeoCities had seventy-five employees and nine hundred thousand editors, which meant seventy-five paid workers along with nine hundred thousand unpaid editors.[108] The volunteers didn't work forty hours per week, but their effort was nonetheless significant because it was absorbed into GeoCities's profit making. The company leveraged the content created by unpaid users to generate more market share and more traffic. In 1999 GeoCities was purchased by Yahoo! for $3.57 billion.[109]

The extensive use of unpaid labor by Internet companies went unchallenged until a group of volunteers at AOL's "Community Leader Program" reported AOL to the Department of Labor, asking the department to investigate whether the company had violated the federal Fair Labor Standards Act. They pointed out that they were treated like any other paid employees, filing time cards, working specific shifts, and so on, and therefore should be compensated.[110] America Online, the largest ISP at the time and a major market actor across the length and breadth of cyberspace, had recruited a large number of volunteers as "community leaders" to perform routine tasks such as answering subscribers' questions, maintaining chat rooms, and offering technical support in exchange for waived or heavily discounted monthly AOL connection fees. At its peak, AOL had up to sixteen thousand volunteers, some as young as twelve years old,[111] compared to twelve thousand paid employees.[112] One former executive estimated that the value of work performed by volunteers was as much as 30 percent of the company's annual revenue,[113] and *Forbes* reported that AOL saved almost $1 billion in expenses from 1992 to 2000.[114] In 2001 the Department of Labor declined to take any action against AOL, reasoning that the agency had limited resources and that it was "inappropriate" for the government to intervene in the dispute between AOL and its volunteers. Later, the group of volunteers filed a class-action lawsuit against AOL, which settled the case for $15 million.

This brief moment when the public questioned the use of unpaid work within social relationships between labor and capital quickly disappeared as the Internet sector increasingly became a site of economic growth. The deployment of consumer labor in the new economy has been described in the business literature with such neologisms as "co-creation," "co-innovation," and "democratization of innovation."[115] The definition of *co-creation* or *co-innovation* here is the creation of value jointly with consumers at the behest of capital. Leading business scholars have started to point out that the future of competition depends on this approach to value creation, one based on a supposed individual-centric co-creation of value between consumers and companies rather than company-centric value creation.[116] This approach goes beyond earlier forms of self-service such as pumping one's own gas or making a withdrawal from an ATM because unpaid consumers are now actively drawn into capital's profit-making pursuits and participate directly and indirectly in the creation of value.

The concept of co-creation was once a business mantra—"users must be treated as co-developers"—at the very heart of many early Web 2.0 projects.[117] The ubiquitous appropriation of unpaid user labor by Internet companies usually is no longer visible today; while its status as labor is effaced, user labor is hailed as typifying a supposed Internet-based culture of participation, democracy, and "open innovation." In the Internet sector today, the incorporation of unpaid labor in profit making has become increasingly standardized in improving companies' competitive advantage.

Unpaid Labor as Covert Strategic Workforce

In the case of the search engine industry, companies depend on unpaid user labor for the most capital- and labor-intensive part of their work—providing feedback on algorithms, creating content, constant testing of new products, and correcting the data in digitized content. One of the most apparent of these tasks is providing feedback on search engine algorithms. Users are unwitting co-developers with engineers, assisting in the refinement of a search engine company's core algorithm technology as they go about their everyday search activities.

On average, Google changes its search ranking algorithm five hundred to six hundred times annually.[118] These changes are based on more than two hundred different ranking factors, including user interaction/user intent, which signals Google to tune the search algorithm.[119] In 2018 Google had devoted about one-third of its workforce—around 30,000 employees out of 98,771—to research and development. This segment of the workforce has responsibility for working on the design of information systems, including its algorithm and new products and services. Along with them, Google might have approximately ten thousand paid quality raters, and an unknown number of paid usability testers, but the most significant group of workers who provide the constant feedback used to improve the algorithm are unpaid users who perform searches every day.

Algorithms are central to search engine businesses, but they cannot be effective without a large quantity of fresh content to index and deliver to users and advertisers; thus, generating original content has long been a major task for search engine businesses. For this, companies again rely heavily on user labor in creating, uploading, sharing, filtering, and commenting, supplemented by acquired proprietary content and partnering with content providers such as NBC Universal, Sony Pictures, and Disney. Take Google's YouTube site for instance. YouTube, which handles more than 1.8 billion unique users each month, is the world's largest video sharing platform and the third-most-visited site on the web after Google search and Facebook. In 2020 more than five hundred hours of video were uploaded to YouTube *every minute*.[120] Although Google doesn't disclose the exact number of YouTube staff, the unit has between one thousand and five thousand employees, according to the company's LinkedIn page,[121] and upwards of ten thousand paid content moderators[122] to deal with this huge amount of content and usage.[123]

Given the enormous scale of the site and the massive amount of work needed to improve its algorithm, functionality, and interface and to upload and filter new content, this is still a relatively small number of full-time workers. Google once admitted that it was overwhelmed by the sheer amount of uploaded YouTube content needing to be evaluated. In a rare moment of transparency, Google Public Policy Manager Verity Harding openly stated in 2015, "We do rely on our one billion-strong community to help us flag violations of our policies."[124] The filtering of media content is one of the most labor-intensive parts of YouTube's business. Since 2012 Google has used volunteers for two different tasks: Trusted Flaggers evaluate and report content that violates the site's guidelines, and YouTube Contributors look after the site's help forum and social media and respond to users. In 2018 YouTube generated more than $15 billion in ad sales. In the same year, Netflix earned $15.8 billion but spent $8 billion creating original content.[125] If YouTube had to pay its one billion volunteers, could it generate $15 billion in revenue?

With its creative deployment and appropriation of unpaid labor, Google was one of the industry's early trendsetters in co-creation. This was manifest as the company employed from its inception the so-called beta business model, which mirrors the open-source community's bug-fixing approach, in which its products are released incomplete and during development. At Google, the motto has long been "Launch early and iterate,"[126] meaning that the iteration process relies on work by users to assist Google in perfecting its products. A product would normally be tested by paid workers or internally by Googlers, but Google decided to release products that are perpetually in beta versions to large numbers of users. According to Jeff Jarvis, this was Google's way of saying, "There are sure to be mistakes here and so please help us find and fix them and improve the product," as the company monitors user activities to see how new "free" products and services are used and which features are rejected and adopted.[127] The logic behind releasing "perpetual beta" products is not to conduct a technical experiment; rather, it is a business strategy to transfer part of the work to unpaid labor.

All of Google's products and services, for instance, Google Maps, Google Translate, and Google Health tap into unpaid labor from around the world. Google has boasted that its translation service was powered by AI, but it was actually a combination of machine learning and volunteer translators. Since 2006 Google volunteers have run the webmaster forum, covering fifteen languages and dealing with fifty thousand threads per year. In 2018 Google revamped and renamed its volunteer program, now the Product Expert Program, with a goal of recruiting volunteers to run Google forums, test beta products, and clean spam on Google Maps by correcting fake listings, bogus reviews, and so on.[128] This volunteer program is organized hierarchically, from community specialist to Silver Product Expert, Gold Product Expert, and Platinum Product Expert, assigning different tasks depending on volunteers' levels of contribution. In exchange for free labor, Google rewards volunteers with "perks" such as testing Google's new products before release, direct feedback to Google employees, and having "special badges."[129]

Imagine how many quality raters, usability testers, translators, and cartographers Google would need to hire to perform these myriad tasks. Instead of paid workers, Google is using the old but familiar community-based business model. This "community" of covert strategic labor has been a vital force in the industry's profit making and development and in the transformation of search engine technologies into one of the most dynamic information industries.[130]

The appropriation of unpaid labor in capitalism is not new; rather, various forms of unpaid labor—by women, prisoners, consumers, and interns—have always been part of the capitalist system. What is new in the search engine industry is the sheer scale and range of unpaid labor taken by capital in our daily lives. An important question needs to be raised: What's the relation between paid and unpaid labor considering that within the very definition of capitalism, workers must sell their labor to the market in order to survive?

As illustrated above, the search engine industry's accumulation process relies on both paid and unpaid labor, which are dynamically intertwined. With automation, mechanization, and routinization, capital has deskilled workers, resulting in the hiring of low-wage processing workers and increasing the RAL as well as the transferring of tasks previously performed by paid workers to users. With capitalists' cut-throat competition and constant restructuring of labor for ongoing accumulation, the combination of a reserve army of labor, appropriation of unpaid labor, and new technologies is driving down wages, increasing exploitation, creating precarious working conditions, and greatly increasing corporate profits.

Several questions remain: Why are people willing to perform voluntary work for Google and the other Internet firms? Users are not merely performing work on behalf of Google's business. Their everyday information-seeking activities are also rewarding in and of themselves, providing entertainment, communication, work, and education. Given that users receive benefits from commercial Internet services, one could argue that users are willing to trade their labor in exchange for services. The question then needs to be shifted from "why?" to "at what price?" The price visitors pay to use those services is to live in a constant state of surveillance in which their moves are gathered, monitored, extracted, and analyzed for corporate gain. Is this a fair trade? The absence or lack of public information provision offers few choices for the public; however, as Chapter 1 illustrated, the choice wasn't absent, it was consciously removed via policy and capital.

Conclusion

Braverman argues that capitalism tends to deskill work so that tasks can be interchangeably performed by any group of workers. This feature of degraded work has been carried into today's Internet sector even though new kinds of skilled work are being generated. No longer are librarians cataloging websites behind the search engine; now thousands upon thousands of quality raters are looking through the web link by link. The common myth of the highly automated search engine industry is that it is generally reliant on highly skilled workers. Yet the need for and use of human labor have by no means been eliminated by automation; on the contrary, these needs have actually intensified. Google deploys an array of highly skilled and educated employees but also has legions of contingent and low-wage processing staff, unpaid users, and volunteer workers who substitute for paid workers. That is how Google and other Internet companies are able to support thousands of highly paid workers and generate billions of dollars of profit. At the same time, even highly skilled workers are not secure because the industry is constantly trying to enlarge its pool of labor through automation and tapping into foreign labor markets. Google's accumulation and growth are mainly attributable not to its algorithm but to its use of unequal, exploitative occupational structures and a large cohort of low-wage and unpaid labor.

Google is not an exception; rather, it reflects today's changing occupational structure, which is due to ongoing competition and the reorganization of labor through automation, standardization, mechanization, and declining working conditions and wages. The challenge today is not to define digital labor but to locate a new opportunity for solidarity among the fragmented working classes who are working on- or offline—search quality raters, domestic care workers, fast-food workers, assembly workers, immigrant farm workers, unpaid domestic labor, logistics workers, Amazon workers, Uber and Lyft drivers, and content moderators—within ever-changing organizations and complex social divisions of labor.

The next question to be examined is how the search engine industry controls its workers and how workers are resisting. Google's current hierarchical labor organization alone is not sufficient to generate over $76 billion in net income.[131] Google is known for its "innovative" labor management, which supposedly is participatory and democratic; however, Chapter 4 will demonstrate that it is firmly ingrained in the historical tradition of capitalist labor management built on the twentieth century's welfare capitalism and Frederick Winslow Taylor's scientific management of the workforce.

Chapter 4

DIGITAL WELFARE CAPITALISM

In March 2020, in response to the global pandemic, Google became the first major tech company to shift its workers to remote work mode and quickly announced that its employees would work from home until the summer of 2021. Google CEO Sundar Pichai wrote, "I hope this will offer the flexibility you need to balance work with taking care of yourselves and your loved ones over the next 12 months."[1] The move was quickly followed by work-at-home announcements from the other Internet companies. This was in stark contrast to the millions of service workers who had to put their lives on the line and fight to demand a $5 per hour hazard pay increase.

Google is known for its search technology, but it has also been long associated with employee welfare, freedom, and engagement. The company has represented a new corporate culture and management that has supposedly reinvented labor management, revolutionized the power relations between labor and capital, and transcended the industrial mode of labor control. This chapter looks at Google's employee relations and how the company controls and manages its workers for its accumulation project.

In the era of the industrial economy, the distinct characteristic of labor management was the "scientific" approach—or "Taylorism," after the works of Frederick Taylor—in which workers were tightly controlled and tasks were highly automated and mechanized based on time and motion studies, as their autonomy was stripped in order to attain maximum productivity.[2] In conjunction with Taylorism, industrial capitalists in the Progressive era of the nineteenth-century also experimented with industrial paternalism, also called welfare capitalism or corporate welfarism as a mechanism for controlling labor by providing welfare programs such as pensions, education, healthcare, and housing. They were intended to increase productivity, curtail the tension between labor and capital, and undermine labor unions. These were the marks of managerial labor control techniques in the era of industrial capitalism.

Yet in contrast to Harry Braverman's thesis of the degradation of work, described in Chapter 3, post-industrial theorists in the 1970s whose ideologies later became the basis for the concept of the "new" economy in the 1990s argued that the new information-based economy had brought about the structural transformation of capitalism.[3] Tayloristic and centralized labor controls were supposed to be no longer applicable because flexible organizations with workers having access to networked computer technologies undermined the logic of Taylorism.[4] In the postindustrial era, it was claimed that skilled workers would be empowered to participate in decision-making processes as they enjoyed more autonomy and flexible working conditions, leaving behind the scientific management and bureaucratic control of the industrial era. At the same time, other scholars emphasized that instead of traditional coercive means of control, new managerial practices adopted corporate culture as a mechanism of social control. According to Gideon Kunda, whose work focuses on the tech industry, corporations adopted a culture of participation, autonomy, self-direction, pleasure of work, and technological solutions as ways for workers to be attached to their work and internalize corporate interests.[5] The sociologists Luc Boltanski and Eve Chiapello observed this reorientation of the corporate value system, describing it as the "new spirit of capitalism"—an ideology that emerged between the 1960s and 1990s to justify and sell capitalism to the masses.[6]

Have the old industrial forms of labor management simply disappeared in the new economy? Are these really new managerial control techniques? And what about Google? The search company seemed to be an exception, showing the possibility of transforming capitalist labor relations by deploying new labor control systems to empower workers' voices, encourage their participation and collaboration, and give them the freedom to explore. Google's economic success was often attributed to its seeming to move away from old ways of management by wholeheartedly embracing these empowering managerial techniques. This chapter, however, challenges the post-industrial theory and argues that Google's seemingly participatory and democratic approaches to labor management are firmly rooted in the historical tradition of industrial capitalist labor control.

The first part of this chapter describes the emergence of corporate welfare in the nineteenth century as forms of labor control within which Google's current labor management should be situated. The second part focuses on Google's specific labor control techniques—modes that facilitate the expansion of capital—and shed light on how work and workers are controlled within the longer history of labor management in capitalism. It shows that, behind the façade of ostensibly worker-oriented and participatory working conditions, Google deploys traditional tactics of scientific management and corporate welfare programs that are in sync with the seemingly bygone era of industrial capitalism.

Workers' Newfound Paradise?

Organic gardens, cafés and well-stocked kitchens, swimming pools, onsite doctors and masseuses, day care, free haircuts, around-the-clock fitness centers, yoga and meditation classes, Wi-Fi–enabled commuter shuttles with private guards, and Google bikes are all part and parcel of the extensive benefits of working at the Googleplex. More than three million square feet in area, the Googleplex occupies a suburban landscape within sunny, bucolic Silicon Valley. This hardly looks like a typical workplace. For several years running, *Fortune* has named Google the best place to work in the United States, and for many young professionals the company is perceived as the archetypal idealized workplace.

With "Passion not Perks" as its motivational tagline, Google is famous for its 20 percent time program, in which its employees are supposedly allowed to spend one day each week working on projects they are passionate about but are outside their primary job duties.[7] The program has morphed over the years, and it's unclear how many Googlers actually use their 20 percent time.[8] Yet it is one of the well-known "perks" of the company's "innovative" policy. Its competitors have followed in Google's footsteps. Facebook boasted about offering free meals, on-site health check-ups, dental care, haircuts, laundry service, an art studio, and more. Apple launched its own version of 20 percent time, allowing some employees to take two weeks to work on their own projects of interest.[9] More recently, Google, Apple, and Facebook have even been offering to freeze the eggs of their female employees.[10] While this chapter focuses on Google, many of the major tech companies in the Valley and other parts of the world have emulated Google's model as they all compete over a small segment of highly desirable workers.

In the Googleplex, it is claimed, employees seem to have autonomy and are able to pursue their curiosity and inspiration as an escape from the drudgery of work. Google management has embedded the maker or do-it-yourself ethos into the Googleplex to encourage technical experimentation and play for their own sake—and has presented it as an alternative to capitalist pursuits. The company has often been portrayed by media as an intellectual playground, a relaxed and informal workplace that fosters curiosity, creativity, and innovation. It has claimed a non-hierarchical, open organization and a bottom-up approach to management instead of a bureaucratic, hierarchically controlled structure; it has hyped employee participation, empowerment, and democratic decision making. Mission, transparency, and voice were ostensibly the main components of Google's corporate culture. The firm's success has often been attributed to this unique management style. Google has long been perceived in the press as reinventing, democratizing, and revolutionizing labor management as it represented an epochal shift in capitalist development.

Google's seemingly idyllic culture and exciting working environment are unthinkable for most workers today, who are barely clinging to their jobs and face grueling working conditions and radical reductions in, if not eradication of, basic employee benefits such as pensions, paid leave, and healthcare coverage.[11] Google's showering of its workers with a host of perks, services, and amenities seems unfamiliar to many ordinary workers, and even anticapitalistic. It could be seen as a unique feature of the new economy. However, US corporations deployed similar forms of welfare capitalism in the late nineteenth and early twentieth centuries to control labor and alleviate labor conflicts driven by the expansion of industrial production. This, in turn, allowed them to avoid government intervention and curtail unionization.

The Rise of Welfare Capitalism

The late nineteenth century was an era of upheaval in the American labor movement. The rapid expansion of industrialization and the emergence of big business with the introduction of large factory systems were accompanied by bitter and intense labor struggles. With the backdrop of the two economic depressions from 1873 to 1878 and 1893 to 1897, which led to widespread unemployment wage cuts and dire conditions for workers. Toward the end of the first depression, workers began staging a series of nationwide strikes and protests against capital's vicious oppression and brutal exploitation. In 1877 the first major nationwide strike, the Great Railroad Strike, broke out on the Baltimore and Ohio Railroad and quickly spread across the country. The 1886 Haymarket incident brought together in a peaceful labor demonstration tens of thousands of overworked and underpaid skilled and unskilled workers demanding "ten hours' wages for eight hours' work" and ended with seven anarchists sentenced to death.[12] During the Homestead strike of 1892, steel workers fought a bloody battle against a mill owned by the Carnegie Steel Company, which tried to reduce wages and break the union.[13] In 1894, workers at the Pullman Palace Car Company factory in Chicago walked out after the company laid off a large number of employees and the American Railway Union (ARU), after failed wage negotiations, led a nationwide strike. Between 1880 and 1900 workers struck nearly 23,000 times, disrupting more than 117,000 companies.[14] Workers fought against corporations via unionization, strikes, sabotage, picketing, high turnover, and absenteeism; they also faced the government, which often backed the companies and sent out the National Guard to break strikes. In response to labor upheaval and acts of resistance, employers attacked labor using a range of tactics including legal injunctions, anti-union open shops, private militias, industrial espionage, strike breakers, blacklisting of union organizers, and mechanization.

In the midst of this labor unrest, capital experimented with a new kind of labor management called *welfare capitalism*, or corporate provision of welfare programs rooted in industrial paternalism to ameliorate labor-capital relations.[15] The practice emerged in the context of increasing unionization and labor resistance, the expanding role of government in industrial affairs, and workplace reforms during the Progressive era.[16] Welfare capitalism was still designed to exert managerial power and enhance production and profit, as was Fredrick Taylor's scientific management theory, whose premise was that human activities could be controlled, measured, and mechanized. But wellfare capitalism emphasized social relations and "human elements" disregarded by Taylorism.[17]

At first, corporate welfare programs were piecemeal because not all industrial capitalists accepted the idea, given that it required heavy capital investment. The historian Daniel Nelson points out that welfare programs often were introduced in geographically remote companies or in industrial sectors such as textile mills where a large number of women were employed.[18] They offered amenities like lunchrooms, social clubs, and organized social events. But there were differences in the way the sexes were treated. Female workers were not considered the main breadwinners and weren't expected to work long-term, so they were not offered pensions, savings programs, or insurance plans.[19] Welfare capitalists inscribed traditional gender roles in private workplaces as factory owners cast themselves in a parental role to "protect" and "nurture" women workers to be good wives and mothers while being wage earners and "taking care" of their workers in exchange for hard work and loyalty.[20]

Welfare capitalism evolved over time, with specifics depending on the firm and its location, the nature of its business, and the composition of its workforce.[21] In general, welfare programs became more common in large firms, which were more inclined to experiment with new labor management systems because they had financial backing, needed to manage a large and diverse workforce, wanted to improve their public image, and—most important—required a stable labor force for industrial production lines.[22] Thus, such companies as National Cash Register, International Harvester, Standard Oil, H. J. Heinz, General Electric, Western Electric, AT&T, Pullman, US Steel, Procter & Gamble, Good Year Tire and Rubber, Eastman Kodak, and Endicott-Johnson were all early adopters and proponents of the welfare approach to the labor problem. Offerings varied by company, encompassing housing, medical services, educational and recreational facilities, gardens, swimming pools, sport teams, boys' and girls' clubs, libraries, educational benefits, cafeterias, stock options, profit-sharing plans, pensions, and sick leave.

Dayton, Ohio was the early twentieth century's equivalent to Silicon Valley, generating the most patents in the United States at that time.[23] One Dayton company in particular, National Cash Register, was known for its expansive welfare programs starting in the late 1800s, established by the first corporate welfare department.[24] The 1899 *Bulletin of the United States Bureau of Labor Statistics* survey on welfare capital firms showed a glimpse of National Cash Register's corporate programs.[25] The company provided fresh aprons and sleevelets with free laundry services and equipped its workspace with luxurious restrooms and lounges furnished with pianos and couches.[26] Fresh towels and soap were provided for free, with shower facilities in each men's bathroom.[27] The company's hygiene department was staffed by a physician and nurses to provide medical aid. Its work floor was considered a model factory, surrounded by a 325-acre park and well-groomed lawn, with rooms that were well-lit and equipped with ventilation and heat.[28] The company also offered classes in English for immigrants and music classes, sewing, cooking, and gardening classes, and financial benefits including profit-sharing and paid vacations. These welfare programs became the model for many other big US corporations including IBM and General Motors. Welfare capitalism went beyond the factory floor, as well. It was not only used to stave off unionization and buy workers' loyalty but also was appropriated for public relations in order to appeal to and appease the public and the government.

In the last quarter of the nineteenth century, as big corporations grew and accumulated enormous wealth and power by controlling markets, exploiting workers, and influencing government in the United States, reform-minded journalists—nicknamed "muckrakers"—and other social reformers began to expose to the public these companies' monopolistic and illegal business practices, abusive treatment of workers, and abhorrent working conditions. Under this scrutiny, it was important for corporations to garner public support in order for them to retain workers, maintain their power, and deflect government regulations. Thus, companies sought PR strategies to create positive images by distributing company magazines lavishly covering their welfare work and sponsoring tours to bring influential academics to their plants.[29] To assuage the public, many corporations extended their welfare programs by building urban parks, town centers, city gardens, and public recreational facilities and participated in neighborhood planning.

Welfare capitalism began to spread more widely in the early twentieth century as national organizations like the National Civic Federation and the League of Social Service promoted the programs.[30] The National Civic Federation, in particular, which included corporations, conservative unions, social reformers, politicians, and academics, established a committee on welfare work in an attempt to systematize welfare programs across industrial sectors.[31] Moreover, institutions of higher education including Bryn Mawr, Smith College, and Yale University began to offer courses on the subject such as "Industrial Service Work" and professionalized welfare work.[32] By 1916, 150 schools offered similar classes related to welfare services.[33] Welfare capitalism was also wrapped up in an Americanization effort intended to assimilate large numbers of immigrants into the US workforce. The Ford Motor Company was an exemplar that developed welfare programs as a way to manage the cheap foreign workers who mended its machines—71 percent of Ford's workers were immigrants, primarily Russians, Romanians, and Austro-Hungarians.[34] The company had consistently suffered from a high workforce turnover rate; Ford's plant in Detroit had a rate of 370 percent in 1913, and sometimes workers simply walked off the job.[35] This frequent turnover was costly to Ford. To stabilize and retain its workforce and increase productivity, the company experimented with internal welfare programs in an effort to solve the human elements, the "labor problem." It extended control of labor processes beyond the factory floor by instituting programs such as savings options, healthcare, and profit-sharing.

One of Ford's most famous programs was the five-dollars-a-day plan, with a reduction of the working day from nine hours to eight, which shocked the world because it was double the average wage at that time, making Ford workers better paid than those in any other industry. But the five-dollar-a-day program wasn't company largesse; rather, it served two functions, both aimed at solving capital's immediate problems. Because mass production requires mass consumption, raising workers' wages was a way to generate higher consumption of automobiles. The other function of the program was to discipline and control workers' behavior so they would be docile on the shop floor and beyond.

Historian Stephen Meyer recounts that the five-dollars-a-day wage was not given to workers as fair pay; rather, it was used as a reward system to motivate them and intervene in their private lifestyles to ensure that they fit into the mechanized work environment for mass production.[36] Employees had to change their behaviors and qualify to earn five dollars per day by meeting particular behavioral criteria established by the company.[37] In order to tackle these tasks, Ford established a Sociological Department at its Highland Park facility in Detroit, where the company conducted investigations on workers, monitoring and detailing their private lives. By 1919 the department had hired hundreds of investigators who visited workers' homes, talked to workers, and documented their spending habits, cleanliness, and sobriety, among other personal details.[38] The Sociological Department used those data to determine eligibility for the five-dollars-a-day program. As Meyer observed, Ford extended its management beyond the shop floor to impact broader social and cultural values and behavior.[39] Although Ford was an example of the times, it was not uncommon for welfare capital firms to use cultural and social values such as family, good morals, individual responsibility, and thrift to discipline their workers.

As capital extended its control to workers' social and private lives and recognized the "human element," there was increasing interest in applied social and behavioral science on the part of corporate America to understand the conditions under which workers could be more efficient and productive. In the highly influential experiments, conducted in the 1920s at the Western Electric Company's Hawthorne plant in Cicero, Illinois, social science was applied to the factory floor and industrial relations to investigate the relationship between productivity and working conditions.

Western Electric was one of the leading companies to endorse welfare capitalism early on, and it refined its approach over time. Beginning in the early twentieth century, the company gradually extended its welfare programs: It offered a pension system, stock options, and a benefits package; opened a hospital and medical department; and established the Hawthorne Club as the center of workers' social activities, with concerts, classes, sports competitions, a club store, and beauty contests.[40] To administer and manage these various programs, Western Electric established a centralized personnel management department akin to today's human resource department. By formalizing a personnel management unit that dealt with discharge, promotion, and benefits, the company was able to exercise bureaucratic power over a large workforce. The emergence of personnel management was one of the essential features of welfare capitalism.[41] Western Electric's Hawthorne plant was one of the sites of new systematic experimentation in human relations.

The company brought in Harvard University professor Elton Mayo and his research team, including Fritz Roethlisberger of Harvard Business School and Clair Turner of the Biology and Public Health Department at MIT, to conduct research on a team of six female relay assemblers under various working conditions over a period of time. Richard Gillespie relates that Mayo's research was funded by Western Electric, AT&T, Rockefeller Foundation grants, and the National Research Council.[42] The research team ran numerous experiments with variables such as illumination, rest periods, working conditions, shift hours, and length of the workday and week to measure their relation to workers' efficiency and productivity. Gillespie points out that the nature of the research was heavily paternalistic as the team also conducted interviews with female workers about their private lives and probed their physical conditions using their visits to the factory hospital to experiment on the relation between the women's personal lives and their productivity, as the researchers applied their backgrounds in psychology, sociology, and anthropology.[43]

According to Mayo's experiment, workers' productivity increased with the improvement of the working environment, but productivity also continued to increase if special improvements in working conditions were removed. Their research claimed that employees' attitudes toward work, their motivation, and their morale could be more important than their actual physical working conditions in increasing efficiency and productivity. This became known as the Hawthorne Effect, in which productivity, performance, and job satisfaction would be improved temporarily when workers felt as if they were valued and receiving attention, and that their employers cared about them.[44] This research has been credited with the development of the industrial labor relations theory, but as Gillespie argues, this scientific knowledge was "discovered" and disseminated within a network of business elites including managers, executives, and social scientists and the particular context of institutional and ideological environments in which a school of labor management was developed.[45] One of the legacies of the Hawthorne experiments was a scientific foundation for capital to move away from coercive management and unilateral paternalistic welfare capitalism and instead adopt "participatory" and "worker-centered" welfare capitalism through personnel management.

Welfare capitalism accelerated during World War I because the war effort required the maintenance of a stable and undisrupted workforce for wartime production. The government also established a Committee on Welfare Work of the Council of National Defense to pressure corporations to adopt welfare programs to ensure labor stability. During the war, workers seemed to make inroads toward exerting their power and improving their working conditions, but this did not last long. Once the war was over, many firms retracted wartime benefits at the very time when workers were struggling to retain their bargaining rights and pay for their basic needs amid postwar inflation. As the workers' struggles intensified, corporations revived their welfare programs to undermine labor's organizing efforts and state welfare programs. Sean Dennis

Cashman documented that, according to the Bureau of Labor Statistics, in 1919, 375 of 431 firms provided various types of medical services, 265 had a hospital, 75 had pension benefits, 80 offered disability benefits, and 152 were equipped with recreational facilities for their workers.[46] In the 1920 survey, 50 percent of 1,500 of the largest US companies had established comprehensive welfare initiatives.[47] This boost in welfare programs also stemmed from and was spurred by the 1917 Russian revolution, as capital feared the possibility of proletarian revolution in the United States.[48]

Along with beefing up welfare, capital also launched repressive open shop campaigns led by the National Association of Manufacturers (NAM) to weaken and break unions across the country. The association mobilized around the slogan of the "American Plan," which claimed that unionization was un-American, and required workers to sign agreements that they would not join a union—the so-called yellow dog contract.[49] The National Association of Manufacturers, along with the US Chamber of Commerce, sought to make the American Plan appealing to the public as they attacked labor. Corporate America deployed a mixture of tactics including both carrots and sticks to promote its interests, and unions began losing ground. The brutality and repression of industrialists against labor were well exposed later by the La Follette Committee's investigation of workers' civil liberties from 1936 to 1939.[50]

The Great Depression of the 1930s brought about a resurgence of labor militancy along with the involvement of the federal government in backing welfare programs as part of New Deal reforms. Some historians argue that welfare capitalism disappeared because of the Depression,[51] but Sanford Jacoby points out that it was simply reshaped in response to the labor movement and political and economic conditions.[52]

Facing the collapsing economy and pressure from labor insurgency, Franklin D. Roosevelt and his New Deal coalition embarked on economic relief programs and became involved in providing state welfare. Far from the radical structural reforms that workers were demanding, the New Deal established a foundation of state welfare programs that later interlocked with corporate welfare programs.[53] Roosevelt's New Deal introduced a number of social policies including the Social Security Act of 1935, followed by the National Labor Relations Act of 1935, also known as the Wagner Act, which gave workers the right to organize, made company unions illegal, promoted fair labor standards, and instituted unemployment compensation, public pensions for the elderly, and a federal minimum wage.

Under the Wagner Act, a range of workers' benefits could now be negotiated via collective bargaining over wages, hours, and working conditions, and the government began to expand state-financed welfare programs. The act had provided a legal platform for the mobilization of workers and union drives by the newly formed Committee for Industrial Organization, which was actively organizing both semi- and unskilled workers, who increasingly replaced skilled craftsmen, under the slogan of "one big union" in industrial factories.

But American business aggressively lobbied to overturn the Wagner Act, and soon after World War II Congress passed the 1947 Taft-Hartley Act to modify the Wagner Act and restrict the power of organized labor, despite labor's mobilization against the Taft-Hartley Act. With Taft-Hartley, non-union companies expanded welfare capitalism as they tried to defeat the new union-organizing drives and compete for worker loyalty. Sanford Jacoby notes that such major firms as Eastman Kodak, Sears Roebuck, Procter & Gamble, DuPont, and IBM refashioned their welfare programs as they competed against unions for worker loyalty, promoting the mutual interests of capital and labor as an alternative to unionism.[54] This new phase of welfare capitalism, supplemented by government welfare programs, was distinct from earlier versions as capital sought to establish a "kinder, gentler sort of paternalism" which emphasized consent rather than control.[55] Although the labor movement grew more militant during the 1950s and 1960s, the private welfare system was sustained by US companies as a tactic to stifle unions. As Jacoby points out, welfare capitalism had to be reshaped between 1930 and 1960 to grapple with both industrial unionism and ascending state welfare programs. In the 1980s and 1990s, spurred by the decline of labor power, global competition, and political economic changes, welfare capitalism once again changed as US businesses deskilled, eliminated, and offshored jobs, demonstrating that "we care" was merely a public relations gimmick used to bolster the public image of the corporations rather than a real change in capital-labor relations.

With this as historical backdrop, the Internet industry exists within a largely union-free environment in the Valley,[56] but it has revived welfare capitalism. Specifically, Google's renewal of welfare capitalism needs to be contextualized and resituated within the long history of corporate welfare as a form of labor control.

Welfare Capitalism 2.0

With growing competition and rapidly changing markets and technologies in the search engine industry, it is vital to have a steady stream of engineers and other professionals who may be tasked with immediate and strategically imperative work objectives. Boltanski and Chiapello describe this group of workers as "cadres": young, educated technical experts of high social status "whose support for capitalism is particularly indispensable for running firms and creating profit."[57] They argue that these workers "aspire to share decision making power, to be more autonomous, to understand managerial policies, to be informed of the progress of business."[58] And for many of these cadres, a high salary is not a sufficient reason to work; the work is supposed be meaningful and contribute to the greater good.[59] In the search engine industry, these cadres are a small segment of workers—including the software engineers, financial analysts, project managers, and related professionals described in the preceding chapter—many of them belonging to the group of workers possessing the mobility to climb the social ladder. In order to retain them for a certain period of time and ensure a continuing supply, Google sells the values of freedom, morality, and public goods as a labor management and accumulation strategy.

Describing itself as "organizing the world's information," Google has long asserted that "you can make money without doing evil"[60] and triumphantly presented its endeavor as a worthwhile alternative career opportunity. Its slick leaders, Larry Page, Sergey Brin, and Eric Schmidt, have public images that are far from tyrannical. They are portrayed more as freedom fighters who challenge and revolt against oppressive regimes such as China and Cuba (as defined by the US government). For young elites, working for such a search engine firm, whose main business is information access, this seems to offer an uncompromised opportunity in which working for capital and pursuing the public good are—for once—mutually and completely compatible. With the rhetorical façade of democracy, freedom of information, and human rights, Google has developed global common values that not only motivate and drive its employees but also extend outward to attract intellectuals, activists, and the public to sympathize with its enterprise. Initially, Google's logic was that when its employees internalized these values Google would have no need to use strict management techniques. As Richard Edwards points out, "The most sophisticated level of control grows out of incentives to workers to identify themselves with the enterprise, to be loyal, committed, and thus self-directed and self-controlled."[61]

Unlike industrial factories that exploit every ounce of a worker's labor to increase profits, Google's management approach has often been praised for the utmost care shown for its employees as well as the common good. The company has long been known for taking care of its workplace and everything within its employees' lives, from meals to laundry to death benefits that include paying the spouse or domestic partner of the deceased 50 percent of his or her salary for ten years. The question raised at this point is: If the nineteenth century's corporate welfare program was created to control labor, curtail labor unions and government intervention, and prevent proletariat revolution, then what is the motivation behind Google's renewing and expanding employee benefits when there are few labor unions and scarce threats of government intervention? Why do companies like Google spend so much money on employee benefits? Some might think that the exploitative nature of the capitalist system has given way and that in the new economy a benign capitalism is truly possible. Yet Google's management techniques illustrate that the new economy carries characteristics of a supposedly bygone era of welfare capitalism. Why? In response to what threat or compulsion? The answer lies in history.

A century ago, National Cash Register president John Patterson, in reference to his company's welfare program, explained, "It pays."[62] Similar practices have been paying off for Google. Its employees are 40 percent more productive than those in the average company.[63] Laszlo Bock, Google's former vice president of People Operations, described it thus: "The important thing to note is that you don't need a lot of money to do what Google has done. If you give people freedom, they will amaze you."[64] Seemingly over-the-top lavish perks and freedom do not contradict capitalist logic; rather, they closely align with capital accumulation by bringing elites into the Google enterprise and are a successful way of hiring and managing a highly skilled workforce. Google's welfare capitalism is a strategy based on economic self-interest; it aims to secure the enthusiastic and intensive labor of the top engineers, programmers, and managers in the world—a scarce commodity easily lured away by the competition.

For instance, Google's mode of management is commonly exemplified by the company's provision of free gourmet food for its regular employees, which receives much positive press coverage. Corporate free food programs are not new; however, Google seems to have brought them to a different level by supplying executives as well as all employees with local, fresh, and organic meals cooked by top chefs and catering to the international tastes of its employees. Though it has often been portrayed as genuine exceptionalism on Google's part, the food program was part and parcel of the company's management strategy. A Google executive once stated that it was a way to increase productivity; employees would not have to leave their workplace for meals, which meant extending working hours.[65] In 2014 Google spent $80 million per year for food, but even that was a net savings. Joe Labombarda, former executive chef at Google's Manhattan office, in an interview with ABC said that the purpose of the free food was to maximize productivity and loyalty.[66] At the turn of the twentieth century, free lunch similarly embodied corporate paternalism; well-fed workers were more productive.[67] Google's free food is not a perk, it is part of a productivity maintenance strategy. In 2011 Google chairman Eric Schmidt put his management technique bluntly:

> The goal is to strip away everything that gets in our employees' way. . . . We provide a standard package of fringe benefits, but on top of that are first-class dining facilities, gyms, laundry rooms, massage rooms, haircuts, car washes, dry cleaning, commuting buses—just about anything a hardworking employee might want. Let's face it: programmers want to program; they don't want to do their laundry. So, we make it easy for them to do both.[68]

He presented this idea as if the purpose of these generous benefits was truly to look after workers' personal growth and interests, but by "strip[ping] away everything" else Google extends employees' working hours by reducing any work interruptions and stoppages. In his 2008 interview with McKinsey & Company, Inc., a management consulting firm, Schmidt also revealed how the company managed productivity and intensity of work, stating:

> You need two things. You have to have somebody who enforces a deadline. In a corporation the role of a leader is often not to force the outcome, but to force execution. Literally, by having a deadline. Either by having a real crisis or creating a crisis. And a good managerial strategy is "let's create a crisis this week to get everybody through this knot hole."[69]

Under industrial capitalism, the speed and intensity of work were coded into new machinery that set the pace of work for working-class labor. Although

Google does not use machinery in a nineteenth-century sense, it does resort to psychological manipulation—techniques of labor control stemming from the early twentieth century welfare firms.

Moreover, Google is now extending its hand over the very lives of its employees beyond its single workplace by appropriating and reshaping the environment and landscape itself. The company expanded its physical footprint, constructing its ambitious new Mountain View, California, corporate campus by adding a forty-two-acre section of NASA's Moffett Field (a former US naval air station) through a long-term lease from the federal government. In 2017 Google began to construct two office buildings totaling 1.1 million square feet for research and development. Its real estate chief, David Radcliffe, remarked that the goal was to make the company headquarters "nurturing and regenerative to the environment, provide a vibrant community and work/life balance for all."[70]

The new campus, called the Bay View Complex, opened in 2022 with much fanfare. According to Google, it is designed on the principle of people-centered sustainability—natural light, renewable power, open space, and greenery—featuring two giant tent-like office buildings with solar panel roofs shaped like dragon scales, a thousand-seat event venue, and a short-term housing complex with two hundred rooms.[71] More than seventeen of the forty-two acres of the Bay View campus are preserved natural areas with wetlands, marsh, trees, and wildlife habitat. Google employees have access to these natural places, which become part of the company's corporate management strategy: a "potential source of inspiration and education."[72] But unlike its proprietary search algorithm, the surrounding natural area is also open to the public, the perfect marriage of natural and sustainably built spaces right out of a utopian sci-fi movie. Such a sublime landscape helps conceal how Google's wealth is being generated and its reliance on exploitative hierarchical labor structures.

Google is also in the midst of seeking approvals from the city of Mountain View for massive company town plans: the Middlefield Park Master Plan and the North Bayshore Plan. Unveiled in 2020, Middlefield Park is a forty-acre project with multiple parks, retail stores, offices, and community space, as well as up to nineteen hundred residential units.[73] The North Bayshore project, Mountain View's largest development proposal ever—slated to take thirty years to complete—develops 127 acres with seven thousand housing units, three million square feet of offices, and thirty-one acres of public parks.[74] Google states that the projects are building on the principles of community, innovation, nature, and economics.[75] Yet these principles camouflage the nature of capital and labor relations in capitalism: The company is reengineering built space where workers, capital, economic and social activities, and infrastructure can be brought together to create conditions for further expansion and capital accumulation.

Google's vision is far from unfamiliar: It replicates a modern-day company town on the model of Pullman, Illinois, Hershey, Pennsylvania, or McDonald, Ohio, along with a corporate culture where there are no boundaries between work and private life and employees will have no reason to leave Google's orbit. For this reason, under the premise of a "flexible and hybrid model" and "community," the company does not need to deploy a traditional tightly controlled management mechanism to expand the boundary of work; rather, Google intends to reshape workers' lifestyles and their physical environment in order to motivate them to voluntarily put in longer hours at the Googleplex, and inscribe its corporate value.

Google's worker-centered and democratic management strategies are typically equated with its overall approach, yet this is not the entire picture. On one level, Google embraces a care-free or hands-off approach to managing its elite employees, seemingly with little direct control over labor processes, which appear to move away from industrial forms of labor control. But on another level, it has adopted, adapted, and extended a form innovated by Western Electric, a method built on science and data for managing its workforce.

Google by Design

Few would question that the search engine business is driven by data, but it is less well understood that this extends to Google's labor management and is an integral part of its organizational culture. The firm has refashioned its human resource functions, mimicking scientific objectivity by applying data across the depth and breadth of its welfare programs. It calls its human resources department People Operations (POps). According to Laszlo Bock, former senior vice president of people operations for Google, POps consists of people from three different backgrounds—one-third of the staff have traditional human resources training, another third come from strategy consulting, and the last third consists of academics from fields as disparate as organizational psychology and physics.[76] The department manages various aspects of its employees' lives and operates on the principle that "All people decisions at Google are based on data and analytics."[77] It claims to distinguish itself from the traditional human resources department in that its decisions are backed by data and science. If Ford had its sociological department and Western Electric had Mayo's research team, Google has POps, where scientists collect detailed data on workers' behaviors and activities through interviews, focus groups, ethnographies, and surveys. As Google explained on its blog in 2012, "We apply science to organizational issues as well."[78] The company thus wants its personnel staff to emulate a science lab by using methods by which everything is observed, measured, and tested. In the interest of increasing workers' productivity, POps has experimented with their seemingly mundane everyday activities—"happiness," lunch lines, and food choices.

In a 2013 *New York Times* interview, Google spokesperson Jordan Newman proudly alluded to Google's overarching management principle as "creat[ing] the happiest, most productive workplace in the world."[79] The connection between workers' happiness and productivity has been studied and broadly embraced by businesses and written about in the business literature,[80] but Google claims to establish this through data and scientific analysis. In 2006 the company created the People Analytics team within POps to observe and measure the emotional states of employees using a mix of quantitative and qualitative data analyses that dissect workers' satisfaction or "happiness" levels and link them to benefits, perks, salaries, talent management, hiring, and all other human resources issues, encompassing many aspects of employees' lives.

The tech journalist Farhad Manjoo corroborated this, writing about how Google uses its employee data tracking system to empirically quantify as many aspects of workers' lives as it can.[81] Manjoo recounts that POps even measured the employee lunch line and found that between three and four minutes was the optimal sweet spot for workers to have time to meet new people but at the same time not "waste time." He writes that the tables, which look like those in high school cafeterias, are considered ideal because the company can put employees in close proximity to each other to spur conversations and share information.[82] As "people walk down between the chairs, they bump into each other—it's actually called a 'Google bump,'" according to John Sullivan, a management professor at San Francisco State University and a workplace consultant.[83] This is no accident; it is Google by design.[84]

Google's interest in the management of its employees has even reached the level of individual diets. Jennifer Kurkoski, who has a PhD in organizational behavior and was part of the People Analytic team, had experimented with changing workers' eating habits. She explained, "When employees are healthy, they're happy. When they're happy, they're innovative."[85] Kurkoski once conducted research on how Google employees could make better food choices by rearranging the location of food, resizing plates, and replacing food containers to reengineer employees' eating behaviors.[86] The objective behind this experiment was to understand ways to "nudge" the food intake and food choices of employees. The irony was that on one hand, Google provides access to free food to increase productivity; on the other, the company has found that it needs to deal with the negative result of providing unlimited access to food at any time, namely, risks to workers' health. This seems like a benign experiment that could be considered an act of true care for workers; however, poor health also directly affects workers' capacity to perform their tasks and ultimately affects Google's bottom line. Stressing a rigorous science, Google presents POps research as transcending the social context in which powerful corporate interests are embedded in the production of scientific knowledge.

People Operations' experimentation with Google's welfare programs stretches beyond the workplace to workers' behavioral psychology. The company has probed the minutiae of diet but also tried to engineer interactions between workers and team dynamics. Bock stated, "We try to bring as much analytics and data and science to what we do on the people side as our engineers do on the product side." He emphasized that Google even has data on productivity based on the relationships between new employees and their managers. He once noted that "when an employee starts on their first day, we have data that says, if the manager shows up and says, 'Hi[,] nice to meet you, you're on my team, we're gonna be working together,' and does a few other things, those people end up 15 percent more productive in nine months."[87] And this is only a minor part of Google's data-driven management. Concerned about employee turnover, which could have a negative effect on its ability to compete, Google even built an algorithm to identify the employees who were most likely to leave based on employee reviews, promotions, and pay histories.[88]

In Bock's words, Google did so to "get inside people's heads even before they know they might leave."[89]

At the same time, it also mines data to modify employees' behavior. Google has emphasized nonhierarchical empowerment of individuals but still decided to institute a hierarchical structure, especially as it grew into a mid-sized and then a large corporation. In order to reconcile this apparent conflict between professed values and actual practices, it needed to convince its engineers that managers were necessary, since they had long been acculturated to the idea that managers were obstacles.[90] The solution was data that justified the benefit of managers to its engineers.[91]

In 2008 Google launched a premier project called Project Oxygen to identify the traits of its highest-performing managers. A team of researchers gathered more than ten thousand observations about managers and their performance reviews, employee feedback surveys, and nominations for top manager awards.[92] The researchers then coded, analyzed, and extracted general patterns from these data and built hypotheses. The analysis resulted in a set of rules called "Eight Good Manager's Behaviors and Three Pitfalls," which was incorporated into Google's management training program. Karen May, Google's vice president of people development, who led the redesign of the employee training program in 2012, summed up the core of Google's new management philosophy: "What's important is that it aligns with our overall business strategy."[93]

In 2012, as a sequel to Project Oxygen, Google launched Project Aristotle in search of the most effective and productive teams. Abeer Dubey, a manager in the People Analytics Division, assembled a team of statisticians, organizational psychologists, sociologists, and engineers to study how teams work across Google worked, which team dynamics were helpful or harmful, and the characteristics of the best teams.[94] According to Julia Rozovsky, a POps analyst, the team spent two years studying more than 180 Google teams, conducting more than 200 interviews, and dissecting more than 250 different team attributes to find out what makes a team effective.[95] We may ask, though, effective for whom and for what purposes? Google's experimentation bears a striking resemblance to the Hawthorne studies of a century earlier: In both, workers are being surveyed, studied, and experimented on as capital searches for ways to control and optimize the labor process. Brian Welle, a psychologist and the director of People Analytics at the company, said, "At Google, you need to engage people not just as subjects, but as experimenters."[96]

Google's supposedly unconventional management style is, thus, far from unconventional; rather, it dances between the paternalistic "we care" worker-centered welfare capitalism and data-driven social and behavioral science and scientific labor management to get inside workers' heads to increase productivity and maintain stability in its workforce. Moreover, these techniques are not exclusively applied to highly skilled and other paid workers. As described in Chapter 3, Google's workforce also includes unpaid user labor, and the company uses the same approach to managing them. The search engine firm has been scientifically managing users for decades, investing enormous capital in research on users as well as giving them "free" services as a form of welfare program on capital's behalf. By espousing welfare programs along with scientific management, Google wants to get inside *all* users' heads—and Google was doing so to unpaid labor long before it got inside its own workers' heads. This is the actual essence of the Google tenet "focus on the user and all else will follow."

Participatory Culture?

Google's efforts to manage its employees and users, encouraging them to believe that it differed from other corporations, seemed to work when there were fewer firms encroaching on its territory of profit. But this image has tarnished in recent years. For one thing, the exploitative ways in which Internet companies generate their wealth has been revealed, and Google's paradise has been shown to be for only a few select workers at the top. For another, even some of its elite workers began to realize that Google's "open" and "democratic" culture was only valid when it helped Google's bottom line.

In recent years there has been increasing resistance from white-collar tech workers within the company who have spoken out against management, challenging Google's labor practices, military contracts, surveillance, and sexual discrimination and racism and demanding that the company live up to its former motto, "Don't be evil." In 2018 more than twenty thousand workers walked off their jobs, protesting against the company's handling of sexual harassment cases and its inadequate policies concerning equity and transparency. In 2019 a group of Google contract workers from a third-party vendor, HCL Technologies, a subsidiary of an Indian contracting company in Pittsburgh, PA—the historic home for radical labor movements including the railroad strike of 1877 and the Homestead steel strike of 1892—formed a union with the United Steel Workers.[97] In January 2020, the Alphabet Workers Union (AWU) was formed with support from the Communications Workers of America. The union is open to all workers including TVCs.

Google is not alone in facing this move toward unionization. Workers in other tech giants like Facebook and Amazon have also been mobilizing to organize unions, and these efforts go back decades. Silicon Valley's wealth was built on the open shop, and the industry has a long history of undermining workers' efforts to organize.[98] For two decades starting in the 1970s until factories were offshored to Asia, workers in semiconductor manufacturing plants fought for unionization and for the dignity of labor; in the 1990s Apple janitorial contract workers called for a boycott of Apple products and joined the nationwide organizing campaign by the Service Employees International Union known as Justice for Janitors, and pressured Apple to sign a contract with the SEIU; in 2019 contract cafeteria workers in tech companies, whose wages started at $35,000 per year, joined the local chapter of Unite Here. Before the creation of the AWU, tech shuttle bus drivers in the Valley and Facebook cafeteria workers—a majority of whom are women and people of color—fought for and succeeded in unionizing. Today, the Amazon warehouse workers' grassroots union drive shows the possibility of a resurgence of labor movements in the United States. Although Google's union of white-collar tech workers is a new development, it is part of this longer history of labor struggles.

In response to its workers' resistance, Google is taking both overt and covert actions to intimidate them. The company began to restrict workplace speech, implementing tighter rules on internal discussion forums and replacing its weekly all-hands meetings, where employees had once been encouraged to ask hard questions, with monthly product launch talks.[99] Using a tactic familiar in corporate America, Google employed the union-busting consulting firm IRI to suppress workers' organizing efforts and urged the government to overturn a 2014 law that allowed workers to use employers' email to organize unions during nonworking time.[100] In 2019 Google fired four engineers who spoke out against management and protested against Google's contracts with US Customs and Border Patrol. After investigating Google's dismissal of these employees, the National Labor Relations Board (NLRB) filed complaints against Google for interfering with workers' legal rights to discuss workplace issues, which are guaranteed by section 7 of the National Labor Relations Act.[101] The Board revealed that Google had secretly operated the anti-union drive "Project Vivian" between 2018 and 2020 to "engage employees more positively and convince them that unions suck."[102]

On one hand, the company is running anti-union drives and tightening up its control over workers behind the scenes, but on the other, Google is also turning up its public relations campaign to promote its slogan "We care." To show the community that it cares, Google announced that it would provide $1 billion for affordable housing in the Bay area as the company expands its multi-million-dollar campus, integrating a large part of downtown San Jose, California. It is casting this extension as a "co-community development" with green space, education, housing, arts, and cultural centers. In an *Ars Technica* interview, Alexa Aren, Google's San Jose development director, recounted that this new venture was "much less the corporate campus" and more like "a resilient neighborhood."[103] This recalls National Cash Register's strategy of promoting the open shop in the nineteenth century as well as creating a benevolent corporate image by commissioning urban planning, city beautification, and arts as part of its "welfare work" program.

Google has not yet established a clear strategy for handling its internal labor unrest, and the question of how Google will respond in the long term to the newly established union remains open. The company is facing intense domestic and international competition and myriad external regulatory pressures, both domestically and internationally. In light of this, it is unclear whether Google will be able to continue to repair and maintain its image of open culture and benign capitalism while operating under an imperative to compete and generate profit.

Conclusion

Google's management practices have long been perceived in the mainstream media as new and exceptional. Contrary to this perception, the company's strategies are the evolution of modes of control that are rooted in industrial capitalism. Scientific management and corporate welfare have, in fact, not disappeared in the new economy, and Google's practices are not radically new. We have seen in this chapter that despite the changing political economy and technology, capital accumulation is still based on the same modes of labor control. Early corporate welfare programs began with selective skilled workers in non-union sectors before they reached a wider segment of workers.[104] In this sense, Google's model resembles an earlier version of welfare capitalism but is designed to target the elite class in non-union tech firms.

Backed by data, science, and the interactive nature of Internet technologies, the current practices of welfare capitalism have a façade of democracy that conceals the exploitative relationship between capital and labor as if capitalism could be built on democratic and participatory ideals. Although Taylorism has been roundly criticized for its dehumanization of workers, a new stage in the historical arc of Taylorism is reemerging that is celebrated today as "scientific" and that has been adopted by Google and other Internet firms. And this time, scientific management is not only being applied to low-level factory workers but to the entire spectrum of elite workers, low-paid labor, and unpaid labor in tech industry as well.

Google has rebranded scientific management and corporate welfare programs rather than transforming power structures. It has been able to extract more surplus value by adapting industrial-era labor control techniques and has built its business on the long suppression of organized labor in Silicon Valley.

In 2018 Google became a trillion-dollar company, but that wealth wasn't accumulated by its search algorithm, as it claims. Rather, it was built on exploitation and control of labor that was rapidly internationalized in the search for new markets and new labor. Next, Chapter 5 scrutinizes the different economic zones of China and the European Union, where US capital is facing the most resistance, to shed light on the conflict among the intercapitalist states over the Internet to illustrate the dynamics of global capitalism.

Chapter 5

MARKET DYNAMICS AND GEOPOLITICS

The search engine industry operates across territorial boundaries as the gateway to the newly established marketplace of the Internet that has been absorbed into the global political economy, enabling the selling of new goods and services and reorganizing the way everyday people live and work. Search has been organized as a social, political, and economic control structure that plays a major role in deepening information markets on a global scale. This fundamental function of search is dominated not by Great Britain, Germany, France, or China but by the US-based search engine industry—primarily Google. American dominance seemingly reaffirms a long-established US-led global information and communication order; however, it has pried open new geopolitical flash points among key global power centers.

Google dominates most of the world with a few exceptions—Russia, South Korea, and China. There are two particularly contentious zones, one with a burgeoning Internet sector and one almost completely bereft of a domestic Internet sector: China, a relatively new and expansionary economic force and the world's second-biggest economy, and the European Union, a longtime US ally as well as its economic competitor and historical political counterweight. In China, where Google has struggled to carve out a foothold in the largest market in the world, the Chinese search engine Baidu dominates. Meanwhile, Europe's dependence on US information systems has benefited the United States; thus, Google's dominance as well as China's emerging tech sector have provoked Europe's anxiety over losing control of strategic emerging Internet sectors to both the United States and China. Given the rivalry between the two nations, the European Union has been asserting its power via the pursuit of a series of regulatory impositions and antitrust cases against Google and other US tech companies and has called for technological sovereignty. Given that these three entities are the largest global economic and trading partners, the clash between power blocs has significant impact on shaping the global Internet. What is the nature of these conflicts? Where is the tension and resistance? This chapter explores both questions.

Information and communication technologies have long been vital for capital's geographical expansion. As Dan Schiller points out, they have been built, rebuilt, and extended over the course of centuries to facilitate the global capitalist system and its expansion by serving cultural and information commodities and services as well as supporting capital flows and global supply chains.[1] Historians have shed light on the link between ICTs and capitalist empires, revealing that the process of construction of global networks has been interlinked with the interests of nation-states, national and transnational corporations, and other political constituents.[2] Dwayne Winseck and Robert Pike point out that global network building has involved not only major imperial power states but also collaboration among states, multinational conglomerates, and international organizations.[3] Thus, they describe this system as a "shared hegemony," though Great Britain was the dominant imperial power in the nineteenth and early twentieth centuries. Ellen Wood's conceptualization of capitalist imperialism is instructive in clarifying this idea. She states, "Today's imperialism is not really about the relation between a capitalist and a non-capitalist world. It has more to do with the relations within a global capitalist system."[4] In other words, capitalism is a system in which the economies of capitalist nation-states are interconnected and unevenly integrated into a global economic system.[5] Thus, the wiring of this global network infrastructure is complex, requiring cooperation from multiple states, different units of capital, and political and social actors while it also meets a range of resistance and obstacles. Since World War II, the United States as capitalist imperial power has been the leading player in constructing global information systems in the sense that it has forged relationships with its subordinate countries by means of both coercion and alliance. This long-standing structure has built the Internet systems; however, the new geopolitics and economics are challenging the existing order. This chapter illustrates the role of geopolitics in the restructuring of the global political economy of the Internet, at the center of which is search.

First, the chapter discusses the historical context in which the United States has ascended and presided over global network infrastructure for decades, while illustrating the instabilities of the US position. The second part demonstrates the current political economic context, in which China has become entrenched in global capitalist markets and has strategically built its domestic Internet market by both drawing in and limiting foreign capital. The Chinese Internet sector has been persistently viewed as state-controlled cyberspace, the "Great Firewall," but the chapter challenges the Western mainstream framework of democracy versus authoritarianism. Taking a critical approach, the chapter illuminates the fact that the growing domestic Internet market in China is inextricably integrated with US-led transnationalizing digital capitalism. Finally, the chapter examines the European Union's uneasiness toward both US and Chinese tech power, its failed attempts to build an alternative to Google, and its renewed efforts to build an EU-based Internet sector and weaponize regulation to shape the global Internet sector.

Unfinished Battle

Within a few hours of Great Britain's declaring war against German imperial ambitions in 1914, it destroyed two German submarine cables that connected Europe and America and began to censor all communications that went through British-controlled cables in order to isolate Germany. This alarmed the United States owing to the lack of sufficient independent communication infrastructure and spurred the country to build its own independent information networks in order to serve their economic interests and promote geographic expansion.[6] The United States attempted several times to build its own communication networks in the interwar years but did not realize these plans until World War II and afterward.

Relatively unscathed by World War I, the United States was in an improved position in its rivalry with the other world powers, as Germany was defeated and Great Britain and France were weakened by the war. After World War II, the United States emerged as the sole capitalist imperial hegemon in the global capitalist system, moved away from its reliance on Great Britain's colonial information system, and began to build its own information infrastructure.[7] The expansion of the information industry played a central role in the country's ascent into a position that today dominates the world via the economic instruments of capitalism. This power has not gone unnoticed by its rivals, however, and its formidable position in the information sphere has been repeatedly assailed over the course of time as geopolitics and economics have changed and interchanged.

In the 1970s the government of President Valéry Giscard d'Estaing of France was troubled by US corporate dominance in computer and information technologies and France's cultural and technical dependence on the United States. The response to US dominance in the computer industry was articulated in the 1978 report *Computerization of Society*, also known as the Nora and Minc Report.[8] The document, commissioned by the French government, warned of American domination in "telematics" as a threat to French sovereignty and economic competitiveness and warned of IBM's dominance in the European information market. The report urgently called for government intervention to counter IBM. It also recommended that the country develop its own information-based industry as well as a comprehensive national strategic policy and investment in national information technology and telecommunication systems.

Also in the 1970s, from a different direction, the Non-Aligned Movement, led by newly independent countries of the global South aspiring to self-determination and galvanized by a mass movement, challenged the United States and the Western information sphere as they recognized the importance of control over information for their economies, cultural independence, and national sovereignty. They demanded a new world information and communication order (NWICO). Mobilized by the Non-Aligned Movement, NWICO, using the venue of UNESCO, called out the structural power imbalance of global information flows and sought out a more equitable, balanced information exchange among sovereign nations.[9] The United States, which had deployed the Free Flow of Information doctrine to support its global expansion, was criticized, and it attacked NWICO.[10]

The Free Flow of Information doctrine, part of the capitalist imperial strategy designed by the US government and corporations, was an economic means to coerce nations of the global south to open their ICT markets. This confrontation between the United States and its Western allies, on one hand, and the global South, on the other, led the United States and the United Kingdom to leave UNESCO in 1984 and 1985, respectively.[11] By the late 1980s the NWICO movement had been defeated by intense pressure from the United States and its allies, which further opened markets in newly decolonized countries.

Thirty years later, in the early twenty-first century, the debates about the unequal global power structure of the new ICT system resurfaced, starting with the World Summit on the Information Society, hosted in Tunis by the International Telecommunication Union. This time the debate concerned the Internet. The Tunis Agenda stated that "all governments have an equal role and responsibilities" with regard to the development of the Internet and policy concerning its use.[12] The summit offered a venue for developing countries to challenge US control and to debate the global disparity in access to information and communication technologies; however, it fell far from achieving its goals.[13] The United States refused to cede control of the Internet Corporation of Assigned Names and Numbers (ICANN), the organization that oversaw the Internet's naming and numbering systems, which at the time was under the control of the US Department of Commerce. The United States agreed to create a new organizational actor, the UN-affiliated Internet Governance Forum, though it would be within the existing ICANN structure. Schiller observes that this was done so that the United States could push back against more drastic reforms that could lessen its control over the Internet.[14] In 2013, however, Edward Snowden's revelations about the mass surveillance program being run by the United States refueled the debates regarding its role in ICANN and its outsized influence over shaping the Internet. The United States faced immense international pressure to relinquish ICANN. The Department of Commerce finally did so, with the caveat that a multi-stakeholder model would be best. The United States made this compromise to avoid turning ICANN over to the International Telecommunication Union, which was the intergovernmental approach for which China, Russia, and a coalition of African and Middle eastern countries had advocated.[15]

The battle over the information and communication sphere is far from over. And today's contention needs to be approached within this historical context, though the actors and their motives may have shifted. The business of search is one such new information domain.

The United States has long recognized the importance of its primacy over information in the maintenance and extension of US-led global capitalism.

President Obama, addressing American innovation in his 2011 State of the Union address, claimed: "What America does better than anyone else is spark the creativity and imagination of our people. We're the nation that put cars in driveways and computers in offices. The nation of Edison and the Wright brothers; of Google and Facebook."[16]

The search engine industry, one of the top new US strategic information industries, has cultivated an entirely new global industry. Led by Google, US tech firms dominate in the sphere of information search, controlling the entry point of the Internet, as they expand the domestic information market, churn out many new products, and aggressively build an extraterritorial information network for the global market. This process of global penetration requires collaboration among nation-states in order to remove barriers to entry, and it faces opposition. Thus, Google's global dominance is not a permanent condition; rather, its continued growth and expansion actually depend heavily on geopolitical and economic forces and the politically organized global markets. In particular, Google has long been struggling to move into China. The firm's inability to do so has often been viewed by the liberal Western media as a struggle between democracy and an authoritarian regime, but the story is far more complex. The following section demonstrates that the development of the Chinese Internet sector is structurally integrated within the existing system of the US-led information order, which relies heavily on transnational capital, and at the same time the Chinese state has been maneuvering around the US-dominated information order and has built a domestic Internet sector that is tightly interlinked with the global economy.

New Challenge: China

The information industry has long been considered to be of strategic importance for China within the wider context of its reintegration into the global capitalist economy.[17] In the 1970s the post-Mao Chinese Communist Party, just emerging from its Cultural Revolution, launched a national campaign in four areas of "modernization," with science and technology being one of the sectors along with agriculture, industry, and national defense. In shifting from Maoist socialism to a more state capital–oriented economy, China had prioritized its IT sectors as driving forces, designated its information industries as one of the pillars of the national economy, and reorganized these sectors into a new zone of economic growth.[18] The former Chinese president Jiang Zemin once stated, "None of the four modernizations would be possible without information."[19] It is therefore important to consider the development of China's ICTs to set the stage for the geopolitics of search in that region.

Starting in the late 1980s, as part of its overall economic reform, China carried out extensive industrial reform policies to develop its domestic information and communication sectors, including the building of national networks, special economic zones, and state-funded technology parks, supporting homegrown software and hardware IT firms, and investing in large-scale state-sponsored ICT infrastructure initiatives.[20] Along with its national push to build information infrastructure, the state made a concerted effort to bolster the commercial use of information technologies at every level of industry, government, and people's everyday lives through a series of state-led informationizing initiatives. These included the Golden Bridge Project, a national public information network called the Golden Gateway, a foreign trade and import and export network, and Golden Card, the national credit card network.[21] Information technologies were adopted across a wide range of sectors, and by the late 1990s the commercial Internet domain made up 76 percent of all domain-name registrations.[22] China announced that 1999 would be "The Year of Getting to the Internet" and soon became the largest IT market in Asia. The Chinese state thus played a central role in the country's reintegration into the global capitalist economic orbit.

While China's accession into the World Trade Organization in 2001 was seen as officially opening up China to foreign capital, as Yu Hong shows, long before that, the Chinese government had facilitated foreign investment and technology transfer in the development of its tech sector via a policy friendly to foreign direct investment and by selectively reducing state investment.[23] In 1994 foreign investment in the Chinese telecommunications sector was already 16.8 percent of total foreign investment.[24] And by early in the twenty-first century such major multinational corporations as IBM, Microsoft, Intel, Alcatel, General Electric, Bell Labs, and General Motors had already established R&D centers in China. As Yuezhi Zhao succinctly put it, China's restructuring of its ICT sectors was a key means for it to open itself to the global capitalist system.[25]

As part of opening up, China's economic policy explicitly encouraged the participation of Chinese private and foreign capital in the development of its

Internet service sectors.[26] Lutao Ning points out, however, that China had two clear strategies for the prized ICT sector: "Attracting in" allowed domestic firms to access large amounts of capital and technical knowhow, while "walking out" facilitated the boost in global competitiveness and integration into the global market. "Attracting in" was a crucial first step toward "walking out."[27]

Yet China's "attracting in" policy didn't mean outright liberalization. Min Tang documents the state's process of implementing carefully crafted multi-tiered regulations concerning ICTs throughout a different economic developmental stage.[28] The ICT sector was protected as a strategic industry, restricting foreign direct investment and causing a majority of such funding to be poured into the ICT manufacturing sector.[29] Meanwhile, the Chinese state had begun to boost domestic tech startups and create the conditions for drawing foreign capital into its nascent tech sectors.

From the 1980s to the 1990s, China launched a series of initiatives to develop its domestic technology base by funding tech-start-ups and offering incentives to foreign capital firms to invest in and locate in China. This involved a high-tech program called 863 that funded R&D at universities in critical areas. The Ministry of Science and Technology kicked off the Torch program to create and support high-tech industrial zones including "incubators" for high tech start-ups[30] and made technology transfer regulations for joint ventures with foreign firms. Many of the projects from 863, the Torch program, and tech industrial zones were spun off as the government functioned as venture capital (VC). By the mid-1990s China recognized that these funding systems were insufficient to develop tech start-ups into a national economic development project, so the state further liberalized the market, establishing both government-financed and university-backed VC firms.[31] In 1998 corporate-backed VC firms were allowed to be established; the following year, the state introduced the regulatory framework for VC investment. This brought VC firms backed by the government, as well as corporate and foreign capital, into the market. Foreign VC firms had been allowed to operate since the 1980s with limited capacity, but by the twenty-first century they had become a major source of financing for tech start-ups.[32] Subsequently, the first dot-com boom brought significant foreign venture capital investment to Chinese tech start-ups as China's Internet sector and global financial capital converged. But direct VC was not the only mechanism for drawing foreign capital.

Domestic and foreign firms also pursued joint ventures and joint research and development of mutually beneficial interest that allowed foreign firms access to the Chinese market and gave Chinese firms access to foreign capital. American Internet firms such as Yahoo!, eBay, Amazon, and Microsoft entered the Chinese market via joint ventures with local companies. Foreign investment in value-added Internet services was restricted by the state, however, so Chinese Internet firms and foreign capital took a different route and began to rely on a system called variable interest entities (VIEs), a workaround in which foreign investment could be utilized to participate in restricted industries such as the Internet and telecommunication sectors but could not directly control the enterprises. The VIE structure is often referred to as the Sina model because it was first deployed in 2000 by the Chinese Internet company Sina. In the VIE structure, two entities are created: One is offshore and the other is in China. Chinese individuals and foreign investors first establish an offshore entity in the Cayman Islands or another tax haven into which they can inject capital; in turn, they can acquire ownership in offshore assets. The Chinese subsidiary sits between the offshore firms and the VIEs. Via a series of contractual agreements with the Chinese subsidiary, the VIEs enable the overseas-listed company to, in effect, run its operations inside China.

In addition to Sina, other major Chinese Internet companies such as Baidu, Tencent, Tudou, Sohu.com, Alibaba, and JD.com listed themselves on the stock markets in the United States, Hong Kong, and Shanghai using the VIE structure.[33] By 2011 the law firm Cadwallader reported in the *Financial Times* that 42 percent of Chinese companies listed on the US stock exchanges were using the VIE structure, with thousands of unlisted companies operating in the same way.[34] The Chinese government remains well aware that many of its Internet firms use VIEs to draw in foreign capital and that foreign capital uses VIEs to invest in the restricted Chinese Internet industry. For a couple of decades, however, China maintained its ambiguous policy stance without clamping down on Chinese companies using the VIE structure in their IPOs. What, then, was the reason for not taking direct action against VIEs to restrict foreign capital in Chinese strategic industries? And on the flip side, US shareholders in Chinese Internet firms face major risks because Chinese courts might not hold that those contractual agreements are legal, according to a report by the US-China Economic and Security Review Commission.[35]

Why, then, did US investors continue to invest in Chinese Internet firms in this manner for two decades?

For the Chinese government, this seemingly ambiguous position allowed for state influence at arm's length, effectively maneuvering between the interests of national and transnational capital and controlling the flow of foreign capital into strategic industries while also providing the party with space to regulate as needed. Meanwhile, the US government calling the VIE structure illegal was an attempt to nudge China at that time to further open its Internet market. At the same time, there was unspoken understanding among transnational capitalists that the Chinese state was unlikely to take any measures that would negatively affect major Internet firms because too many firms rely on VIEs, involving massive financial stakes across the sector. In early 2015 the Chinese Ministry of Commerce released a draft law revising its Foreign Investment Law to favor transnational capital by legalizing VIEs so that foreign investors would have ownership rights in Internet industries along with telecommunications and education industries.[36] The draft law was never implemented, but the issue of VIEs resurfaced with escalating tensions between the United States and China. In 2021 the China Securities Regulatory Commission proposed new rules for overseas IPOs but did not ban the use of VIEs. Chinese companies that sought to list abroad via VIE could use them but would now be required to follow compliance procedures.[37] The Chinese state signaled assurances of foreign capital's continued investment in China's Internet sectors, but at the same time, with this move, it legitimized its ability to intervene as needed.

The state has been instrumental in managing the flow of capital, establishing home-grown industries, and working in tandem with transnational capital to allow it to be deeply interwoven into the development of the Chinese Internet industry. Since the integration with global capitalism, the Chinese state has been navigating between private and public actors and between transnational and national interests while creating space for domestic industries within US-led digital capitalism—something that postwar western Europe has so far failed to achieve. Zhao underscores the state's active participation in absorbing foreign capital and its ability to negotiate with transnational capital on specific terms of entry.[38] Within this context, Google's counterpart Baidu emerged.

The Rise of Baidu

Baidu was co-founded in 2000 by Robin Li and Eric Xu, Chinese nationals educated in the United States. In 1999 the two raised $1.2 million in seed money from the Silicon Valley VC firms Integrity Partners and Peninsula Capital and returned to China.[39] On January 18, 2000, with that seed money and using the VIE structure, Baidu was incorporated in the Cayman Islands as Baidu .com. In 2005 Goldman Sachs, Piper Jaffray, and Credit Suisse First Boston underwrote Baidu's IPO and listed it on the NASDAQ stock exchange. Baidu's IPO was considered the biggest opening on NASDAQ since the dot-com peak of 2000. Soon afterward, Baidu secured another $10 million from two other US venture capital firms, Draper Fisher Jurvetson and IDG Technology Venture.[40] The 2010 Report to Congress of the US-China Economic and Security Review Commission stated that Baidu's initial majority investors were Americans and American firms.[41] Google, Baidu's competitor in China, even bought a 2.6 percent share of Baidu in 2005—and sold the shares for a 1,100 percent return as the company started its own operations in China. Baidu embraced Google's investment. Baidu CEO Robin Li stated, "Google is a leader in the global Internet industry and its investment will help investors appreciate the value of a search engine provider like Baidu."[42] In fact, in 2015 Google offered $1.6 billion to gain control over the Chinese search market, but ultimately Baidu rejected Google's takeover attempt.[43] At the time Baidu was filing its IPO the majority of its shares were held by financial institutions and mutual funds including Baillie Gifford & Co., Price (T.Rowe) Associates, Inc., Oppenheimer Funds, Inc., and Capital Research Global Investors. Baillie Gifford, Price (T.Rowe) Associates, and others were also top shareholders of Google.

Baidu was far from an exception. Early Chinese Internet startups were nurtured by both the Chinese state and transnational capital, in particular US venture capital. One of Baidu's early accumulation strategies was aggressively building partnerships with domestic as well as foreign IT companies that wanted to break into the Chinese information market. In 2006 Baidu struck a deal with MTV to provide original television and music programs to Baidu and share advertising revenue, entered into a cooperative agreement with Nokia, and worked with Intel to develop search services. In 2010 the company teamed up with Providence Equity Partners, one of Hulu's investors, to inject $50 million into the creation of video platform iQiyi, and later acquired

Providence Equity Partners' stake in the platform. Now iQiyi is the largest streaming service in China.[44] Baidu established a joint venture with Japan-based Rakuten to operate a business-to-consumer online shopping service in the Chinese market. In 2011 Baidu partnered with Dell to develop mobile phones with its own mobile operating system to target the Chinese market, which was then dominated by Apple and the Chinese company Lenovo—itself the buyer of IBM's PC business. While not all early strategic partnerships were successful, the series of partnerships, along with the drawing of foreign capital, facilitated Baidu's embedding itself deeply into the global tech sectors and expanding its Internet business.

The rise of Baidu in China has often been attributed by the Western media to Google's partial withdrawal from China in 2010 and Chinese government policies favoring Chinese-owned companies. After Google moved its operations to Hong Kong, Baidu was supposed to fully monopolize the Chinese search market with little competition. This prediction was only partly correct. By no means has the search engine market in China stabilized, although Baidu seemingly dominates it. Baidu was and is facing serious competition among other fast-growing homegrown Chinese Internet firms fueled by global capital, so its continuing dominance in search is far from assured in the rapidly changing Chinese information landscape.

Fierce Competition

China's search engine market quickly evolved and became crowded. One of Baidu's early major competitors was Qihoo, founded in 2006 by a former Yahoo! executive and initially backed by the VC firm Sequoia Capital,[45] which was also a major backer of Google. In addition to Sequoia, Qihoo was supported by both Chinese and foreign VC firms such as IDG Ventures, Highland Capital Partners, Trustbridge Partners, and the Chinese private equity firm CDH. The company was known for being China's largest antivirus software vendor, but it launched a search engine called so.360.cn, then used it in place of Google as the search engine on its portal.

In the beginning Qihoo gradually chipped away at Baidu's search market share, and Baidu responded by blocking Qihoo from access to its products and services. Baidu also took legal action against Qihoo 360, claiming that the latter violated its robot exclusion protocol by indexing its web content without permission.[46] In response to the lawsuit, Qihoo argued that Baidu's actions violated China's anti-monopoly laws.[47] To ease the tension between these competitors, the Internet Society of China, a government-backed trade group, stepped in and in 2012 got search companies and other Internet firms including Baidu, Qihoo 360, Tencent, and Sina to agree to sign a self-regulation pact including a code of conduct to maintain fair competition.[48] This self-regulation could be seen as weakening the role of the Chinese state in the new market-oriented economy, but it was part of the state's neoliberal strategy, whereby the party distances itself from the market yet is able to maintain its influence and strategically facilitate commercialization processes.

Trailing Qihoo was Sogou, a subsidiary of the web portal Sohu and a longtime player in the Chinese search market. Sohu was the first Chinese-language search engine and portal in China. The company was founded in 2004 by ChaoYang Zhang, who received his PhD in experimental physics from MIT in 1993. Zhang left his position as MIT's liaison officer for China and returned to China in order to start his own company, Internet Technologies China (which later changed its name to Sohu), with help from MIT Media Lab director Nicholas Negroponte—the evangelist for One Laptop per Child—and Edward Roberts of MIT's Sloan School of Management.[49] Sogou held a solid 10 percent share of the search market—good enough for third place in the market—but it wasn't able to sustain growth. Thus, in 2013 Sogou made a deal with Tencent, which invested US$448 million for a 36.5 percent stake in the company. Tencent had originally partnered with Google, but in 2009 it had replaced Google services with its own Soso search platform; now Tencent merged Soso into Sogou.[50] After that Sogou became a distant second behind Baidu in terms of market share. In 2021 Tencent completely acquired and absorbed Sogou into its WeChat platform with its more than 1.2 billion users—80 percent of China's total population—to directly challenge Baidu.

Meanwhile, in 2013 e-commerce giant Alibaba rolled out its general search engine, called Aliyun or Alibaba Cloud Search, the same brand as its mobile operating system. Aliyun's cloud computing division offered the basic features of search (Internet, news, images, and maps) and competed directly with Baidu.[51] This was not the first time Alibaba had ventured into the search market. In 2010 it had partnered with Microsoft and launched the shopping search engine Etao.com;[52] at the same time, Yahoo! owned 40 percent of Alibaba. And in 2014 in order to tackle China's growing mobile search market, Alibaba formed a joint venture called Shenma with the Chinese browser developer UCWeb, which in 2021 was the third most widely used mobile search engine. In 2019 ByteDance, backed by Kohlberg Kravis Roberts, SoftBank Group, Sequoia Capital, General Atlantic, and Hillhouse Capital Group (the owner of social media app TikTok), also jumped into the search market, launching Toutiao Search and scooping up engineers from Google, Bing, and Baidu.[53]

Given this political economic context, the growth of a competitive search market in China can't be seen only from the perspective of the insulated "Great Firewall" managed by the Chinese state, which censors search engines. This market evolved within the context of China's infusion of transnational capital through attracting in and walking out. Instead of seeing the sector only as part of the Chinese state's censored media, therefore, Chinese search engine companies should also be seen as what Lianrui Jia and Dwayne Winseck describe as "capitalist enterprises" that operate under an expansionist imperative and are highly integrated into the global capitalist market.[54]

As Chinese Internet firms have looked to diversify their accumulation strategies, they have, like US firms, moved into each other's territories of search, social media, browsers, mobile phones, music, games, video, e-commerce, the "Internet of things," cloud computing, and autonomous cars, all predicated on continuing commodification and commercialization of the Internet. China's dynamic and fluid search market is increasingly fragmented as new players continue to enter it.

As the company faces intense competition on multiple fronts, Baidu's main revenue source, online ads via search, has been steadily declining. To survive and maintain its market primacy, Baidu needed to find a new growth sector, and so it pivoted its strategy toward AI because China is poised to lead the global AI market, which is expected to grow to $554.3 billion by 2024.[55] Baidu's reorientation of its business to AI was also done to seize an opportunity in responding to China's new economic developmental phase. Facing intense economic pressure from the United States and its allies, China has accelerated the restructuring of its economic base to pursue self-reliance by moving up the value chain from low-end labor-intensive manufacturing industries to high-tech-driven industries and upgrading its industrial sectors by incorporating advanced information technologies such as AI, big data, cloud computing, and semiconductors. As part of the new economic initiative, the Chinese government selected AI as one of the strategic areas for emerging industries in its Thirteenth National Five-Year Plan (2016). The government released a policy document in 2017, the Next Generation Artificial Intelligence Development Plan, aiming for AI to be the driving force for China's industrial upgrading and economic restructuring to move up the value chain.[56] In pursuing this goal, the state drew in major domestic tech companies to develop its domestic AI industry.

Baidu is considered one of the largest AI companies in the world. Its new slogan is "All in AI," putting it into all its core products and services in order to gain a competitive advantage and racing to develop cloud services, mobile platforms, smart speakers, and autonomous cars. Baidu has filed for more AI patents than any other Chinese company, and has been granted 2,682 patents as of October 2020.[57] The company has poured a great deal of capital into its autonomous vehicles, testing its Apollo self-driving platform in China and the United States, and it has shored up partnerships with Microsoft, Intel, BMW, Ford, Volvo, and Volkswagen. Baidu's autonomous car, brought to the road first in China, has driven more miles than any of its competitors.

Given the ever-intense domestic and global capitalist rivalries within China, along with rapid technological change, Baidu's dominant position in search and its future growth in the Internet sector continue to be challenged. Thus, Baidu is compelled to seek not only sectorial expansion to reduce its dependence on ads but also "walking out" toward a geographical expansion of its business; meanwhile, Google's efforts to cultivate the world's largest market continue unabated.

Baidu Going Out and Google Coming In

Baidu's transnational ambitions go back to 2007, when the company launched its search service in Japan. The company chose Japan because of its cultural similarities and the use of Chinese characters in the Japanese language. After eight years the service came to an end because Baidu wasn't able to make a dent in its competition against incumbents Yahoo! Japan and Google. Yet this experience has not deterred Baidu's global expansion effort. Baidu has since made a series of forays into emerging markets, targeting Southeast Asia, South

America (Brazil), and the Arabic-speaking regions (particularly Egypt).[58] It also eyed the European market, working with the tourism administrations of Denmark, Finland, Norway, and Sweden to target China's outbound tourism market, thus directly competing with Google Maps and Apple Maps. However, Baidu has been struggling to expand outside China, meeting with many losses, and it has shut down some of its international operations including in those Brazil. The company's business is still quite limited in China and faces barriers and constraints in operating within US-led digital capitalism.

Although Baidu has had to retract a large part of its global expansion efforts for the moment, for its survival and growth the company cannot afford to abandon the global market. Baidu continues to operate a couple of major R&D centers abroad. Its research lab, the Institute of Deep Learning, which opened in Silicon Valley in 2013, recruited Andrew Ng, a leading AI researcher who previously worked on deep learning at Google. The R&D center—located close to the offices of Apple, Motorola, Amazon, Google, and Microsoft—recruits top engineers, taps into US academic institutions, and develops AI.[59] Its second Silicon Valley R&D center is the home of a division of Baidu's Intelligent Driving Group, which focuses on its Apollo platform. The company has already obtained a permit to test its self-driving car in California and is poised to compete against Google's Waymo and General Motor's Cruise.[60]

While Baidu has struggled at home and abroad, its competitor Google has continued to attempt to capitalize on the billion Internet users in China. Neither of Google's domestic competitors, Microsoft Bing and Yahoo!, have ever had a strong foothold in the Chinese search market. Can US-based transnational capital give up on the world's largest and fastest-growing Internet market? The answer is absolutely not.

In 2010 Google announced that it was exiting China and moving its servers to Hong Kong because of an alleged Chinese cyberattack on more than thirty different companies, including Google's servers. After Google's announcement, a Microsoft spokesman stated that the company had no plans to move out of or redirect its operations in China. Then Microsoft CEO Steve Ballmer wrote in a blog post about the importance of China for his company and stated its position thus: "We have done business in China for more than twenty years and we intend to stay engaged, which means our business must respect the laws of China."[61] Microsoft remained silent about censorship and the whole hacking incident, not wanting to damage its long-term relationship with

China. From Microsoft's perspective, this was a business opportunity with one less competitor.

One year after Google relocated its servers to Hong Kong, Microsoft's Bing search engine tried to seize the opportunity by teaming up with Baidu. The partnership was intended to capture English-language search, which had a 5 percent market share in China, while abandoning the Chinese-language search market. To pursue this partnership, Microsoft complied with Chinese law, stating that "as part of this partnership, Bing will incorporate certain filtering technologies and processes to ensure that we are in compliance with local laws."[62]

Google search, Facebook, and Twitter are not accessible in China, but Microsoft's Bing has continued to operate its service on the mainland, though the company holds less than 1 percent of the Chinese search market. Search is only one of many pieces of its business there, however. In fact, Microsoft has been present in China since 1992, and the company once hired former secretary of state Henry Kissinger to advise on political strategy to open up the Chinese market.[63] In 1995 Microsoft set up its R&D in China and established its fourth R&D center in Shanghai in 2019, signaling its continuing commitment to the Chinese market. Although it had to respond to the Trump administration's pressure and was forced to cut ties with Huawei, the company warned the US government that the restrictions on Chinese tech firms would eventually hurt US interests, indicating the importance of the Chinese market for Microsoft.[64] In fact, in the midst of the Huawei fiasco, Microsoft has been quietly expanding its cloud business in China by operating through the Chinese company 21Vianet.

How about Google? It entered the Chinese market in 2005, gaining more than 35 percent of the search market by number of users by the time it moved operations to Hong Kong in 2010. In the mainstream media, Google's "withdrawal" from the mainland Chinese market was attributed purely to the company's extraordinarily high moral ground in refusing to abide by the Chinese government's censorship policy. But did Google really give up on the world's largest growth market because of its self-claimed business principle "Don't be evil"? The answer is no.

In fact, Google never actually left China. The company itself dismissed the popular claim that it had left the country; in 2012 Daniel Alegre, Google's president of the company's Asia-Pacific operations at the time, stated:

> We never left China, and we continue to believe in the market. . . . It's a very vibrant Internet market. We have some of the best employees at Google and we continue to grow not only our revenue but also our headcount in the country.[65]

Google was praised for its "idealistic" act of leaving China to protest and evade government censorship, and it was true that it started to deliver its main search service through servers in Hong Kong instead of from mainland China.[66] But it was well known that Google kept its R&D operations, offices, and ad business in Beijing and Shanghai; in addition, it didn't cease its other business ventures—like music, maps, online shopping services, and the AdMob mobile ad platform—until much later, and for different reasons. According to the *New York Times*, in August 2018 Google had more than seven hundred employees in China.[67]

As a matter of fact, as Reuters reported, Google had shifted its business strategy in China, targeting display advertising, particularly centered around China's growing export firms, which wanted access to global consumers and mobile businesses.[68] Given the country's heavy reliance on exports, as much as Google needs the growing Chinese market, Chinese firms also need Google, which reaches 90 percent of Internet users worldwide via its ad network.

Considering these mutual interests, it was no surprise that Google refocused on rapidly growing Chinese exporters who were eager to reach out to overseas markets. In 2016 Sundar Pichai, chief executive officer of Google, reaffirmed Google's interests in China in his public remark: "I care about servicing users globally in every corner. Google is for everyone. . . . We want to be in China serving Chinese users."[69]

The company maintained Google Adwords Experience Centers in Shenzhen, Songiang, Zhengzhou, Tianjin, Dalian, Shanghai, Guiyang, Changsha, Dongguan, Guangzhou, Foshan, and Zhongshan to train Chinese companies how to use Google platforms for their overseas marketing.[70] As part of its agreement to open its Shanghai center in 2016, Google offered to train five hundred Songjiang-based companies and two thousand e-commerce professionals and to generate jobs for the local area.[71] In 2015 Google also established a company called Pengji Information Technology in Shanghai's pilot Free Trade Zone. In his interview with the *Wall Street Journal* in 2015 Sergey Brin said, "We already do quite a lot of business in China, although it has not been an easy country for us."[72] In 2017 Google opened its AI center in Beijing—its first AI research center in Asia—and reintroduced several products such as Android apps Files Go and Translator through Baidu's, Xiaomi's, and Huawei's third-party app stores, and also invested in China's second-largest online retailer, JD.com.

From early on, Google had had no intention of giving up its efforts to gain market share in the world's largest Internet market. After only six months, the company quietly turned off its much-publicized anti-censorship service in China—though it continued to criticize the Chinese government's censorship in public. Considering Google's desperate and persistent efforts to gain a foothold in the Chinese market, the 2018 revelation by the *Intercept* of Google's censored search engine project for China, called Dragonfly, shouldn't have been a surprise; the company defended Dragonfly, saying that a censored Google service is a better option for Chinese people than Baidu.[73] Google abandoned Dragonfly owing to pressure from the Trump administration and its own employees. Yet the firm's further attempts to access the Chinese market have become more complicated and uncertain with the heightening of the geopolitical rivalry between China and the United States over tech supremacy.

American capital's struggles to capture the largest Internet market, and China's increased ability to maneuver within the US-centric information system, have been irritants to the United States. The Trump administration drew much attention for banning Chinese tech platforms from the US market, but the United States and US-based transnational corporations have long been engaged in restricting Chinese firms' access to the US tech sector and obstructing China's attempts to promote its indigenous technology standards in the international arena.[74] The Biden administration's positioning as a global moral leader against authoritarian regimes has continued and broadened its predecessor's policies. The administration expanded the list of Chinese companies banned from US investment under the premise of national security and human rights. As of 2021 the blacklist included fifty-nine firms.[75] The Biden administration vowed to take a hard line toward China, shifting its strategy from Trump's unilateralism to enlisting "digital alliances" to counter China. But this "decoupling," after decades of integration of the US and Chinese economies within and through their respective technology sectors, comes with mounting challenges. As Ming Tang demonstrates, the decades of integration between the US and China have brought about a deep interdependence, from hardware to software to capital investment.[76] In 2021 the

US Chamber of Commerce released a report stating that the costs related to such a decoupling would be about $190 billion.[77]

Acknowledging the potential collateral damage, US Treasury Secretary Janet Yellen said that the United States would decouple from China in selective areas to protect its national security and economic interests, but she expressed concerns about a full decoupling on the technological front.[78] Along these lines, former Google CEO Eric Schmidt, who chairs the National Security Commission on Artificial Intelligence, joined with Alphabet's Jared Cohen to form and co-chair the China Strategy Group in the fall of 2020. A leaked report by the group stated that "a degree of 'technological bifurcation' in the US and Chinese tech sectors" is in America's interest and recommended building a " plurilateral coalition" that includes Japan, Germany, France, Great Britain, Canada, the Netherlands, South Korea, and Finland.[79] In February 2021, Schmidt, testifying alongside Microsoft president Brad Smith during a Senate Armed Services Committee hearing, warned that China's economic and technology power was a threat to US economic competitiveness and urged the Congress to focus on boosting the US tech sector through public and private partnerships, which meant that the public would subsidize corporate growth.[80] This is a common self-serving argument from the US tech sector, but the influence of tech elites on US policy is undeniable.

As the United States retools its policy toward China, the Chinese party-state is doing the converse, and it has further bolstered its core technologies to move away from a low-wage, labor-intensive economy and reduce its dependence on foreign semiconductor chips, software, and advanced materials in a move that will reshape its political economy and the global power structures of the future.

The question remains, what degree of bifurcation between the two countries could the United States and China afford without damaging domestic and transnational capital for their shared accumulation process? Amid tensions with the United States, China began to craft and impose new technology regulations on the Internet sector. In 2020 the Chinese financial tech company Ant, affiliated with Alibaba, had its IPO listing suspended in Shanghai and Hong Kong under new draft rules for online micro-lending. And the following year the Cyberspace Administration of China removed the Chinese ride-hailing giant DiDi from domestic app stores because of violations of data protection rules right after its landmark listing on the New York Stock Exchange. Meanwhile, in 2021, China released a new data protection, storage, and security law and the following year revised its 2008 anti-monopoly law, which was aimed at the Internet sector. From the Western media's perspective, this was just one big heavy-handed crackdown by the authoritarian regime over its tech sector.[81] Yet China has been focused specifically on three major areas that are vital for the growth of the Internet sector—antitrust, data security, and fintech—as it aims to rein in selective tech companies. China's intention was not merely to crack down on its tech giants or decouple from foreign capital, but rather to construct clear Internet regulations (which are still under development) in order to create stable market conditions for domestic and global capital in general.[82] Moreover, China is also nudging its Internet giants through regulations and subsidies to shift their consumer-facing businesses to high value-added industrial sectors.[83] For long-term economic development, China is willing to take short-term losses to ensure a well-functioning Internet market and promote new industrial policies centered around advanced technologies.

Meanwhile, on the other side of the world, the European Union, where Google dominates 90 percent of the market, is poised to regulate Google's market power, signifying the intensification of intercapitalist competition on the Atlantic front.[84]

Europe: The Old Challenge

Countering Google

Transnational capital based in the United States is confronting serious obstacles in China. Yet Google, in particular, also faces vicissitudes in Europe despite its overwhelming domination of Europe's search engine market. Since World War II, Europe has had a long history of struggles to challenge US dominance in the information sphere, but it has not been able to build a globally competitive information economy or even autonomous information systems. In fact, Europe's dependence on US information systems has benefited both the United States and US capital. Google's global dominance and the emergence of China's Internet sector in the global arena have again renewed Europe's attempts to rebuild a home-grown Europe-based Internet sector.

The full story of Europe's failed attempts to establish a thriving, multifaceted information industry independent of and competitive with the United States, both individually and within the framework of the European Union, has never fully been told. It started in the immediate postwar period and has impacted digital computers, satellites, data communication networks, and today's Internet systems and applications; competitive tensions pertaining to search must be placed in this larger context.

In 2005, during the French-German ministerial conference, French president Jacques Chirac warned about the dangers of losing the "power of tomorrow" and stated, "We must take the offensive and muster a massive effort."[85] Chirac was responding to US dominance in the Internet industry and to Google in particular. At the conference, Chirac, alongside German chancellor Gerhard Schröder, endorsed a proposal to build a Franco-German Internet search engine called Quaero (Latin for "I Seek"). Later that month, following the conference, Chirac self-servingly declared, "Culture is not merchandise and cannot be left to blind market forces. We must staunchly defend the world's cultural diversity against the looming threat of uniformity. Our power is at stake."[86]

With urgency, France and Germany initially agreed to provide $1.3 billion to $2.6 billion over five years in order to build an alternative search engine.[87] Technology companies based in Europe such as Thomson, France Télécom, Siemens, and Deutsche Telekom also contributed to the project.[88] Yet this effort was far from successful in mobilizing European countries to counterbalance Google; it ended rather ignobly when Germany dropped out of the project in 2007.

According to the *New York Times*, the main reason for Germany's departure from the project was a disagreement regarding the format of the search engine, with German engineers pursuing a text-based engine and French engineers favoring a multimedia version.[89] Yet this is merely part of the story. It was the German government under its new chancellor Angela Merkel—from the Christian Democratic Union, which had just defeated Gerhard Schröder's Social Democratic Party—that shifted Germany's position and dropped the project.[90] This was because many of the German participants did not want it to be seen as anti-Google, since many considered Google's technology to be beneficial at that time.[91] Rooted in its historical legacy, France was overtly anxious about US dominance of new information spheres and the enrichment of US digital capital at the expense of France; for its part, the German government aspired to ally itself with the United States to be part of the global digital capitalist system.

In 2007, soon after Germany pulled out of the project, its Ministry of Economics and Technology launched the search research project Theseus. Theseus focused on developing new technologies for Internet services based on semantic web technologies, which linked information together via metadata through partnerships with sixty academic institutions and private industry.[92] Hendrik Luchtmeier, a spokesman for the ministry, distinguished Theseus from Quaero, stating that Theseus would not develop a search engine per se, but would support private companies and research organizations working in fields including search technologies and advanced communication networks.[93] By aiding private IT companies and the public institutions supporting them, the German government intended to build a domestic information sector that would have capacity to compete in and be an integral part of the global information market. The Theseus program, one of Germany's biggest research projects in the field of ICTs, was the main part of its "Digital Germany 2015" initiative, whose goal was to further incorporate ICTs throughout the entire German economy.[94] The economic minister at the time, Michael Glos, spoke openly of about Theseus's economic agenda, stating, "New forms of acquiring, searching for and evaluating Internet-based information are of strategic importance for the German governments . . . With Theseus we want to improve Germany and Europe's ability to compete and reach a top position in IT and communications technology."[95] Neither Quaero nor Theseus, however, has succeeded in countering Google's market dominance. Though there were several attempts by the European Union and EU-based tech companies, none came to fruition. In tandem with these efforts, the European Union had mobilized a new cultural front, Europeana, to challenge Google.

Along with the announcement of Quaero in April 2005, Chirac and the premiers of Germany, Spain, Italy, Poland, and Hungary also sent a letter to the president of the European Commission and recommended that the European Union create a digital library to make Europe's cultural heritage accessible for all. This was a state-centered response to Google Book Search, which had embarked on a project to digitize books, maps, newspapers, paintings, photographs, government documents, and other cultural artifacts from around the world. Jean-Noël Jeanneney, who was the head of the Bibliothèque nationale de France from 2002 to 2007, called out Google's book project as a bid for supremacy based on privileging American culture and privatizing public resources.[96] Europeana was the answer to this supposed attack on French and European culture.

An initiative of the European Commission, Europeana aggregates resources from European national libraries, museums, and archives. It was originally part of a larger initiative of the European Commission's five-year economic strategy, called European Information Society 2010, and was meant to build a Europe-based digital marketplace to stimulate the continent's economy.[97] The strategy was launched in 2005 to foster economic growth and job creation by prioritizing information sectors within a single European information market and to provide EU investment in research on information-related sectors.[98] Given this context, Europeana was not only focused on European Union's cultural agenda but also on its political and economic aims of boosting EU-centered information industries. And the chosen vehicles for achieving this were public-private partnerships to digitize cultural materials. Following in the footsteps of US capital, the European Union moved into its cultural realms, which had not been fully captured by capital, to turn them into a marketplace. Digitization was the first step in this process.

To launch the European Information Society, the European Union called for member states to join forces to build regional information sectors by recruiting cultural institutions, though it did so unevenly. Digitization and the organization of digitized information are expensive, onerous processes that require enormous financing, extensive technical expertise, and a developed digital infrastructure. Few institutions in Europe could afford the cost or had the technical capacity to compete with and outpace Google, especially amid widespread austerity policies. The European Union made clear that it would not pay for the actual digitization work, which was left to individual member nations and institutions. Many European cultural institutions, such as national and university libraries in Italy, Austria, Spain, Ireland, and Great Britain, therefore allied with Google, which was willing to digitize their collections to speed up the process. Google's offer was enticing for many European institutions because it meant the company would digitize the materials free of charge in exchange for adding the digitized materials to Google Book Search as well as Europeana.

France was the exception among European countries in defying any alliance with Google and challenging US dominance of European information sectors. In 2009 president Nicolas Sarkozy vowed to spend $1.08 billion toward digitization of the content of French museums, libraries, and cinematographic heritage organizations.[99] He warned that he would not allow Google to "carry out a massive literary land grab on French and other European literature."[100] Sarkozy stated, "We won't let ourselves be stripped of our heritage to the benefit of a big company, no matter how friendly, big or American it is"[101] and further vowed, "We are not going to be deprived of what generations and generations have produced in the French language just because we weren't capable of funding our own digitization project."[102]

The plan was for France to use existing digital collections within the Gallica project, which digitized national collections, and challenge Google. Sarkozy emphasized the importance of public-private partnerships in digitizing his nation's cultural works. France aimed to build up Gallica's collections by partnering with French publishers and private companies.[103] This public-private partnership was a step toward exploitative privatization of public resources. France's overarching concern was to erode US dominance in the information market and reserve France's cultural heritage for French commercial interests, not to attack capitalist development of information provision.

In December 2009, after France had said no to Google—the president of a French publishing industry group had called it "cultural rape"[104]—and decided to pursue its own digitization project, Minister of Culture Frédéric Mitterrand, nephew of former president François Mitterrand, and Google executive David Drummond met in Paris to discuss France's concerns. In a *New York Times* interview, Bruno Racine, president of the Bibliothèque nationale de France (2007–2016), asserted the "necessity of a partnership with the private sector in order to secure the capital needed for vast digitization projects."[105] Racine's position shifted from that of his predecessor, Jean-Noël Jeanneney, who had been a fierce opponent of Google Books. France left the door open for Google to be part of the public-private partnership. According to a diplomatic cable made public by WikiLeaks, the reason Mitterrand altered his position was that it would cost $1.5 billion and require technical expertise to digitize fourteen million works in the library, and Google had agreed to create jobs in France and open a scanning facility in Lyon as part of its digitization agreement with the University of Lyon.[106]

By January 2010 France had succumbed to working with Google on the digitization of books at its national library, but it insisted that it would not allow

Google to have legal control over digitized materials. Google was demanding exclusive control over the works for a period of twenty to twenty-five years. Mitterrand stated, "Google came to Europe with the attitude of a conqueror, and many opened the door to it by signing deals which I find unacceptable, [that] are based on excessive confidentiality, impossible exclusivity, and a casual, even one-sided approach to copyright. . . . We will propose to them . . . to exchange files without confidentiality or exclusivity, in total transparency and with total respect for copyright."[107]

France aspired to control its own information and culture and insisted that Google drop the exclusivity clauses in the agreement.[108] Yet before the French government's official announcement of the partnership with Google, the Bibliothèque Municipale in Lyon had forged a deal allowing Google to digitize its entire book collection and to give the company the commercial rights to the works for twenty-five years.[109] It became the first library in France to partner with Google to digitize books.

France had led Europe in voicing its opposition to US control over information and culture, but there were signs that France was gradually having its information sphere taken over by US-based transnational capital and marching toward the privatization of its own cultural materials. In 2013 the Ministry of Culture announced a public-private partnership between the Bibliothèque nationale de France and US-based ProQuest to digitize more than seventy thousand books, two hundred thousand sound recordings, and other documents in the public domain. The European public domain advocacy organization Communia pointed out that ProQuest would retain ten-year exclusive agreements allowing the private company to host and commercialize the digitized collections while limiting online access during the period of digitization.[110]

American capital was not merely going after a segment of culture; it was eyeing the entire span of cultural spaces in France and Europe more widely to bring them into their profit-making realm. The Google Cultural Institute, launched in 2011, aimed to digitize cultural materials from museums and archives around the world and gobble them up into its business of information.[111] The Google Cultural Institute established its headquarters in Paris to preemptively occupy the untapped cultural information sphere as it swallowed French symbols of culture from the Eiffel Tower to Versailles to the Paris Opera and even street art into Google's digital territory.

Battlefield

American capital devoured a massive reservoir of culture that would be a new source of profit-making, but not without opposition. Google's relentless advances into Europe's cultural and information spheres have stirred Europe's deep-seated anxiety over US information dominance. But the battle is not merely between European and US-based capital; it is also between US rivals. Much of the US-based Internet capital was looking for competitive advantage extraterritorially by making use of European legal authority in the jurisdiction of the European Union. As a result, Europe turned into a major battlefield for US inter-capitalist rivalries.

In 2010 the European Commission, the European Union's executive body and the twenty-seven-nation bloc's antitrust authority, officially opened an antitrust case against Google, which concerned whether the company was penalizing its competitors in search rankings. The case was initiated by four companies based in Europe: the French legal search engine Ejustice.fr, 1PlusV (the parent company of Ejustice.fr), the UK-based Foundem, and Germany-based Ciao!, which was owned by Microsoft at the time of the case. These four companies filed official complaints with the European Union, stating that Google's search algorithm had had significant negative consequences for their website traffic. On the surface, it seemed that the case had been brought to protest against Google's dominance in the European market. In point of fact, though, as Nicolas Petit, a professor of competition law at the University of Liege, Belgium, pointed out, "Everyone understands here in Brussels that it's Microsoft versus Google."[112] At the time of the investigation, Microsoft was one of the leading lobbyists in Europe, with more than $5 million spent in 2014.[113] Close behind Microsoft, Google spent between $3.94 million to $4.23 million in 2014.[114]

Backed by its lobbying efforts, Microsoft was one of the leading companies behind numerous EU antitrust complaints against Google, doing so to object to Google's giving preference to its own services and advertisers in search rankings. Microsoft used several lobbying groups as fronts to urge the European Commission to probe Google's business practices. The *Financial Times* uncovered the fact that Foundem was supported by the Initiative for a Competitive Online Marketplace, a Microsoft-backed lobbying group.[115]

In addition to Foundem, Ciao!—formerly a longtime Google AdSense partner, but acquired by Microsoft in 2008 and sold in 2012 to LeGuide Group, the European online shopping guide—initially took its antitrust case to the German competition authority but moved it to the European Commission to have legal standing throughout Europe. In March 2011 Microsoft itself filed a formal complaint with the commission, stating that Google had engaged in an unfair, anticompetitive "pattern of actions."[116] TripAdvisor, a travel review website, also joined the EU competition complaints against Google. TripAdvisor, along with Microsoft, was one of the founding members of FairSearch, which was created after Google had acquired flight-booking software program ITA in 2010. Members of FairSearch also include other major US-based Google competitors Expedia, Hotwire, Kayak, and Oracle.

In April 2013 the European Commission concluded that Google may have breached antitrust rules and could have fined the company as much as 10 percent of its annual worldwide revenue,[117] but it allowed Google to submit a proposal to address its concerns. Soon afterward, however, Google's rivals pressured the commission to reject Google's proposal, which promised to label Google's own services and show links to rival services in its search results. FairSearch's chief counsel Thomas Vinje harshly criticized Google's proposal, saying that it merely reaffirmed the company's monopoly.[118] Under pressure from the lobbying groups backed by US tech firms, the European Union made Google agree to further concessions to settle the case. In February 2014, Google agreed to alter the way its search results displayed competitors' links, seemingly putting an end to the three-year antitrust probe and avoiding a heavy fine.

Yet along with the US tech firms, European capital also mobilized opposition to Google's proposed settlement with the European Union. A group called the Open Internet Project, supported by the German media giant Axel Springer, the leading French mobile media group Internet Lagardère Active, and twelve hundred European digital companies, lobbied the commission to revisit its decision concerning the Google settlement.[119] More than thirty publishers from the European Association of Newspapers also requested that the European Union reject Google's proposal, arguing that the settlement would secure Google's dominance and continue to stymie competition.[120] Arnaud Montebourg, France's Minister of Economy at the time, compared Google to "a new East India Company" seeking to ravage European wealth.[121] The German Economy Minister, Sigmar Gabriel, even called for breaking up Google's monopoly, asking to "re-establish the sovereignty of law by ruling that Google can no longer simply bypass European standards."[122]

In 2014 Europe's fear of US dominance was reignited with Edward Snowden's exposure of the US National Security Agency (NSA) and its secret global surveillance programs. Given the scale of such activities and the fact that the NSA collected data directly from the servers of major Internet firms including Microsoft, Google, Apple, Yahoo!, and others, EU member states were looking to tighten the reins on Google and other US Internet firms.

Despite Google's vehement denials, there were several reports of the company's collaboration with and close ties to the NSA.[123] After Snowden's news broke, Google quickly turned up its PR machine as it and other US Internet firms recognized that NSA's Prism program would cost their businesses, which rely heavily on international markets. For example, IBM spent a billion dollars to build a data center outside the United States to assure its international clients that their data would be safe from US government surveillance.[124] Microsoft now offers foreign customers the option of storing their data on servers outside the United States.[125] The company opened data centers in Germany and strategically put Deutsche Telecom in charge of the data centers' operations.[126]

In 2015 the EC Commissioner for Competition, Margrethe Vestager, formerly the finance minister of Denmark, renewed the European Union's charges against Google's dominance in search and officially opened a second investigation of Google and its Android mobile operating system. This time, the European Commission charged the company with anticompetitive behavior because it required mobile manufacturers to pre-install Google products and services. In the following year, the European Union brought a third antitrust case against Google for favoring its own shopping services and using its dominant market position to prevent the display of ads from competitors.[127]

It is interesting that in 2016, in the midst of this ardent battle Microsoft, one of Google's most outspoken opponents, suddenly agreed to a pact with Google to drop all pending regulatory complaints against each other. And Microsoft withdrew from its memberships in FairSearch and Initiative for a Competitive Online Marketplace, the two lobbying groups in which Microsoft had been deeply involved to support antitrust actions against Google's search business in Europe.[128] Microsoft's new attitude toward Google was a practical move given that this long, draining legal battle had no guarantee of financial or market gains, but more important, it was more an indication of shifts in business priorities. Microsoft was repositioning itself by moving into cloud computing and artificial intelligence, which are built on "big data." Therefore, the company shifted its lobbying priorities in Europe, particularly toward data-related policy such as privacy and data protection.[129] It needed to forge relationships with major competitors such as Google to lobby against the European Union's data protection rules, which impacted the entire industry. The heavy hitter Microsoft had moved on, but there were plenty of Google competitors remaining on both sides of the Atlantic to continue challenging the company. In 2017, under EU competition chief Margrethe Vestager, Google was hit with a record $2.7 billion fine for the promotion of its own shopping service, with its rivals demanding stronger regulatory measures. Subsequently, in 2019, the European Union fined Google $5 billion for using Android OS to embed other Google services and $1.7 billion for abusing its dominant position in online advertising. Far from retreating from reining in US tech giants, Brussels continues forging ahead with full force.

The current president of the European Commission, Ursula von der Leye, is poised to take a leading role in global tech regulation including AI, big data, privacy, antitrust, and facial-recognition technology. The European Union reappointed Margrethe Vestager as its competition chief and bestowed on her a new title, Executive Vice President for a Europe Fit for the Digital Age. Vestager invigorated oversight of the tech industry and garnered hefty fines from US tech giants including Google and Apple; her new position extends her power across digital sectors in which tech firms are heavily invested, including finance and automobiles. Moreover, US tech firms are not the only objects of scrutiny by EU authorities. Member states have also demanded that the European Union look into Chinese state-owned companies acquiring EU assets as China increases its footprint in Europe.[130] China's total foreign direct investment (FDI) in the European Union—which includes mergers and acquisitions and greenfield FDI—had risen from €7.6 billion in 2013 to over €$44 billion in 2016, outpacing European FDI in China.[131] Since its peak, mergers and acquisitions FDI has declined due to China's regulatory control over outbound capital, geopolitical tensions, and the COVID-19 pandemic, but greenfield FDI—where a company establishes a subsidiary in a foreign country—has increased from an average of 6.5 percent of total FDI to 20 percent in 2020.[132] The United Kingdom, Germany, and France accounted for 50 percent of China's total FDI in the EU market in 2020.[133] The European Union sees China as a new rival; however, it has not ruled out China as a new potential strategic ally hedging against the United States and as a partner in building the EU tech sector.

In 2019 the Chinese equipment vendors Huawei and ZTE held more than 40 percent of the EU market.[134] Amid the trade dispute between the United States and China during the Trump administration, the United States pressured the European Union to ban Huawei, the leading supplier of 5G technologies, from participating in the development of European 5G infrastructure. The US government was even considering funding European rivals Nokia and Ericsson as alternative 5G suppliers.[135] Nokia and Ericsson were caught in the crossfire. Along with Great Britain, Sweden had banned Huawei and ZTE as 5G equipment suppliers. State-owned China Mobile, the world's biggest wireless carrier, shrank its 5G equipment contracts with foreign suppliers from 11 percent of total contracts awarded in 2020 to 5.4 percent in 2021. The Swedish vendor Ericsson faced the biggest cut; it was the sole foreign supplier in 2020, but its China Mobile contract was reduced in 2021 to 1.9 percent of the total of 5.4 percent. Meanwhile, the Finnish telecom company Nokia took the major share of the Chinese contracts awarded to foreign companies, at 3.5 percent of an estimated $6 billion.[136]

So far Europe hasn't shown a united front in responding to US pressure to drop Chinese telecom vendors. Germany, France, and other European countries, defying the United States, have refused to exclude Huawei in building out their 5G networks. But the Biden administration, under the self-serving principle of fighting against "tech-autocracies," quickly tried to rebuild alliances by renewing transatlantic relationships, creating the EU-US Trade and Technology Council to extend bilateral trade in the tech sector, and, to isolate China further, also shored up its alliances with South Korea, Japan, and Taiwan.[137] Presenting a new agenda for the newly formed council, EU foreign affairs minister Josep Borrell made assurances that this new alliance was not meant to exclude or isolate China from the economic and tech sectors, stating, "We need China."[138]

The European Union is pushing dual strategies: leading global tech regulatory regimes as well as creating an EU-based information industry to respond to China and the United States. So far, the European Union doesn't have its own tech behemoths to compete with these, but it is increasingly weaponizing its regulatory power to challenge the US and Chinese Internet sectors. According to a 2019 survey, the majority of global tech policy was coming from either the European Union or from EU member states.[139] In 2018 a major data protection policy called the General Data Protection Regulation was implemented across the European Union. It was designed to protect EU citizens' personal data from tech companies and organizations. Violators would be fined up to $23 million or 4 percent of their global revenue, whichever was higher. The regulation was viewed as a model for other countries struggling to figure out ways to limit personal data collection by the tech industry. In 2021 the European Commission overhauled its Internet regulations and proposed the Digital Services Act and the Digital Markets Act. The former focuses on the online advertising industry while the latter deals with market power and global tech giants that are considered gatekeepers hindering new entries into the market. These expansive proposals aim to tame the Silicon Valley tech giants and create more competitive market conditions for EU-based companies.

Yet by no means are Google and US tech companies merely on the defensive regarding these new European Internet rules and regulations. They are aggressively engaging in lobbying efforts. Google has the most extensive lobbying operation in Brussels and in major European capitals, and its business operations in Europe have expanded over the years. In 2012 Google opened a Berlin office in Unter den Linden, the European Union mecca for lobbyists. In 2013 according to *Der Spiegel*, Google began to build its lobbying network of PR professionals, activists, and academics.[140] The newspaper noted that a former Google lobbyist worked for the German Foreign Ministry, where he co-organized a conference along with Aarhus University, Human Rights Watch, and the Humboldt Institute for Internet and Society on the theme of Internet and Human Rights.[141] This is one of Google's more artful tactics; as the company attempts to mobilize activists, academics, and government officials to pursue the twin virtues of "human rights" and "Internet freedom," to which few would object, this actually is an attempt to shield its corporate interests. In 2021 the *Financial Times* reported that a leaked internal Google document revealed that the company's lobbying strategies were to remove "unreasonable constraints" on Google's business model and shift the political discourse regarding the proposed EU Digital Services Act and Digital Marketing Act in Brussels, stressing that these regulations would economically impact Europeans and limit the potential of the Internet.[142] According to a 2021 *Transparency International* report, Google was the top lobbying spender that year and had the most meetings with members of the European Parliament.[143] In 2020 Google spent €5.75 million on lobbying in the European Union, and combined with Amazon, Facebook, and Apple, US tech lobbying budgets reached €19 million, or $23 million, and have increased almost threefold since 2014.[144] Margarida Silva of *Corporate Europe Observatory* noted that "the budgets are really unrivaled—we've never seen this kind of money being spent by companies directly."[145]

For the European Union, regulatory influence alone is not sufficient to curtail US and Chinese tech power. The European Union intends to build its own digital economy and is setting up a €100 billon sovereign wealth fund to back European-based tech companies in their competition against Google, Facebook, and Amazon.[146] The German government has pushed for cloud independence and a European-based cloud network called Gaia-X to challenge Amazon Cloud, and France has joined this effort. In a 2019 German-French joint meeting, France's Economy and Finance Minister, Bruno Le Maire, said: "We want to establish a safe and sovereign European data infrastructure, including data warehouses and data pooling and develop data interoperability." Germany's Minister for Economic Affairs, Peter Altmaier, said that this cloud computing initiative would help Europe "regain" its "digital sovereignty."[147] In 2021 the European Commission launched an initiative called the EU Startup Nations Standard, which seeks to create friendly conditions for startups to catch up with the United States and China. By 2022, twenty-five European countries had joined this initiative. The questions for the European Union are, against the encroachment of the United States and China, will the European Union be able to maneuver between the two global power blocs (which are its largest trading partners) and national, European bloc, and transnational capital interests? In what ways will its regulatory forays limit or restrict the development of an EU-based tech sector?

Conclusion

This examination of search elucidates that the Internet is at the leading edge of the transnational capitalist market system and has turned into a major geopolitical, economic, and intercapitalist fissure. Google's struggles in moving into the Chinese Internet market have been persistently seen as an "intranet" managed by China, whose dynamic Internet sector is tightly intertwined not only with the global Internet market but also with global capitalism.

China's far-reaching success in building its domestic Internet sector, which is undercutting the long-time dominance of US-centric Internet systems and services, has escalated anxiety in the United States, driving the its aggressive policy, from tariffs to restrictions on investment in Chinese tech companies, investing in domestic technologies, and rearranging its global alliances. Amid tensions between the United States and China, the European Union, a major arena for US rivals, is leveraging its position and asserting its power by setting up new global Internet regulations. The rivalry between the United States, the European Union, and China over the Internet, which has been woven into the global political economy, animates the restructuring of US-led digital capitalism.

Because the United States is determined to maintain its dominant position, the Biden administration swiftly brought up the familiar virtues of "democracy," "freedom," and "human rights," which obfuscate its real objectives. It is certain that the US government and major US firms such as Google will continue to push to maintain and shape the Internet in their favor. This cross-border inflection isn't about "a battle between the utility of democracies and autocracies in the 21st century," as Biden claims.[148] The conflict is about which capitalist states and which capital will have the upper hand in controlling the Internet, the axis of global capitalism today. The United States continues to attempt to keep China and the European Union within the US-led global capitalist system. At the same time, the counterpressures are intensifying as the new geopolitical landscape, accompanying the changing power structure of transnational capitalism, enters a phase of global power realignment and political economic dynamics that will further disrupt US-led global digital capitalism.

CONCLUSION

As of this writing, the coronavirus pandemic is still ravaging the planet and has disrupted the global capitalist economy. The pandemic has revealed an undeniable cruelty of the capitalist economic system, which bleeds public institutions and resources—libraries, healthcare, education, the US postal system, and public transportation—to a state of anemia that has disproportionately affected poor and working-class areas both in the United States and the global South, where there are few basic protections or social safety nets. Yet in the midst of this pandemic, which has killed millions of people, capitalist governments and elites have "reopened" the economy. Former Google CEO Eric Schmidt told investors in 2020, "Use the opportunity of the crisis to reconfigure and ensure the decisions you make now make you stronger when this lifts—in a year or maybe less."[1] In order to seize new opportunities for accumulation, Google and other tech companies have quickly asserted that they care about people, as their PR machines have churned out an upbeat response to the coronavirus. Google and Apple, which are competitors in many sectors, showed their willingness to collaborate to build "contact tracing" apps for the coronavirus; meanwhile, the tech giants are ready to accelerate the commercialization, commodification, and corporatization of public health to profit from the pandemic. Schmidt opined that COVID should make people more "grateful" for Big Tech once and for all.[2]

This response from the tech sector brings one back to this book's starting point. Google tells the public that search is a free service because it cares, but the development of search has been shown to have been largely socialized by taxpayers, and the basis of the massive wealth of the industry has been extracted from public resources and workers.[3]

Search is ubiquitous in people's social lives. Humans are predisposed to be inquisitive. This basic domain of information searching used to be either informal or contained within the public sphere, where it was managed by nonmarket entities such as libraries and other cultural and educational institutions. Yet capital has gradually pried open and reorganized those institutions into commercial zones. The development of the search function with Internet connectivity in the 1990s seemed to show new possibilities for accessing and organizing information, and for bringing the pieces of the information domain that had moved to the market back into the public sphere. New technical capabilities for accessing and distributing information and the absence of a fully developed market-based model used on the Internet offered opportunities for cultural institutions to expand their influence in shaping information provision for the public good.

Despite its democratic potential and wondrous technical affordances, however, the search function has instead been reorganized by capital and transformed into a new commodity. Under state policies that encouraged capital to carefully structure the Internet into new economic growth zones, capital persistently innovated search engine technologies not to meet social needs but to construct a profit-making information enterprise whereby Google and other tech companies resorted to an advertising-based business model. But, this commodification of search has *not* taken place within deliberative public debates, nor is it a product of democratic consensus. Rather, capital-driven digitization of search is predicated on destruction and robbing of public resources—the process of "accumulation by dispossession."[4]

The search engine industry has ravaged the public information commons, establishing new sites for profit making and engulfing the remaining nonmarket information domains, and it has become the leading edge of the information economy. In the past generation, ordinary people's information activities have almost completely migrated away from a patchwork of libraries, the Yellow Pages, newspapers, magazines, community, friends, family, and acquaintances and toward the transnational Internet-based information retrieval system. This shift has spurred new practices in social and cultural life expressed in terms of efficiency, democracy, and technological breakthroughs, yet it deepens market logics and is far removed from democratic information provision. By annexing public information provision and controlling information infrastructure, capital has gained a stranglehold on the information space and has turned search into a global industry. Our basic search activities are now solely dependent on the market. Fundamental information provision has been transformed into a lucrative market controlled by US-based multinationals.

Despite Google's 90 percent market share in many countries around the globe, there is intense competition. This drives cost-cutting, lowering of wages, and technical innovation. As Anwar Shaikh notes, "the profit motive is inherently expansionary," so firms compete against each other.[5] In order to maintain its dominance while facing intense competition from multiple directions, Google has sought to expand its influence in markets across the economy, weaving itself into every information and communication sector and beyond and shaping the political economy of the Internet. Google, Facebook, Microsoft, Amazon, and Apple dominate their own areas, but the sectoral lines no longer exist as they compete, bleed into each other's territories domestically and internationally in search of new profit sites, and propel new capital accumulation projects.

Under this competitive pressure, to speed up the production process, control its position, and grow, Google's search business impels efforts to reconstitute global network infrastructures to outbid competitors as it fights to shave milliseconds from Internet traffic and places cables in new territories. The depth and breadth of network infrastructure constructed by Google and its US internet competitors, allying with local and regional telecom companies, illustrates how much of the world is integrated into transnationalized digital capitalism.

This titanic global search business requires particular occupational structures and labor controls for its ongoing competition, accumulation, and growth. The persistent myth of big tech has been that it would create a large quantity of well-paid occupations and lead to the disappearance of mundane low-wage work. On the contrary, capitalism's further integration of digital technologies has not, in fact, evaded the deskilling and degradation of work; rather, it has extended it as it continues to introduce and instill technical and organizational innovations to reorganize labor processes to increase productivity and profit. This has resulted in the growth of low-wage work and incorporation of unwaged labor. The search industry reflects this trend. The occupational structure of the highly automated and science-based company Google, for instance, consists of a small number of skilled and well-paid workers at the top, along with a mass of low-wage process workers and users who perform unpaid work. The bottom is expanding, defying the common notion that the new information economy will distribute wealth and reduce poverty.

Google's exploitative labor structure was initially camouflaged from the public since it was outsourced and fragmented widely over the network. Meanwhile, Google has long been portrayed in the media very favorably as defying its capitalist logic by empowering workers and seemingly relinquishing capital's control over labor.

In this era of austerity, when many workers struggling for survival are willing to accept wage cuts simply to hang on to their jobs, Google has been perceived as going against the grain by offering a system in which capitalism could be compatible with democratic ideals. The search business seems on the surface to have departed from industrial capitalism; however, Google shows characteristics similar to those of industrial enterprises, hierarchical labor organization, and the nineteenth-century labor control mechanisms. Relations between labor and capital at Google firmly ally with its corporate accumulation strategies by artfully applying the renewed welfare capitalism management techniques of the industrial era and combining them with the premise of "objective" science and big data. Google's "worker-centered" corporate management strategies show no signs of altering but, rather, actually deepening capitalist social relations.

Buttressed by its expansive global infrastructure, a global army of workers, and an exploitative labor structure and management, Google has impressively captured the most profitable and dynamic internet sector. Yet its success has also recast the strategic economic importance of information flows and communication networks in the expansion of global capitalism, which has reignited geopolitical rivalries. Despite the global dominance of the US internet giants, the evolution of search shows that the US information regime faces mounting challenges. This is because of structural changes to the political economy and a new geopolitics of information and communication including China's reentry into the worldwide capitalist system and Europe's renewed efforts to shape the global information sphere.

Although the Western media portray the Chinese Internet sector in terms of freedom, human rights, censorship, and authoritarianism on the web, this rhetoric conceals the changing political economy of the Internet. China's successful creation of a home-grown Internet industry that is substantially integrated into the global political economy is restructuring US-led global capitalism. China's advancement in critical technologies, which Europe hasn't been able to achieve, spurred a new rivalry between the United States and China. The former is aggressively engaged in safeguarding its primacy. To counter China, the US government has been mobilizing its political economic power. It is not only placing a range of sanctions against Chinese tech actors, creating barriers to entry, but is also flexing its muscles to arrange economic alliances, for example, pursuing a deal with the European Union for a joint investment in critical Internet sectors from AI and semiconductors to supply chains.[6] The United States has to keep the European Union within its economic sphere of influence if it is to contain China. Meanwhile, Europe is on a tightrope and looking for a strategic balance between China and the United States to serve its own interests and assert its power by writing new rules and regulations for the Internet. The United States has even showed signs of willingness to restrain its domestic tech giants in order to accommodate Europe's assertion of new regulatory policies from corporate taxes to antitrust measurements and privacy.

This new geopolitical conflict animates the restructuring of digital capitalism in which all three of these major players are trying to reconfigure the Internet industry to serve their own interests as well as to renew global capital accumulation. For the United States, maintaining its tech supremacy is vital to its global power yet is a very complicated business. Deeply transnationalized global capitalism doesn't consist merely of major power states and multinational corporations; it is a system wherein multiple states, domestic capital, and local social and political actors are in a complex and ever-shifting relationship. Thus, the questions are: How and to what extent will the United States and China pursue their own interests without disrupting vital markets and destabilizing the shared project of the global capitalist system? How will Europe push new regulatory regimes without hurting its domestic capital, navigate between the economic poles of its two major rivals, build its own Internet sector to better compete within the bloc and globally, and keep a united front among all twenty-seven member nations? How and in what ways will these super-economic powers collaborate to privilege transnational (as opposed to domestic) capital and navigate domestic political and social interests? And how will various states manage as the ground continues to shift under their feet?

These questions pose the ultimate conundrum for the global powers, yet these questions are at odds with the United States' self-appointed role in guarding technological democracy. Answering them gets us no closer to reorganizing the Internet to be a truly democratic, shared resource managed outside the marketplace or addressing the growth imperative of capitalism that brought the exploitation of public resources and workers. Where, then, is the hope for a democratic and emancipatory world when even the most basic function of search is being controlled and appropriated by capital? What are the possibilities for organizing a society where democratic information provision is possible?

The answer lies not in choosing between Google and another venture capital–funded search engine such as DuckDuckGo, or merely implementing various privacy tools developed by the US State Department and corporations, or negotiating with corporations and capitalist states to tweak capitalism to be gentler and kinder. Exposing corporate greed, demanding accountability, implementing government regulations, and breaking up giant corporations are vital moves toward a more equitable society, and these are hopeful steps. But merely altering corporations' behavior to make them more socially responsible or moral, or creating more competitive markets by breaking up the giants, is not sufficient to reverse capitalist social relations.

If the history of search offers a lesson, the commodification of our basic search activities wasn't an imperative or a natural progression. It tells us that search can be de-commodified and reorganized as a global public good. If capital and capitalist states were mobilized to reorganize basic social and information provision into markets, the force of collective opposition lies with labor. Vivek Chibber underscores that capitalism as an economic system exists through exploitation of the majority working class, but at the same time, this majority can be the organizing force against capital, a force that challenges capitalist social relations.[7] There are signs of hope in local, national, and international arenas where collective action by the working class in different sectors is resisting capitalism, which dispossesses, displaces, and brutalizes ordinary people and strips away basic public resources. Where are the points of struggle?

In 2022, more than a thousand coal miners in Alabama who were struggling to afford basic necessities went on a five-month strike demanding living wages and basic benefits; more than two thousand food couriers organized by *Los Deliveristas Unidos*, a loose network of immigrant workers demanding better working conditions, marched in Times Square in New York; and Uber and Lyft drivers pressured Congress to pass the Protect the Right to Organize Act, which would allow contractors to unionize.[8] In 2020, 250 million people in India participated in a general strike to protest against repressive agricultural reforms that sought to deregulate and further open up the sector to corporations;[9] and in Colombia, protesters around the country, in part mobilized by Colombia's National Strike Committee—made up of indigenous people, students, and trade unions—were in the streets against a regressive tax bill and to demand economic and educational equity as well as police reforms.[10]

However dispersed or fragmented they are, these are the forces that can dismantle the myth of corporate controlled digital capitalism—which persistently promises quality jobs, democracy, equality, fairness, and universal knowledge to people—and digital capitalism which insidiously generates further exploitation and injustice.

NOTES

Introduction

1. "Alphabet Cash on Hand," *Macrotrends*, https://www.macrotrends.net/stocks/charts/GOOGL/alphabet/cash-on-hand.

2. "$25 Billion to Vaccinate the World," *Public Citizen*, May 24, 2021, https://www.citizen.org/article/25-billion-to-vaccinate-the-world/.

3. American Innovation and Choice Online Act, S. 2992, 117th Congress, 2nd sess., introduced in the Senate October 18, 2021, https://www.congress.gov/bill/117th-congress/senate-bill/2992/text/.

4. Open App Markets Act, S. 2710, 117th Cong., 2nd sess., introduced in the Senate August 11, 2011, https://www.congress.gov/bill/117th-congress/senate-bill/2710/actions.

5. Ryan Tracy, "Tim Wu, Big Tech Critic, Named to National Economic Council," *Wall Street Journal*, March 5, 2019, https://www.wsj.com/articles/tim-wu-big-tech-critic-named-to-national-economic-council-11614954821.

6. See Matthew Hindman, *The Myth of Digital Democracy* (Princeton: Princeton University Press, 2009); Lucas Introna and Helen Nissenbaum, "Shaping the Web: Why the Politics of Search Engines Matter," *Information Society* 16, no. 3 (2000): 169–185; Eszter Hargittai, "Do You 'Google'? Understanding Search Engine Use Beyond the Hype," *First Monday* 9, no. 3 (2003), https://firstmonday.org/article/view/1127/1047; Alexander Halavais, *Search Engine Society* (Cambridge, MA: Polity, 2009); Siva Vaidhyanathan, *The Googlization of Everything (and Why We Should Worry)* (Berkeley: University of California Press, 2011).

7. Elizabeth Van Couvering, "Search Engine Bias: The Structuration of Traffic on the World-Wide Web" (PhD diss., London School of Economics, 2010); Paško Bilić, "A Critique of the Political Economy of Algorithms: A Brief History of Google's Technological Rationality," *TripleC: Cognition, Communication, Co-operation* 16, no. 1 (2018), 315–331; Christian Fuchs, "Google Capitalism," *TripleC: Cognition, Communi-

cation, Co-operation 10, no. 1 (2012): 42–48; Micky Lee, *Alphabet: The Becoming of Google* (London: Routledge, 2019); Frank Pasquale, *The Black Box Society: The Secret Algorithms That Control Money and Information* (Cambridge, MA : Harvard University Press, 2015).

8. Joseph Johnson, "Global Digital Population as of January 2021," *Statista*, April 7, 2021, https://www.statista.com/statistics/617136/digital-population-worldwide/.

9. Jessica Clement, "Most Popular Websites Worldwide from 1993 to 2020, by Highest Number of Monthly Visits," *Statista*, February 5, 2021, https://www.statista.com/statistics/1175389/most-popular-websites-monthly-visits/.

10. "Digital Advertising Spending Worldwide from 2019 to 2024," *Statista*, May 28, 2021, https://www.statista.com/statistics/237974/online-advertising-spending-worldwide/.

11. Joseph Johnson, "Annual Revenue of Alphabet from 2017 to 2020, by Segment," *Statista*, February 2, 2021, https://www.statista.com/statistics/633651/alphabet-annual-global-revenue-by-segment/.

12. Shanhong Liu, "Microsoft Corporation Search Ad Revenue 2016–2021," *Statista*, August 3, 2021, https://www-statista-com.stanford.idm.oclc.org/statistics/725388/microsoft-corporation-ad-revenue/.

13. Matt Egan, "2008: Worse Than the Great Depression?," *CNN Business*, August 14, 2014, https://money.cnn.com/2014/08/27/news/economy/ben-bernanke-great-depression/index.html.

14. Robert Lenzner, "The 2008 Financial Collapse Was Worse Than 1929, Geithner Insists," *Forbes*, June 22, 2014, https://www.forbes.com/sites/robertlenzner/2014/06/22/the-2008-financial-collapse-was-worse-than-1929/?sh=735218cf5f35.

15. Staci D. Kramer, "Obama: 'We'll Renew Our Information Superhighway,'" *CBS News*, December 8, 2008, https://www.cbsnews.com/news/obama-well-renew-our-information-superhighway.

16. Lance Whitney, "Obama Dines with Jobs, Zuckerberg, Other Tech Honchos," *CNET*, February 18, 2011, http://www.cnet.com/news/obama-dines-with-jobs-zuckerberg-other-tech-honchos/.

17. Capital accumulation is defined by having at least a portion of surplus-value reinvested and converted to new capital to produce more surplus-value. See Chapter 6 David Harvey, *The Limits of Capital* (London; New York: Verso, 2006).

18. Office of the President of the United States, "Issues: Technology," accessed January 1, 2020, https://web.archive.org/web/20090805221222/http://www.whitehouse.gov/issues/technology/.

19. White House Office of the Press Secretary, "White House to Launch Digital Promise Initiative," September 16, 2011, http://www.whitehouse.gov/the-press-office/2011/09/16/white-house-launch-digital-promise-initiative.

20. Matt Joseph, "How President Obama Shaped the Future of Digital Health," *TechCrunch*, July 27, 2016, https://techcrunch.com/2016/07/27/how-president-obama-shaped-the-future-of-digital-health/.

21. Barack Obama, "Writing the Rules for 21st Century Trade," The White House, February 18, 2015, https://obamawhitehouse.archives.gov/blog/2015/02/18/president-obama-writing-rules-21st-century-trade.

22. Executive Office of the President's Council of Advisors on Science and Technology, "Report to the President: Ensuring Long-Term U.S. Leadership in Semiconductors," January 2017, https://obamawhitehouse.archives.gov/sites/default/files/microsites/ostp/PCAST/pcast_ensuring_long-term_us_leadership_in_semiconductors.pdf.

23. National Intelligence Council, "Global Trends 2030: Alternative Worlds," December 2021, https://info.publicintelligence.net/GlobalTrends2030.pdf.

24. Vijay Prashad, "Trade and Tensions Between the U.S. and China," *Monthly Review Online*, August 3, 2020, https://mronline.org/2020/08/03/trade-and-tensions-between-the-u-s-and-china/.

25. Samm Sacks, Statement Before the House Energy and Commerce Committee Subcommittee on Communications and Technology, "Telecommunications, Global Competitiveness, and National Security," 115th Cong., 2nd sess., May 16, 2018, 19 https://purl.fdlp.gov/GPO/gpo113871.

26. Nick Bastone, "A Wall Street Firm Figured Out How Much Money Google Will Sacrifice by Cutting off Huawei," *Business Insider*, May 24, 2019, https://www.businessinsider.com/wall-street-estimates-google-lost-revenue-huawei-ban-2019-5.

27. Asa Fitch and Stu Woo, "The U.S. vs. China: Who Is Winning the Key Technology Battles?" *Wall Street Journal*, April 12, 2020, https://www.wsj.com/articles/the-u-s-vs-china-who-is-winning-the-key-technology-battles-11586548597; Audrey Cher, "'Superpower Marathon': U.S. May Lead China in Tech Right Now—But Beijing Has the Strength to Catch Up," *CNBC*, May 17, 2020, https://www.cnbc.com/2020/05/18/us-china-tech-race-beijing-has-strength-to-catch-up-with-us-lead.html.

28. Outline of the People's Republic of China's 14th Five-Year Plan for National Economic and Social Development and Long-Range Objectives for 2035, *Xinhua News Agency*, March 12, 2021, https://cset.georgetown.edu/wp-content/uploads/t0284_14th_Five_Year_Plan_EN.pdf.

29. United States Innovation and Competition Act of 2021, S. 1260, 117th Cong., 1st sess., passed in the Senate June 8, 2021, https://www.congress.gov/bill/117th-congress/senate-bill/1260.

30. The America Competes Act of 2022, U.S. House of Representatives Committee on Science, Space, and Technology, https://science.house.gov/americacompetes.

31. Bjarke Smith-Meyer, Lili Bayer, and Jakob Hanke Vela, "EU Officials Float €100B Boost for European Companies." *Politico*, August 22, 2019, https://www.politico.eu/article/exclusive-european-commission-leaked-plans/.

32. Robert McChesney, "The Political Economy of Global Communication," in *Capitalism and the Information Age*, ed. Ellen Wood, John Bellamy Foster, and Robert McChesney (New York: Monthly Review Press, 1998), 1–26.

33. Vincent Mosco and Andrew Herman, "Critical Theory and Electronic Media," *Theory and Society* 10 (1981): 869–896.

34. Janet Wasko, "The Study of the Political Economy of the Media in the Twenty-First Century," *International Journal of Media and Cultural Politics* 10, no. 3 (2014): 259–271.

35. Shoshana Zuboff, *The Age of Surveillance Capitalism: The Fight for a Human Future at the New Frontier of Power* (New York: Public Affairs, 2019); Boutang Moulier, *Cognitive Capitalism* (Cambridge, UK: Polity, 2021); Manuel Castells, *The Rise of the Network Society* (Oxford: Wiley-Blackwell, 2009); Nick Srnicek, *Platform Capitalism* (Cambridge, UK: Polity, 2017).

36. Dan Schiller, *Digital Depression: Information Technology and Economic Crisis* (Urbana: University of Illinois Press, 2014), 8–9.

37. Ellen Wood, "Capitalism's Gravediggers," *Verso*, January 14, 2016, https://www.versobooks.com/blogs/2313-ellen-meiksins-wood-capitalism-s-gravediggers/.

38. Ellen Wood, "Modernity, Postmodernity or Capitalism?," *Review of International Political Economy* 4, no. 3 (1997): 550.

39. The theory of crisis is central to understanding capitalism and reveals the internal contradictions within capitalism. Scholars agree that capitalism has a tendency toward periodic crisis; however, there is disagreement about the reasons for these crises. See Giovanni Arrigh, "Toward a Theory of Capitalist Crisis," *New Left Review* 1/111 (September–October 1978): 3–24; Robert Brenner, *The Economics of Global Turbulence: The Advanced Capitalist Economies from Long Boom to Long Downturn, 1945–2005* (London: Verso, 2006); David Harvey, "Crisis Theory and the Falling Rate of Profit," in *The Great Financial Meltdown of 2008: Systemic, Conjunctural or Policy Created?*, ed. Turan Subasat (Northampton, MA: Edward Elgar, 2016).

40. Robert Brenner, "The World Economy at the Turn of the Millennium Toward Boom or Crisis?," *Review of International Political Economy* 8, no. 1 (Spring 2001): 7–16.

41. David Harvey, *The New Imperialism* (Oxford: Oxford University Press, 2003), 87.

42. Dan Schiller, "Power Under Pressure: Digital Capitalism in Crisis," *International Journal of Communication* 5 (2011): 924–941.

43. Robert McChesney, *Digital Disconnect: How Capitalism Is Turning the Internet Against Democracy* (New York: New Press, 2013).

44. Paul Baran and Paul Sweezy, *Monopoly Capital: An Essay on the American Economic and Social Order* (New York: Monthly Review Press, 1966).

45. Howard Botwinick, *Persistent Inequalities: Wage Disparity Under Capitalist Competition* (Chicago: Haymarket, 2021); Michael Roberts, *The Long Depression: How It Happened, Why It Happened, and What Happens Next* (Chicago: Haymarket, 2016); Anwar Shaikh, *Capitalism: Competition, Conflict, Crises* (New York: Oxford University Press, 2016).

46. Rhys Jenkins, "Transnational Corporations, Competition and Monopoly," *Review of Radical Political Economics* 21, no. 4 (December 1989): 12–32.

47. Richard Bryan, "Monopoly in Marxist Method," *Capital and Class* 9, no. 2 (1985):72–92; Jenkins, "Transnational Corporations."

48. Janine Berg, Marianne Furrer, Ellie Harmon, Uma Rani, and M. Six Silberman, *Digital Labour Platforms and the Future of Work: Towards Decent Work in the Online World* (Geneva: International Labor Organization, 2018); Christian Fuchs, "Labour in Informational Capitalism," *Information Society* 26, no. 3 (2010): 176–196; Nick Dyer-Witheford, *Cyber-Proletariat: Global Labour in the Digital Vortex* (London: Pluto, 2015).

49. See, e.g., Trebor Scholz, *Digital Labor: The Internet as Playground and Factory* (New York: Routledge, 2013); Lilly Irani, "Difference and Dependence among Digital Workers: The Case of Amazon Mechanical Turk," *South Atlantic Quarterly* 114, (2015): 225–234; Christian Fuchs and Sebastian Sevignani, "What Is Digital Labour? What Is Digital Work? What's Their Difference? And Why Do These Questions Matter for Understanding Social Media?" *TripleC: Cognition, Communication, Co-operation* 11, no. 2 (2013): 237–292; Valerio De Stefano, "The Rise of the 'Just-in-Time Workforce': On-Demand Work, Crowdwork and Labour Protection in the 'Gig Economy,'" *Comparative Labor Law and Policy Journal* 37 (2015): 461–471; Mark Graham, Isis Hjorth, and Vili Lehdonvirta, "Digital Labour and Development: Impacts of Global Digital Labour Platforms and the Gig Economy on Worker Livelihoods," *Transfer: European Review of Labour and Research* 23, no. 2 (May 2017): 135–162; Alex Rosenblat, *Uberland: How Algorithms Are Rewriting the Rules of Work* (Oakland: University of California Press, 2018); Mark Graham and Jamie Woodcock, *The Gig Economy: A Critical Introduction* (Cambridge, UK: Polity, 2020).

50. James Cortada, *The Digital Hand: How Computers Changed the Work of American Manufacturing, Transportation, and Retail Industries* (Oxford: Oxford University Press, 2004); James Cortada, *The Digital Hand,* vol. 3, *How Computers Changed the Work of American Public Sector Industries* (Oxford: Oxford University Press, 2007).

51. Kim Nash, "Amazon, Alphabet and Walmart Were Top IT Spenders in 2018," *Wall Street Journal,* January 17, 2019, https://www.wsj.com/articles/amazon-alphabet-and-walmart-were-top-it-spenders-in-2018-11547754757.

52. Dan Schiller, "Labor and Digital Capitalism," in *The Routledge Companion to Labor and Media,* ed. Richard Maxwell (London: Taylor & Francis, 2015), 3–17; Ursula Huws, *Labour in Contemporary Capitalism: What Next?* (London: Palgrave Macmillan, 2019).

53. Maurizio Lazzarato, "Immaterial Labor," in *Radical Thought in Italy: A Potential Politics,* ed. Paolo Virno and Michael Hardt (Minneapolis: University of Minnesota Press, 1996), 133–149; Michael Hardt and Antonio Negri, *Empire* (Cambridge, MA: Harvard University Press, 2001).

54. Tiziana Terranova, "Free Labor: Producing Culture for the Digital Economy," *Social Text* 18, no. 2 (2000): 33–58.

55. Mosco and Herman, "Critical Theory," 883–889; Harry Braverman, *Labor and Monopoly Capital: The Degradation of Work in the Twentieth Century* (New York: Monthly Review Press, 1998).

56. Braverman, *Labor and Monopoly Capital,* 393.

57. Michael Burawoy, *Manufacturing Consent: Changes in the Labor Process Under Monopoly Capitalism* (Chicago: University of Chicago Press, 1980); P. K. Edwards, "Understanding Conflict in the Labour Process: The Logic and Autonomy of Struggle," in *Labour Process Theory*, ed. David Knights and Hugh Willmott (London: Macmillan), 125–152.

58. Stuart Brandes, *American Welfare Capitalism, 1880–1940* (Chicago: University of Chicago Press, 1976); Lizabeth Cohen, *Making a New Deal: Industrial Workers in Chicago, 1919–1939* (New York: Cambridge University Press, 1990); Sanford Jacoby, *Modern Manors: Welfare Capitalism since the New Deal* (Princeton: Princeton University Press, 1997).

59. Herbert Schiller, *Who Knows: Information in the Age of the Fortune 500* (Norwood, NJ: Ablex, 1981), 7.

60. Anthony Smith, *The Geopolitics of Information: How Western Culture Dominates the World* (London: Faber & Faber, 1980).

61. Ryan Heath, "China's Tech Authoritarianism Too Big to Contain," *Politico*, November 20, 2020, https://www.politico.com/news/2020/11/20/chinas-tech-authoritarianism-438646.

62. Yuezhi Zhao, "The Challenge of China: Contribution to a Transcultural Political Economy of Communication for the Twenty-First Century," in *The Handbook of Political Economy of Communication*, ed. Janet Wasko, Graham Murdock, and Helena Sousa (Chichester, West Sussex: Wiley-Blackwell, 2011), 558–582; Yu Hong, *Networking China: The Digital Transformation of the Chinese Economy* (Urbana: University of Illinois Press, 2017); Min Tang, "From 'Bring-in' to 'Going Out': Transnationalizing China's Internet Capital through State Policies," *Chinese Journal of Communication* 13, no. 1 (2019): 27–47; Hong Shen, "Across the Great (Fire) Wall: China and the Global Internet" (PhD diss., University of Illinois, Urbana-Champaign, 2017).

63. Dwayne Winseck, "The Geopolitical Economy of the Global Internet Infrastructure," *Journal of Information Policy* 7 (2017): 228–267.

64. Wood, *Empire of Capital*, 130.

65. See ibid., 89–117.

Chapter 1. Searching for Profits

1. Janet Abbate, *Inventing the Internet* (Cambridge, MA: MIT Press, 1999).

2. Laurie Flynn, "With Goto.com's Search Engine, the Highest Bidder Shall Be Ranked First," *New York Times*, March 16,1996, http://www.nytimes.com/1998/03/16/business/with-gotocom-s-search-engine-the-highest-bidder-shall-be-ranked-first.html?pagewanted=2&src=pm.

3. Vincent Mosco, *The Political Economy of Communication* (London: Sage, 2009), 132.

4. Immanuel Wallerstein, *Historical Capitalism* (London: Verso, 1983), 27.

5. Christoph Hermann, *The Critique of Commodification: Contours of a Post-Capitalist Society* (New York: Oxford University Press, 2021), 41.

6. See ibid., Chapter 3, "The Politics of Commodification in the Critique of Commodification." The chapter explains neoliberalism's strategies of commodification.

7. Janet Wasko, "The Study of the Political Economy of the Media in the Twenty-First Century," *International Journal of Media and Cultural Politics* 10, no. 1 (2014): 261.

8. Mosco, *Political Economy*, 144.

9. David Harvey, "The 'New' Imperialism: Accumulation by Dispossession," *Socialist Register* 40 (2004):74.

10. Matt Crain, *Profit over Privacy: How Surveillance Advertising Conquered the Internet* (Minneapolis: University of Minnesota Press, 2021), 11.

11. Jean-Charles Rochet and Jean Tirole, "Platform Competition in Two-Sided Markets," *Journal of the European Economic Association* 1, no. 4 (2003): 990–1029.

12. Elizabeth Van Couvering, "The Political Economy of New Media Revisited: Platformisation, Mediatisation, and the Politics of Algorithms," *Proceedings of the 50th Hawaii International Conference on System Sciences*, 2017, https://scholarspace.manoa.hawaii.edu/bitstream/10125/41374/paper0225.pdf.

13. Nizar Abdelkafi, Christian Raasch, Angela Roth, and R. Srinvasan, "Multi-Sided Platforms," *Electron Markets* 29 (2019): 553–559.

14. José-Marie Griffiths and Donald W. King, "US Information Retrieval System Evolution and Evaluation (1945–1975)," *IEEE Annals of the History of Computing* 25, no. 3 (2002): 35–55.

15. For an in-depth history of pre-web search engines, see Dale J. Vidmar and Connie J. Anderson-Cahoon, "Internet Search Tools: History to 2000," in *Encyclopedia of Library and Information Science*, ed. John D. McDonald and Michael Levine-Clark (Boca Raton, FL: CRC Press, 2018), 2516–2525.

16. Elizabeth Van Couvering, "Search Engine Bias: The Structuration of Traffic on the World-Wide Web" (PhD diss., London School of Economics, 2010), 96–97.

17. "On the Origins of Google," National Science Foundation, August 14, 2004, http://www.nsf.gov/discoveries/disc_summ.jsp?cntn_id=100660.

18. "The Stanford Integrated Digital Library Project," National Science Foundation, http://www.nsf.gov/awardsearch/showAward?AWD_ID=9411306.

19. Robert H. Zakon, "Hobbes' Internet Timeline 25 Growth," accessed May 3, 2020, https://www.zakon.org/robert/internet/timeline/#.

20. Dan Schiller, *Digital Capitalism: Networking the Global Market System* (Cambridge, MA: MIT Press, 1999).

21. Claire-Lise Benaud and Sever Bordeianu, *Outsourcing Library Operations in Academic Libraries: An Overview of Issues and Outcomes* (Englewood, CO: Libraries Unlimited, 1998), 19.

22. This has also led to the erosion of the First Sale Doctrine, the traditional balance in US copyright law and the pillar on which libraries are built so that they can legally buy and lend copies of copyrighted works. There is a robust literature on the history and future of First Sale. See, e.g., Ruth A. Reese, "The First Sale Doctrine in

the Era of Digital Networks," *Boston College Law Review* 44, no. 2 (2003): 577–652, http://lawdigitalcommons.bc.edu/bclr/vol44/iss2/9.

23. Barbara Becker and Oliver Gassmann, "Corporate Incubators: Industrial R&D and What Universities Can Learn from Them," *Journal of Technology Transfer* 3, no. 4 (2006): 469–483.

24. Derek Bok, *Universities in the Marketplace: The Commercialization of Higher Education* (Princeton: Princeton University Press, 2009), 12.

25. Clark Kerr, *The Great Transformation in Higher Education, 1960–1980* (Albany: State University of New York Press, 1991).

26. Bruce Kogut, *The Global Internet Economy* (Cambridge, MA: MIT Press, 2003), 6.

27. Sam Ro, "Venture Capital Funding Is Nowhere Near the Levels We Saw During the Dot-Com Bubble," *Business Insider*, April 10, 2014, http://www.businessinsider.com/historical-venture-capital-funding-2014-4.

28. Shane Greenstein, *How the Internet Became Commercial: Innovation, Privatization, and the Birth of a New Network* (Princeton, NJ: Princeton University Press, 2017), 752–757.

29. Brent Goldfarb, Michael Pfarrer, and David Kirsch, "Searching for Ghosts: Business Survival, Unmeasured Entrepreneurial Activity and Private Equity Investment in the Dot-Com Era," Robert H. Smith School Research Paper No. RHS 06–027, October 12, 2005, http://dx.doi.org/10.2139/ssrn.825687.

30. Ro, "Venture Capital Funding."

31. Brian McCullough, *How the Internet Happened: From Netscape to the iPhone* (New York: Liveright, 2019), 135.

32. Brent Goldfarb and David Kirsch, "Small Ideas, Big Ideas, Bad Ideas, Good Ideas: 'Get Big Fast' and Dot Com Venture Creation," Robert H. Smith School Research Paper No. RHS-06–049, November 2006, https://papers.ssrn.com/sol3/papers.cfm?abstract_id=946446.

33. Christopher Nerney, "The Up and Coming," *Network World*, April 20, 1998, 57–58.

34. Phil Carpenter, *EBrands: Building an Internet Business at Breakneck Speed* (Boston: Harvard Business School Press, 2000), 197.

35. Julia Pitta, "!&#$%.com," *Forbes*, August 23, 1999, 77.

36. Ian Chaston, *Entrepreneurial Management in Small Firms* (Los Angeles: Sage, 2009), 67.

37. Karen Angel, *Inside Yahoo! Reinvention and the Road Ahead* (New York: Wiley, 2002), 39.

38. Phil Carpenter, *EBrands*, 192.

39. "Yahoo! Ends Netscape Partnership," *CBS*, May 22, 1998, https://www.cbsnews.com/news/yahoo-ends-netscape-partnership/.

40. Angel, *Inside Yahoo!*, 124.

41. Anne Callery and Deb Tracy Proulx, "Yahoo! Cataloging the Web," *Journal of Internet Cataloging* 1, no. 2 (2009): 57–64, https://www.tandfonline.com/doi/abs/10.1300/J141v01n01_06.

42. Joan Rigdon, "Yahoo! IPO Soars in First Day, But Honeymoon May Not Last," *Wall Street Journal*, April 15, 1996, https://www.wsj.com/articles/SB849504268462964500.

43. Ken Yamada, "Yahoo Soliciting Advertisers for Internet Directory Service," *Computer Reseller News*, August 7, 1995, 54.

44. Van Couvering, "*Search Engine Bias*," 97–98.

45. John McDonough and Karen Egolf, *The* Advertising Age *Encyclopedia of Advertising* (New York: Routledge, 2015), 804.

46. John A. Deighton, "The Future of Interactive Marketing," *Harvard Business Review* 74, no. 6 (November–December 1996): 151–160, https://www.hbs.edu/faculty/Pages/item.aspx?num=7213/.

47. Fernando Bermejo, *The Internet Audience: Constitution and Measurement* (New York: Peter Lang, 2007), 183.

48. Joseph Turow, *The Daily You: How the New Advertising Industry Is Defining Your Identity and Your Worth* (New Haven, CT: Yale University Press, 2011).

49. "Another Engine Takes Ads by the Click," *CNET*, May 22, 1996, http://news.cnet.com/Another-engine-takes-ads-by-the-click/2100-1033_3-212736.html.

50. Turow, *Daily You*, 51.

51. Debra Williamson, "Early Internet Days Perilous," *AdAge*, March 28, 2005, http://adage.com/article/75-years-of-ideas/early-internet-days-perilous/102660/.

52. Bermejo, Internet Audience, 178.

53. Kim Cleland, "Media Buying and Planning: Marketers Want Solid Data on Value of Internet Ad Buys: Demand Swells for Information That Compares Media Options," *Ad Age*, August 3, 1998, http://adage.com/article/news/media-buying-planning-marketers-solid-data-internet-ad-buys-demand-swells-information-compares-media-options/64931/.

54. Janice Maloney, "Yahoo: Still Searching for Profits on the Internet," *Fortune*, May 26, 2013, http://fortune.com/2013/05/26/yahoo-still-searching-for-profits-on-the-internet-fortune-1996/.

55. Van Couvering, "*Search Engine Bias*," 102–114.

56. David Kleinbard, "The $1.7 Trillion Dot.com Lesson," *CNN Money*, November 9, 2000, http://money.cnn.com/2000/11/09/technology/overview/.

57. Robert Brenner, "New Boom or New Bubble?" *New Left Review* 24 (January 2004), http://newleftreview.org/II/25/robert-brenner-new-boom-or-new-bubble.

58. Joseph Menn, "77% of Advertising on the Web Is Bought by Dot-com," *Los Angeles Times*, September 6, 2000, https://www.latimes.com/archives/la-xpm-2000-sep-06-fi-16112-story.html; Eileen Colkin, "Web Ads Upend Industry Practices," *InformationWeek*, June 13, 2005, 54–56.

59. Peter Gumbel, "E-Commerce (A Special Report): Selling Strategies—Advertising—Ads Click: According to a Major New Survey, Some Types of Online Advertising May Deliver the Goods, After All," *Wall Street Journal*, October 29, 2001, http://search.proquest.com/docview/398941244?accountid=14026.

60. Owen Gibson, "Cash from Clicking," *Guardian*, April 8, 2002, http://www.theguardian.com/media/2002/apr/08/mondaymediasection9.

61. Angel, *Inside Yahoo!*, 195.

62. "Engine Sells Results, Draws Fire," *CNET*, June 21, 1996, https://www.cnet.com/news/engine-sells-results-draws-fire/.

63. Flynn, "Goto.com's Search Engine."

64. Danny Sullivan, "GoTo Sells Positions," *Search Engine Watch*, March 2, 1998, https://web.archive.org/web/20140222030839/http://searchenginewatch.com/article/2066843/GoTo-Sells-Positions.

65. Ibid.

66. Saul Hansell, "Clicks for Sale: Paid Placement Is Catching on in Web Searches," *New York Times*, June 4, 2001, http://www.nytimes.com/2001/06/04/business/clicks-for-sale-paid-placement-is-catching-on-in-web-searches.html/.

67. According to TechCrunch, the idea of selling keywords did not originate with Bill Gross's GoTo.com. It came from Scott Banister's Submit-it service, which helped website owners submit their URLs to search engines and directories. See "Bubble Blinders: The Untold Story of the Search Business Model," *TechCrunch*, August 29, 2010, https://techcrunch.com/2010/08/29/bubble-blinders-the-untold-story-of-the-search-business-model/.

68. Brad Geddes, *Advanced Google AdWords* (Indianapolis, IN: Wiley, 2010), 2–6.

69. Adam Goodman, "Small Advertisers Feel the Pinch as GoTo.com Defends Price Increase," *Search Engine Guide*, May 10, 2001, https://web.archive.org/web/20071123133001/http://www.searchengineguide.com/andrew-goodman/small-advertisers-feel-the-pinch-as-goto-defends-price-increase.php.

70. Geddes, *Advanced Google AdWords*, 3–4.

71. John Battelle, *The Search: How Google and Its Rivals Rewrote the Rules of Business and Transformed Our Culture* (New York: Portfolio, 2006), 112.

72. Sergey Brin and Larry Page, "The Anatomy of a Large-Scale Hypertextual Web Search Engine," *Computer Networks and ISDN Systems* 30, nos. 1–7 (1998): 107–117, https://www.sciencedirect.com/science/article/abs/pii/S016975529800110X.

73. Douglas Edwards, *I'm Feeling Lucky: The Confessions of Google Employee Number 59* (Boston: Houghton Mifflin Harcourt, 2011), 60.

74. Shivanshu Rastogi, Zubair Iqbal, and Prabal Bhatnagar, "Search Engine Techniques: A Review," *MIT International Journal of Computer Science and Information Technology* 2, no. 2 (2013): 56–57.

75. Ibid.

76. Van Couvering, "*Search Engine Bias*," 99.

77. Ken Auletta, *Googled: The End of the World as We Know It* (New York: Penguin, 2009), 63.

78. Nick Srnicek, *Platform Capitalism* (Cambridge, UK: Polity, 2017), 84.

79. David Vise and Mark Malseed, *The Google Story* (New York: Delacorte, 2005), 98.

80. Battelle, *Search*, 124.

81. Cookies are small pieces of code that websites deliver to a visitor's browser and stick around as the person visits other sites.

82. Crain, *Profit over Privacy*, 70.

83. Ibid.

84. Crain, *Profit over Privacy*, 69–72; Turow, *Daily You*, 57–60.

85. Federal Trade Commission, *Privacy Online: A Report to Congress*, June 1998, https://www.ftc.gov/sites/default/files/documents/reports/privacy-online-report-congress/priv-23a.pdf.

86. Ginny Marvin, "Google AdWords Turns 15: A Look Back at the Origins of a $60 Billion Business," *Search Engine Land*, October 25, 2015, https://searchengineland.com/google-adwords-turns-15-a-look-back-at-the-origins-of-a-60-billion-business-234579.

87. Mindy Charski, "Google's Ad Program Stresses Simplicity," *ZDNet*, August 23, 2000, https://www.zdnet.com/article/googles-ad-program-stresses-simplicity/.

88. Auletta, *Googled*, 63.

89. Will Oremus, "Google's Big Break," *Slate*, October 13, 2013, http://www.slate.com/articles/business/when_big_businesses_were_small/2013/10/google_s_big_break_how_bill_gross_goto_com_inspired_the_adwords_business.html.

90. Benjamin Edelman, Michael Ostrovsky, and Michael Schwarz, "Internet Advertising and the Generalized Second-Price Auction: Selling Billions of Dollars Worth of Keywords," *American Economic Review* 97, no. 1 (2005): 246.

91. Mark Levene, *An Introduction to Search Engines and Web Navigation* (Hoboken, NJ: John Wiley, 2010), 154.

92. Saul Hansell, "Google Wants to Dominate Madison Avenue, Too," *New York Times*, October 20, 2005, http://www.nytimes.com/2005/10/30/business/yourmoney/30google.html?pagewanted=al.

93. David Vise and Mark Malseed, *The Google Story* (London: Macmillan, 2005), 90.

94. Shuai Yuan, Ahmad Zainal Abidin, Marc Sloan, and Jun Wang, "Internet Advertising: An Interplay Among Advertisers, Online Publishers, Ad Exchanges and Web Users," *arXiv*, July 2012, 3–4.

95. John Battelle, "Interview with Google's Chief Business Officer Omid Kordestain," *John Battelle's Search Blog*, October 26, 2005, http://battellemedia.com/archives/2005/10/titans_column_omid_kordestani.php.

96. Kunur Patel, "Google Takes Mobile Ads to 1 Million More Advertisers," *Advertising Age*, June 7, 2012, http://adage.com/article/digital/google-takes-mobile-ads-1-million-advertisers/235211/.

97. Brian Morrissey, "Today in History: Google Buys Applied Semantics," *Digiday*, April 23, 2013, https://digiday.com/media/today-in-history-google-buys-applied-semantics/.

98. Federal Trade Commission, *Federal Trade Commission Closes Google/DoubleClick Investigation*, December 20, 2007, https://www.ftc.gov/news-events/press-releases/2007/12/federal-trade-commission-closes-googledoubleclick-investigation.

99. Brett Crosby, "The Path to Acquisition," Stanford University Technology Venture Program, February 13, 2008, http://ecorner.stanford.edu/authorMaterialInfo.html?mid=1905.

100. Sarah Lacy, "Analyzing Google's Analytics Strategy," *Business Week*, November 14, 2005, https://web.archive.org/web/20120712101340/http://www.businessweek.com/stories/2005-11-14/analyzing-googles-analytics-strategy.

101. Ibid.

102. Lionel Sujay Vailshery, "Market Share of Leading Web Analytics Technologies Worldwide in 2021," *Statista*, September 15, 2021, https://www.statista.com/statistics/1258557/web-analytics-market-share-technology-worldwide.

103. "Celebrating 95 Years of Innovation," Nielsen, 2017, https://sites.nielsen.com/timelines/our-history/.

104. Steven Levy, "Secret of Googlenomics: Data-Fueled Recipe Brews Profitability," *Wired*, May 22, 2009.

105. De Liu, Jianqing Chen, and Andrew Whinton, "Current Issues in Keyword Auction," in *Business Computing*, ed. Gediminas Adomavicius and Alok Grupa (Bingley, UK: Emerald, 2009), 73.

106. Crain, *Profit over Privacy*, 63.

107. Michael Indergaard, *Silicon Alley: The Rise and Fall of a New Media District* (New York: Routledge, 2004), 48.

108. Tim O'Reilly, "What Is Web 2.0? Design Patterns and Business Models for the Next Generation of Software," *Communication Strategies* 1, no. 1 (2001): 21.

109. Loren Fox, "DoubleClick Climbs to the Top of the Ad World," *Upside*, February 2000, 59.

110. John Battele, "The Advertising System," *John Battele's Search Blog*, April 9, 2007, http://battellemedia.com/archives/2007/04/the_advertising_operating_system.php.

111. "Useful Responses Take Many Forms," Google, https://www.google.com/search/howsearchworks/responses/.

112. Michael Zimmer, "The Externalities of Search 2.0: The Emerging Privacy Threats When the Drive for the Perfect Search Engine Meets Web 2.0," *First Monday* no. 13, 3 (2008), https://journals.uic.edu/ojs/index.php/fm/article/view/2136/1944>#author.

113. "History of Google Algorithm Updates," *Search Engine Journal*, https://www.searchenginejournal.com/google-algorithm-history/.

114. Edwards, *I'm Feeling Lucky*, 281.

115. Frank Pasquale, *The Black Box Society: The Secret Algorithms That Control Money and Information* (Cambridge, MA: Harvard University Press, 2015).

116. Tripp Mickle and Keach Hagey, "Google Misled Publishers and Advertisers, Unredacted Lawsuit Alleges," *Wall Street Journal*, January 14, 2022, https://www.wsj.com/articles/google-misled-publishers-and-advertisers-unredacted-lawsuit-alleges-11642176036.

117. Jane Chung, "Big Tech, Big Cash: Washington's New Power Players," *Public Citizen*, March 21, 2021, https://www.citizen.org/article/big-tech-lobbying-update/.

118. Mark Sullivan, "Google's Anti-Tracking Move Is Good for Privacy, and Even Better for Google," *Fast Company*, March 4, 2021, https://www.fastcompany.com/90610781/google-third-party-cookies-tracking-advertising.

119. Tony Smith, "Marx, Technology, and the Pathological Future of Capitalism," in *The Oxford Handbook of Karl Marx*, ed. Matt Vidal, Tony Smith, Tomás Rotta, and Paul Prew (New York: Oxford University Press, 2019), 341–359.

120. Tony Smith, "Technology and History in Capitalism: Marxian and NeoSchumpeterian Perspectives" in *The Constitution of Capital: Essays on Volume One of Marx's Capital*, ed. Ricardo Bellofiore and Nicola Taylor (New York: Palgrave Macmillan), 224.

121. David Harvey, *Marx, Capital and the Madness of Economic Reason* (New York: Oxford University Press, 2018), 119.

Chapter 2. Situating Search

1. Yochai Benkler, *The Wealth of Networks: How Social Production Transforms Markets and Freedom* (New Haven: Yale University Press, 2006).

2. Robert McChesney, *Digital Disconnect: How Capitalism Is Turning the Internet Against Democracy* (New York: New Press, 2013).

3. Ibid.; Nikos Smyrnaios, *Internet Oligopoly: The Corporate Takeover of Our Digital World* (Bingley, UK: Emerald, 2018); Nick Srnicek, *Platform Capitalism* (Cambridge, UK: Polity, 2017).

4. John Bellamy Foster and Robert McChesney, *The Endless Crisis: How Monopoly-Finance Capital Produces Stagnation and Upheaval from the USA to China* (New York: Monthly Review Press, 2017), 67–72.

5. Anwar Shaikh, *Capitalism: Competition, Conflict and Crisis* (New York: Oxford University Press, 2016), 211.

6. Willi Semmler, "On the Classical Theory of Competition, Value, and Prices of Production," *Australian Economic Papers* 23, no. 42 (1984): 136.

7. Richard Bryan, "Monopoly in Marxist Method," *Capital and Class* 9, no. 2 (1985): 72–92.

8. Rhys Jenkins, "Transnational Corporations, Competition and Monopoly," *Review of Radical Political Economics* 21, no. 4 (December 1989): 15–16.

9. Kim Moody, "Labour and the Contradictory Logic of Logistics," *Work Organization, Labour and Organization* 3, no. 1 (2019): 81.

10. David Harvey, *The Limits of Capital* (London: Verso, 2018), 379.

11. Dwayne Winseck, "The Geopolitical Economy of the Global Internet Infrastructure," *Journal of Information Policy* 7 (2017): 228–267.

12. Gary Fields, *Territories of Profit: Communications, Capitalist Development, and the Innovation of G.F. Swift and Dell Computer* (Stanford, CA: Stanford University Press, 2004).

13. Tim Wu, *The Master Switch: The Rise and Fall of Information Empires* (New York: Knopf, 2010), 280.

14. Joseph Schumpeter, *Capitalism, Socialism and Democracy* (London: Routledge, 2013).

15. David Harvey, *Marx, Capital and the Madness of Economic Reason* (New York: Oxford University Press, 2018),120.

16. Matt McGee, "Google's New Philosophy: We're a Portal," *Search Engine Land*, September 9, 2010, http://searchengineland.com/googles-new-philosophy-were-a-portal-50216.

17. Claire Cain Miller, "Media Decoder: Google Says It Will Buy Frommer's for Content," *New York Times*, August 14, 2012, https://archive.nytimes.com/query.nytimes.com/gst/fullpage-9C0DEFDD1F38F937A2575BC0A9649D8B63.html.

18. See Alphabet Inc., Form 10-K, December 31, 2021, https://www.sec.gov/Archives/edgar/data/1652044/000165204422000019/goog-20211231.htm#i0ef93c820da04204a9c5a49f49a3b2eb_16.

19. United States of America v. Google LLC (1:20-cv-03010), https://www.justice.gov/opa/press-release/file/1328941/download.

20. Ibid.

21. Daisuke Wakabayashi and Jack Nicas, "Apple, Google and a Deal That Controls the Internet," *New York Times*, October 25, 2020, https://www.nytimes.com/2020/10/25/technology/apple-google-search-antitrust.html.

22. Nils-Gerrit Wunsch, "Number of Alphabet (Google) Patent Families Worldwide by Filing Year from 1999 to 2019, by Legal Status," *Statista*, August 20, 2010, https://www.statista.com/statistics/1033921/number-of-alphabet-google-patents-by-filing-year-and-status-worldwide/.

23. Jenkins, "Transnational Corporations,"15–16.

24. Jessica Clement, "Number of Active Advertisers on Facebook from 1st Quarter 2016 to 3rd Quarter 2020," *Statista*, January 28, 2022, https://www.statista.com/statistics/778191/active-facebook-advertisers/.

25. Jordan Novet, "Amazon Has a $31 Billion a Year Advertising Business," *CNBC*, February 2, 2022, https://www.cnbc.com/2022/02/03/amazon-has-a-31-billion-a-year-advertising-business.html.

26. Alexandra Bruell, "Amazon Surpasses 10 Percent of U.S. Digital Ad Market Share," *Wall Street Journal*, April 2, 2021, https://www.wsj.com/articles/amazon-surpasses-10-of-u-s-digital-ad-market-share-11617703200.

27. Daisuke Wakabayashi, "Google Aims to Be the Anti-Amazon of E-Commerce. It Has a Long Way to Go," *New York Times*, March 27, 2021, https://www.nytimes.com/2021/03/27/technology/google-shopping-amazon.html.

28. Jay Greene, "Look Out, Google: Amazon's Eyeing Your Turf," *Cnet*, May 24, 2013, https://www.cnet.com/tech/services-and-software/look-out-google-amazons-eyeing-your-turf/.

29. Suzanne Vranica, "Amazon Puts a Dent in Google's Ad Dominance," *Wall Street Journal*, April 4, 2019, https://www.wsj.com/articles/amazons-rise-in-ad-searches-dents-googles-dominance-11554414575.

30. Ibid.

31. "Leading Amazon Advertisers in the United States in 2020, by Advertising Spending," *Statista*, December 7 2021, https://www-statista-com.stanford.idm.oclc.org/statistics/1241378/amazon-advertisers/.

32. Geoff Colvin, "AT&T Has Become a New Kind of Media Giant," *Fortune*, March 21, 2019, https://fortune.com/longform/att-media-company/.

33. Claire Miller, "Revenue and Profit Rise at Google, but Mobile Is a Persistent Challenge," *New York Times*, January 30, 2014, http://www.nytimes.com/2014/01/31/technology/revenue-and-profit-rise-at-google-but-mobile-struggles-continue.html.

34. Vittorio Hernandez, "Google's Eric Schmidt Foresees Android Smartphone Users to Hit 2 Billion in Next 2 Years; Gives Thumbs up to New Motorola Gadgets," *International Business Times*, April 17, 2009, https://www.ibtimes.com.au/googles-eric-schmidt-foresees-android-smartphone-users-hit-2-billion-next-2-years-gives-thumbs-new.

35. Tim Bradshaw and Patrick McGee, "Apple Develops Alternative to Google Search," *Financial Times*, October 28, 2020, https://www-ft-com.stanford.idm.oclc.org/content/fd311801-e863–41fe-82cf-3d98c4c47e26.

36. Ibid.

37. Kif Leswing, "Apple's Privacy Change Is Poised to Increase the Power of Its App Store," *CNBC*, March 19, 2021, https://www.cnbc.com/2021/03/19/apples-privacy-change-could-increase-the-power-of-its-app-store.html.

38. Patrick McGee, "Apple's Privacy Changes Create Windfall for Its Own Advertising Business," *Financial Times*, October 17, 2021, https://www.ft.com/content/074b881f-a931–4986–888e-2ac53e286b9d.

39. "Leading Facebook Mobile Advertisers in the United States in 1st Quarter 2020, by Advertising Spending," *Statista*, October 19, 2021, https://www.statista.com/statistics/1112274/us-facebook-mobile-advertisers-ranked-by-ad-spend/.

40. Felix Richter, "Facebook's Growth Is Fuelled by Mobile Ads," *Statista*, July 25, 2019, https://www.statista.com/chart/2496/facebook-revenue-by-segment/.

41. Garett Sloane, "How Header Bidding Wars Led to a Google Antitrust Case and Claims of Collusion with Facebook," *Ad Age*, January 25, 2025, https://adage.com/article/digital/how-header-bidding-wars-led-google-antitrust-case-and-claims-collusion-facebook/2307586.

42. The State of Texas, et al. v. Google LLC, https://www.texasattorneygeneral.gov/sites/default/files/images/admin/2020/Press/20201216percent20COMPLAINT_REDACTED.pdf.

43. Ryan Whitwam, "Samsung Has Android Under Its Heel, and There's Nothing Google Can Do About It," *Extreme Tech*, March 20, 2013, http://www.extremetech.com/

computing/151140-samsung-has-android-under-its-heel-and-theres-nothing-google-can-do-about-it.

44. Bureau of Industry and Security, "Entity List," https://www.bis.doc.gov/index.php/policy-guidance/lists-of-parties-of-concern/entity-list.

45. Shelly Banjo and Mark Bergen, "The Trade War Didn't Stop a Google and Huawei AI Collaboration," *Bloomberg*, April 1, 2019, https://www.bloomberg.com/news/articles/2019–04–01/the-trade-war-didn-t-stop-a-google-and-huawei-ai-collaboration.

46. Kiran Stacey and James Politi, "Google Warns of US National Security Risks from Huawei Ban," *Financial Times*, June 6, 2019, https://www.ft.com/content/3bbb6fec-88c5–11e9-a028–86cea8523dc2.

47. Amir Efrati, "Samsung Sparks Anxiety at Google," *Wall Street Journal*, February 25, 2013, http://online.wsj.com/news/articles/SB10001424127887323699704578324220017879796.

48. Dan Frommer and Rani Molla, "Why Google Is Spending $1.1 Billion to 'Acqhire' 2,000 HTC Engineers," *Vox*, September 21, 2017, https://www.vox.com/2017/9/21/16338500/google-htc-pixel-phone-mixed-reality-team-acquisition.

49. Vincent Mosco, *To the Cloud: Big Data in a Turbulent World* (Boulder, CO: Paradigm, 2014), 143.

50. Ibid., 123–174.

51. "Gartner Says Global IT Spending to Reach $3.8 Trillion in 2019," *Gartner*, January 28, 2019, https://www.gartner.com/en/newsroom/press-releases/2019-01-28-gartner-says-global-it-spending-to-reach-3–8-trillion.

52. Joey Roulette, "Elon Musk's SpaceX Inks Satellite Connectivity Deal with Google Cloud," *Verge*, May 13, 2021, https://www.theverge.com/2021/5/13/22433982/elon-musk-spacex-Internet-connectivity-deal-google-cloud.

53. "Vendor Market Share in Cloud Infrastructure Services Market Worldwide 2017–2021," *Statista*, October 29, 2021, https://www.statista.com/statistics/967365/worldwide-cloud-infrastructure-services-market-share-vendor/.

54. "This Is IT: Federal Cloud Spending to Top $8 Billion in FY 2021," *Bloomberg Law*, August 20, 2021, https://news.bloomberglaw.com/tech-and-telecom-law/this-is-it-federal-cloud-spending-to-top-8-billion-in-fy-2021.

55. Vivek Kundra, "Federal Cloud Computing Strategy," The White House, February 8, 2011, https://obamawhitehouse.archives.gov/sites/default/files/omb/assets/egov_docs/federal-cloud-computing-strategy.pdf.

56. Mosco, *To the Cloud*, 137–147.

57. Lee Fung, "Google Hedges on Promise to End Controversial Involvement in Military Drone Contract," *Intercept*, March 1, 2019, https://theintercept.com/2019/03/01/google-project-maven-contract/.

58. Ibid.

59. Sundar Pichai, "AI at Google: Our Principles," *Google Blog*, June 7, 2018, https://blog.google/topics/ai/ai-principles/.

60. Cade Metz, "Amazon's Invasion of the CIA Is a Seismic Shift in Cloud Computing," *Wired*, June 18, 2013, https://www.wired.com/2013/06/amazon-cia/.

61. Kate Conger, David E. Sanger, and Scott Shane, "Microsoft Wins Pentagon's $10 Billion JEDI Contract, Thwarting Amazon," *New York Times*, October 25, 2019, https://www.nytimes.com/2019/10/25/technology/dod-jedi-contract.html.

62. Ibid.

63. Victoria Albert, "Amazon Sues over $10 Billion Pentagon Contract Awarded to Microsoft," *CBS* News, November 22, 2019, https://www.cbsnews.com/news/amazon-microsoft-pentagon-contract-amazon-sues-over-10-billion-pentagon-contract-awarded-to-microsoft/.

64. Scott Shane and Karen Weise, "Trump Says He May Intervene in Huge Pentagon Contract Sought by Amazon," *New York Times*, July 18, 2019, https://www.nytimes.com/2019/07/18/us/politics/trump-amazon-defense-department-contract.html.

65. Naomi Nix and Anthony Capaccio, "Pentagon Moves to Split Cloud Deal Between Microsoft, Amazon," *Bloomberg*, July 21, 2021, https://www.bloomberg.com/news/articles/2021–07–06/pentagon-scraps-10-billion-cloud-contract-award-to-microsoft.

66. Joseph Tsidulko, "Microsoft Wins $1.76 Billion Services Contract for Military as JEDI Decision Looms," *CRN*, January 17, 2019, https://www.crn.com/news/cloud/microsoft-wins-1–76-billion-services-contract-for-u-s-military-as-jedi-decision-looms.

67. Makena Kelly, "Microsoft Secures $480 Million HoloLens Contract from US Army," *Verge*, November 28, 2018, https://www.theverge.com/2018/11/28/18116939/microsoft-army-hololens-480-million-contract-magic-leap.

68. Klint Finley, "Microsoft CEO Defends Army Contract for Augmented Reality," *Wired*, https://www.wired.com/story/microsoft-ceo-defends-army-contract-augmented-reality/.

69. Reuven Cohen, "Google Announces Cloud Infrastructure Service: Google Compute Engine," *Forbes*, July 28, 2012, http://www.forbes.com/sites/reuvencohen/2012/06/28/google-announces-google-compute-engine-iaas/.

70. Cade Metz, "Google's Bold Plan to Overthrow Amazon as King of the Cloud," *Wired*, March 24, 2014, http://www.wired.com/2014/03/urs-google-story/.

71. Tariq Shaukat, "Investing in Google Infrastructure, Investing in Nevada," *Google Cloud*, July 1, 2019, https://cloud.google.com/blog/products/infrastructure/investing-in-google-infrastructure-investing-in-nevada.

72. Jordan Novet, "Google's Capital Expenditures Doubled in 2018, the Fastest Growth in at Least Four Years," *CNBC*, February 4, 2019, https://www.cnbc.com/2019/02/04/googles-capital-expenditures-doubled-in-2018.html.

73. Christopher Mims, "Google, Amazon, Meta and Microsoft Weave a Fiber-Optic Web of Power," *Wall Street Journal*, January 15, 2022, https://www.wsj.com/articles/google-amazon-meta-and-microsoft-weave-a-fiber-optic-web-of-power-11642222824.

74. Thomas Freeman and Jason Warner, "What's Important in the Data Center Location Decision," *Area Development*, Spring 2011, http://www.areadevelopment.com/siteSelection/may2011/data-center-location-decision-factors2011–62626727.shtml.

75. Steven Levy, *In the Plex: How Google Thinks, Works, and Shapes Our Lives* (New York: Simon & Schuster, 2011), 182.

76. Ariel Schwartz, "Google Reveals Data Center 'Manhattan Project,'" *Fast Company*, April 2, 2009, https://www.fastcompany.com/1257936/google-reveals-data-center-manhattan-project.

77. Steven Levy, "Google Throws open Doors to Its Top-Secret Data Center," *Wired*, October 17, 2012, http://www.wired.com/2012/10/ff-inside-google-data-center/.

78. "Discover Our Data Center Locations," Google Data Center, https://www.google.com/about/datacenters/locations/.

79. "Revenue Distribution of Alphabet from 2015 to 2018, by Region," *Statista*, February 5, 2020, https://www.statista.com/statistics/266250/regional-distribution-of-googles-revenue/.

80. Maureen Farrell, Benoit Faucon, and Summer Said, "Google Weighs Unusual Bid with Giant Oil Firm Aramco to Rev up the Saudi Tech Sector," *Wall Street Journal*, February 1, 2018, https://www.wsj.com/articles/google-parent-alphabet-and-aramco-in-talks-to-build-tech-hub-in-saudi-arabia-1517495498?mod=e2tw&page=1&pos=2.

81. David Morris, "Tim Cook and Sergey Brin Met with the Saudi Crown Prince in Silicon Valley," *Fortune*, April 8, 2018, https://fortune.com/2018/04/08/tim-cook-and-sergey-brin-met-with-the-saudi-crown-prince-in-silicon-valley/.

82. "Saudi Arabia: Google Must Halt Plans to Establish Cloud Region," *Amnesty International*, March 26, 2021, https://www.amnesty.org/en/latest/news/2021/05/google-must-halt-plans-to-establish-cloud-region-in-saudi-arabia/.

83. "Azure Datacenter," Microsoft, https://azure.microsoft.com/en-us/resources/videos/azure-datacenter/.

84. Ross Wilkers, "Microsoft Cloud Infrastructure Spend Totals $1B per Month," *Washington Technology*, May 12, 2017, https://washingtontechnology.com/articles/2017/05/12/microsoft-cloud-investments.aspx.

85. "Global Datacenters, Threat, Vulnerability, and Risk Assessment," Microsoft, https://servicetrust.microsoft.com/ViewPage/datacentertvra.

86. Rich Miller, "Amazon Plans Epic Data Center Expansion in Northern Virginia," *Data Frontier*, November 6, 2017, https://datacenterfrontier.com/amazon-plans-epic-data-center-expansion-in-northern-virginia/.

87. "Amazon Atlas," Wikileaks, https://wikileaks.org/amazon-atlas/.

88. Khalid Al Rumaihi, "The Middle East Needs a Technological Revolution. Start-Ups Can Lead the Way," World Economic Forum, April 2, 2019, https://www.weforum.org/agenda/2019/04/the-middle-east-needs-a-technological-revolution-start-ups-can-lead-the-way/.

89. Jordan Novet, "Amazon's Cloud Is Big Enough to Be the Fifth-Largest Business Software Company in the World," *CNBC*, February 3, 2018, https://www.cnbc.com/2018/02/03/aws-is-the-fifth-biggest-business-software-company-in-the-world.html.

90. "Facebook Data Center Location," Data Center Location, accessed February 2021, https://datacenterlocations.com/facebook/.

91. Sebastian Moss, "Apple Will Spend More Than $10bn on US Data Centers over 5 Years," *Data Center Dynamics*, January 18, 2018, https://www.datacenterdynamics.com/news/apple-will-spend-more-than-10bn-on-us-data-centers-over-5-years/.

92. Paul Mozur, Daisuke Wakabayashi, and Nick Wingfield, "Apple Opening Data Center in China to Comply with Cybersecurity Law," *New York Times*, July 12, 2017, https://www.nytimes.com/2017/07/12/business/apple-china-data-center-cybersecurity.html.

93. Nick Statt, "Google is Poaching Qualcomm and Intel Engineers for Its New Chip Design Team," *Verge*, February 11, 2019, https://www.theverge.com/2019/2/11/18220436/google-pixel-ai-chips-team-division-bengaluru-india-hiring.

94. Jeff Hecht, "Undersea Data Monster: A Hong Kong-to-L.A. Submarine Cable Will Move 144,000 Gigabits Per Second," *IEEE Spectrum* 55, no. 1 (2018), 10.1109/MSPEC.2018.8241732.

95. Urs Hölzle, "The Google Gospel of Speed," Google, January 2012, https://www.thinkwithgoogle.com/future-of-marketing/digital-transformation/the-google-gospel-of-speed-urs-hoelzle/.

96. Ibid.

97. Steven Olenski, "Amazon Found Every 100ms of Latency Cost Them 1% in Sales," *Forbes*, November 10, 2016 https://www.forbes.com/sites/steveolenski/2016/11/10/why-brands-are-fighting-over-milliseconds/?sh=f12d8c24ad33.

98. Drew FitzGerald and Spencer E. Ante, "Tech Firms Push to Control Web's Pipes," *Wall Street Journal*, December 16, 2013, https://www.wsj.com/articles/no-headline-available-1387239940.

99. Prajakta Joshi, "Introducing Network Service Tiers: Your Cloud Network, Your Way," *Google Cloud*, August 23, 2017, https://cloud.google.com/blog/products/gcp/introducing-network-service-tiers-your-cloud-network-your-way.

100. "Building One of the Highest-Capacity Cables in the US for the Los Lunas Data Center," Facebook, https://www.facebook.com/notes/los-lunas-data-center/building-one-of-the-highest-capacity-cables-in-the-us-for-the-los-lunas-data-cen/1966776986928849/.

101. Kevin Salvadori, "Building backbone network infrastructure," Facebook, March 2, 2019, https://engineering.fb.com/connectivity/fiber-optic-cable/.

102. "Swift Fin Traffic & Figures," Swift, https://www.swift.com/about-us/discover-swift/fin-traffic-figures.

103. Deb Richmann, "Could Enemies Target Undersea Cables That Link the World?," *AP News*, March 30, 2018, https://apnews.com/c2e7621bda224e2db2f8c654c9203a09.

104. See Daniel Headrick, *The Invisible Weapon: Telecommunications and International Politics, 1851–1945* (Oxford: Oxford University Press, 2012); Dwayne Winseck and Robert Pike, *Communication and Empire: Media, Markets, and Globalization, 1860–1930* (Durham, NC: Duke University Press, 2007).

105. United Nations Conference on Trade and Development, "Digital Economy Report, 2019: Value Creation and Capture; Implication for Developing Countries," September 4, 2019, https://unctad.org/en/PublicationsLibrary/der2019_en.pdf.

106. Ibid.

107. "Cisco Visual Networking Index: Forecast and Trends, 2017–2022 White Paper," Cisco, 2019, https://web.archive.org/web/20220205065052/https://www.cisco

.com/c/en/us/solutions/collateral/executive-perspectives/annual-internet-report/white-paper-c11-741490.pdf.

108. Doug Brake, "Submarine Cables: Critical Infrastructure for Global Communications," Information Technology and Innovation Foundation, April 2019, http://www2.itif.org/2019-submarine-cables.pdf.

109. Rich Miller, "More Than $8 Billion in Subsea Cable Investment in the Pipeline," *Data Center Frontier*, June 16, 2021, https://datacenterfrontier.com/more-than-8-billion-in-subsea-cable-investment-in-the-pipeline/.

110. International Cable Protection Committee, "Submarine Cables and BBNJ," August 2016, https://www.un.org/depts/los/biodiversity/prepcom_files/ICC_Submarine_Cables_&_BBNJ_August_2016.pdf.

111. Dan Schiller, *Digital Capitalism: Networking the Global Market System* (Cambridge, MA: MIT Press, 1999), 46–49.

112. Winston Qiu, "Complete List of Google's Subsea Cable Investments," Submarine Cable Networks, July 9, 2019, https://www.submarinenetworks.com/en/insights/complete-list-of-google-s-subsea-cable-investments.

113. Jayne Miller, "Google's Trans-Atlantic Dunant Cable Plans to Make Waves," *Telegeography*, June 24, 2018, https://blog.telegeography.com/google-first-private-trans-atlantic-cable-non-telecom-dunant.

114. Joel St. Germain, "Why Is Ashburn the Data Center Capital of the World?," Data Centers, August 29, 2019, https://www.datacenters.com/news/why-is-ashburn-the-data-center-capital-of-the-world.

115. "HAVFRUE/AEC-2," Submarine Cable Networks, https://www.submarinenetworks.com/en/systems/trans-atlantic/havfrue.

116. List of Transatlantic Cables Connecting America and Europe, Submarine Cable Networks, https://www.submarinenetworks.com/trans-atlantic.

117. Tanwen Dawn-Hiscox, "Aqua Comms Plans Havfrue, Transatlantic Cable Network Funded by Facebook, Google," *Data Center Dynamics*, January 16, 2018, https://www.datacenterdynamics.com/news/aqua-comms-plans-havfrue-transatlantic-cable-network-funded-by-facebook-google/.

118. Nicole Starosielski, *The Undersea Network* (Durham, NC: Duke University press, 2015).

119. Eva Dou and Drew FitzGerald, "Google, Facebook Build a Data Highway to Asia—Financed by a Chinese Developer," *Wall Street Journal*, March 17, 2017, https://www.wsj.com/articles/google-facebook-build-a-data-highway-to-asiafinanced-by-a-chinese-developer-1489575605.

120. Department of Justice, "Team Telecom Recommends That the FCC Deny Pacific Light Cable Network System's Hong Kong Undersea Cable Connection to the United States," June 17, 2020, https://www.justice.gov/opa/pr/team-telecom-recommends-fcc-deny-pacific-light-cable-network-system-s-hong-kong-undersea.

121. David Shepardson and Andrea Shalal, "US Approves Google Request to Use Segment of US–Asia Undersea Cable," *Reuters*, April 8, 2020, https://www.reuters

.com/article/us-usa-trade-china-telecommunications/google-wins-u-s-doj-backing-to-use-segment-of-u-s-asia-undersea-cable-idUSKCN21Q2TP.

122. Vijay Prashad, "In the Ruins of the Present," *Tricontinental Working Document* no. 1, March 1, 2018, https://thetricontinental.org/working-document-1/.

123. Marry Ann Azevedo, "As Billions Flow into Latin America, Its Start-up Scene Scales," *CrunchBase*, October 9, 2019, https://news.crunchbase.com/news/as-billions-flow-into-latin-america-its-startup-scene-scales.

124. Will Calvert, "Google Selects Equinix for Submarine Cable Landing Station in LA," *Data Center Dynamics*, February 13, 2019, https://www.datacenterdynamics.com/news/google-selects-equinix-submarine-cable-landing-station-la/.

125. Helen Yaffe, *We Are Cuba! How a Prevolutionary People Have Survived in a Post-Soviet World* (New Haven, CT: Yale University Press, 2020).

126. John Paul Rathbone, "Google Strikes Deal to Bring Faster Web Content to Cuba," *Financial Times*, March 28, 2019, https://www.ft.com/content/338bab00-5000-11e9-9c76-bf4a0ce37d49.

127. U.S. Department of State, *Cuba Internet Task Force: Final Report*, Bureau of Western Hemisphere Affairs, June 19, 2019, https://www.state.gov/cuba-Internet-task-force-final-report.

128. Herbert Schiller, *Living in the Number One Country: Reflections from a Critic of American Empire* (New York: Seven Stories, 2000), 84–48.

129. Dan Swinhoe, "Google's Equiano Cable Lands in Togo," Data Center Dynamics, March 18, 2022, https://www.datacenterdynamics.com/en/news/googles-equiano-cable-lands-in-togo/.

130. Drew FitzGerald, "Facebook Investment in Africa to Expand Internet Capacity Moves Ahead," *Wall Street Journal*, May 14, 2020, https://www.wsj.com/articles/facebook-investment-in-africa-to-expand-Internet-capacity-moves-ahead-11589465142?mod=searchresults_pos1&page=1.

131. Jayne Miller, "This Is What Our 2019 Submarine Cable Map Shows Us About Content Provider Cables," *Telegeography*, March 19, 2019, https://blog.telegeography.com/this-is-what-our-2019-submarine-cable-map-shows-us-about-content-provider-cables.

132. Lester Benito Garcia, "Malbec Subsea Cable Connects Argentina and Brazil with the Rest of the World," Facebook, https://engineering.fb.com/2021/11/11/connectivity/malbec-subsea-cable/.

133. Yevgeniy Sverdlik, "Amazon's Cloud Arm Makes Its First Big Submarine Cable Investment," *Data Center Knowledge*, Mary 13, 2016, https://www.datacenterknowledge.com/archives/2016/05/13/amazons-cloud-arm-makes-first-big-submarine-cable-investment.

134. Ben Treynor Sloss, "Expanding Our Global Infrastructure with New Regions and Subsea Cables," *Google Cloud Blog*, January 15, 2018, https://cloud.google.com/blog/topics/inside-google-cloud/expanding-our-global-infrastructure-new-regions-and-subsea-cables.

135. Ibid.

136. Yevgeniy Sverdlik, "Google and Level 3 Interconnect Network Backbones," *Data Center Knowledge*, February 8, 2016, http://www.datacenterknowledge.com/archives/2016/02/08/google-and-level-3-interconnect-network-backbones.

137. "Google Cloud," Google, https://cloud.google.com/cdn/docs/locations.

138. "Why Cloud Infrastructure Matters," AWS, https://aws.amazon.com/about-aws/global-infrastructure/.

139. "Azure Regions," Microsoft, https://azure.microsoft.com/en-us/global-infrastructure/regions/.

140. Mike Masnick, "Google Fiber Is Official; Free Broadband up to 5 Mbps, or Pay for Symmetrical 1 Gbps," *Techdirt*, July 26, 2012, https://www.techdirt.com/2012/07/26/google-fiber-is-official-free-broadband-up-to-5-mbps-pay-symmetrical-1-gbps/.

141. Matt Hamblen, "Taxpayers Subsidizing Google Fiber Project," *Computer World*, September 7, 2012, https://www.computerworld.com/article/2492159/taxpayers-subsidizing-google-fiber-project.html.

142. Eric Johnson, "America Desperately Needs Fiber Internet, and the Tech Giants Won't Save Us," *Recode*, January 10, 2019, https://www.recode.net/2019/1/10/18175869/susan-crawford-fiber-book-Internet-access-comcast-verizon-google-peter-kafka-media-podcast.

143. Jon Brodkin, "AT&T Sues Louisville to Stop Google Fiber from Using Its Utility Poles," *Ars Technica*, February 25, 2016, https://arstechnica.com/tech-policy/2016/02/att-sues-louisville-to-stop-google-fiber-from-using-its-utility-poles/.

144. Susan Crawford, "Google Fiber Was Doomed from the Start," *Wired*, March 14, 2017, https://www.wired.com/2017/03/google-fiber-was-doomed-from-the-start.

145. Joseph Cotterill, "Cabling Africa: The Great Data Race to Serve the 'Last Billion,'" *Financial Times*, January 31, 2021, https://www.ft.com/content/adb1130e-2844-4051-b1df-a691fc8a19b8.

146. Alexandra Wexler, "Facebook Pushes into Africa," *Wall Street Journal*, October 8, 2019, https://www.wsj.com/articles/facebook-pushes-into-africa-1539000000.

147. Olivia Solon, "'It's Digital Colonialism': How Facebook's Free Internet Service Has Failed Its Users," *Guardian*, July 27, 2017, https://www.theguardian.com/technology/2017/jul/27/facebook-free-basics-developing-markets.

148. Behrooz Morvaridi, "Capitalist Philanthropy and Hegemonic Partnerships," *Third World Quarterly* 33, no. 7 (2012):1191–1210.

149. Tom Warren, "Microsoft Wants to Close the Rural Broadband Gap with TV White Spaces," *Verge*, July 11, 2017, https://www.theverge.com/2017/7/11/15953310/microsoft-rural-airband-broadband-strategy.

150. Kori Hale, "Microsoft Wants to Become Africa's Internet Plug," *Forbes*, October 17, 2019, https://www.forbes.com/sites/korihale/2019/10/17/microsoft-wants-to-become-africas-Internet-plug/.

151. Larry Page, "G Is for Google," Google, August 10, 2015, https://www.blog.google/inside-google/alphabet/google-alphabet/.

152. "Alphabet Inc. Form 10-K," December 31, 2021, https://www.sec.gov/Archives/edgar/data/1652044/000165204422000019/goog-20211231.htm#i0ef93c820da04204a9c5a49f49a3b2eb_16.

Chapter 3. Laboring Behind Search

1. Keren Dagan, "Google's Search Engine Is the 21st [Century] Infrastructure," *Webnomea*, June 11, 2010, https://web.archive.org/web/20160320151425/http://Webnomena.com/2010/06/11/googles-search-engine-is-the-21st-infrastructure/.

2. Ursula Huws, "Material World: The Myth of the Weightless Economy," *Socialist Register* (1999): 29–56.

3. Harry Braverman, *Labor and Monopoly Capital: The Degradation of Work in the Twentieth Century* (New York: Monthly Review Press, 1998).

4. Fabiane Santana Previtali and Cílson César Fagiani, "Deskilling and Degradation of Labour in Contemporary Capitalism: The Continuing Relevance of Braverman," *Work Organisation, Labour and Globalisation* 9, no. 1 (2015): 76–91.

5. Braverman, *Labor and Monopoly Capital*, 267.

6. Ibid.

7. Fred Magdoff and Harry Magdoff, "Disposable Workers: Today's Reserve Army of Labor," *Monthly Review*, April 2004, https://monthlyreview.org/2004/04/01/disposable-workers-todays-reserve-army-of-labor/.

8. "The State of Working America," *Economic Policy Institute*, January 15, 2015, http://stateofworkingamerica.org/great-recession.

9. The White House Office of the Press Secretary, *Remarks by the President on the Economy—Kansas, City, MO*, July 30, 2014, http://www.whitehouse.gov/the-press-office/2014/07/30/remarks-president-economy-kansas-city-mo.

10. US Bureau of Labor Statistics, *Employment Situation*, November 2019, https://web.archive.org/web/20191116111239/https://www.bls.gov/news.release/pdf/empsit.pdf.

11. US Bureau of Labor Statistics, *Alternative Measures of Labor Underutilization for States, 2019 Annual Averages*, https://web.archive.org/web/20200219081618/https://www.bls.gov/lau/stalt.htm.

12. David Ruccio, "Reserve Army—Pandemic Edition," *Monthly Review*, May 14, 2020, https://mronline.org/2020/05/14/reserve-army-pandemic-edition/.

13. Mary Pascaline, "Cisco Layoffs: Company to Dismiss Nearly 14,000 Employees, Report Says," *International Business Times*, August 17, 2016, http://www.ibtimes.com/cisco-layoffs-company-dismiss-nearly-14000-employees-report-says-2402973.

14. "HP: Number of Employees 2010–2022," Macrotrends, https://www.macrotrends.net/stocks/charts/HPQ/hp/number-of-employees.

15. "HP Inc.'s New CEO Unveils Plan to Cut up to 9,000 Jobs," *Associated Press*, October 4, 2019, https://apnews.com/article/san-francisco-technology-us-news-business-ca-state-wire-e941d59f132146db892d15f41cb56e25/.

16. "IBM: Number of Employees 2010–2022," Macrotrends, https://www.macro trends.net/stocks/charts/IBM/ibm/number-of-employees.

17. Alison Griswold, "Microsoft Layoffs Would Be the Fourth-Biggest in Tech's Modern History," *Slate*, July 18, 2014, http://www.slate.com/blogs/money box/2014/07/18/microsoft_cuts_18_000_jobs_it_s_the_fourth_biggest_tech_layoff _ever.html.

18. "Microsoft to Cut up to 18,000 Jobs," *Associated Press*, July 17, 2014, https:// www.politico.com/story/2014/07/microsoft-job-cuts-nokia-109035.

19. "Microsoft: Number of Employees 2010–2022," Macrotrends, https://www .macrotrends.net/stocks/charts/MSFT/microsoft/number-of-employees.

20. "AT&T: Job Cuts to Nowhere," *Seeking Alpha*, October 27, 2020, https://seeking alpha.com/article/4381550-t-job-cuts-to-nowhere.

21. "AT&T: Number of Employees 2010–2022," Macrotends, https://www.macro trends.net/stocks/charts/T/at-t/number-of-employees.

22. Kay Roger, "Layoffs in Tech Now a Permanent Feature," *Forbes*, February 6, 2014, http://www.forbes.com/sites/rogerkay/2014/02/06/layoffs-in-tech-now-a -permanent-feature/.

23. Macy Bayern, "Engineers Dominate the List of Most In-Demand Tech Jobs in Silicon Valley," *Tech Republic*, December 13, 2019, https://www.techrepublic.com/ article/engineers-dominate-the-list-of-most-in-demand-tech-jobs-in-silicon-valley/.

24. Ken Auletta, *Googled: The End of the World as We Know It* (New York: Penguin, 2009), xii.

25. Statista Research Department, "Number of Full-Time Alphabet Employees from 2008 to 2016, by Department," *Statista*, July 7, 2022, https://www.statista.com/ statistics/219333/number-of-google-employees-by-department/.

26. Brian L. Yoder, "Engineering by the Numbers," *American Society for Engineering Education*, 2017, https://engineering.asu.edu/wp-content/uploads/2019/01/2017 -Engineering-by-Numbers-Engineering-Statistics.pdf.

27. "Help Wanted: Google Hiring in 2011," *Google Blog*, January 25, 2011, http:// googleblog.blogspot.com/2011/01/help-wanted-google-hiring-in-2011.html.

28. Mike Swift, "Google Dominates Web sector," *Mercury News*, April 17, 2012, https://www.mercurynews.com/2012/04/17/google-dominates-web-sector/.

29. George Avalos, "Tech Jobs in Bay Area Surpass Dot-com Era's Peak," *Mercury News*, August 24, 2016, http://www.mercurynews.com/2016/08/17/tech-jobs-in-bay -area-surpass-dot-com-eras-peak/.

30. Anaele Pelisson and Avery Hartmans, "The Average Age of Employees at All the Top Tech Companies, in One Chart," *Business Insider,* September 17, 2017, https:// www.businessinsider.com/median-tech-employee-age-chart-2017–8.

31. Madeline Wells, "Here's How Much Silicon Valley Tech Workers Actually Make," *SF Gate*, June 27, 2019, https://www.sfgate.com/technology/article/Silicon-Valley -tech-workers-companies-salary-pay-14047115.php.

32. Rani Molla, "Facebook, Google and Netflix Pay a Higher Median Salary Than Exxon, Goldman Sachs or Verizon," *Recode*, April 30, 2018, https://www.recode.net/2018/4/30/17301264/how-much-twitter-google-amazon-highest-paying-salary-tech.

33. "Rankings of the States 2016 and Estimates of School Statistics," National Education Association, May 2017, http://www.nea.org/assets/docs/2017_Rankings_and_Estimates_Report-FINAL-SECURED.pdf.

34. Michael Hansen, "Which States Might Experience the Next Wave of Teacher Strikes?" Brookings Institute, April 13, 20118, https://www.brookings.edu/blog/brown-center-chalkboard/2018/04/13/which-states-might-experience-the-next-wave-of-teacher-strikes/.

35. This number is even more complicated because the NSF expanded its definition of the STEM workforce to include such occupations as healthcare, construction trades, installation, maintenance and repair, and production. See 2019 Science and Engineering Indicators, https://ncses.nsf.gov/pubs/nsb20212#:~:text=By%20including%20workers%20of%20all,total%20U.S.%20workforce%20in%202019.

36. Marcus Wohlsen, "Silicon Valley Creating Jobs, but not for Everyone," *Wired*, August 3, 2012, http://www.wired.com/business/2012/08/silicon-valley-creates-jobs-but-not-for-everyone/.

37. Dara Kerr, "Reddit's Visitors Skyrocket in 2012 with 37 billion Page Views, *CNET*, December 31, 2012, https://www.cnet.com/tech/services-and-software/reddits-visitors-skyrocket-in-2012-with-37-billion-page-views/.

38. Walter Chen, "4 Secrets to Silicon Valley's Productivity," *Business Insider*, June 1, 2012, http://www.businessinsider.com/4-secrets-to-silicon-valleys-productivity-2012-6.

39. Joint Venture Silicon Valley, "2020 Silicon Valley Index," San Jose, California, https://jointventure.org/download-the-2020-index.

40. Ibid.

41. Eduardo Porter, "Tech Is Splitting the U.S. Work Force in Two," *New York Times*, February 4, 2019, https://www.nytimes.com/2019/02/04/business/economy/productivity-inequality-wages.html.

42. Muzaffar Chishti, Sarah Pierce, and Jessica Bolter, "The Obama Record on Deportations: Deporter in Chief or Not?," Migration Policy Institute, January 26, 2017, https://www.migrationpolicy.org/article/obama-record-deportations-deporter-chief-or-not.

43. US Citizenship and Immigration Service, *H-1B Fiscal Year (FY) 2015 Cap Season*, http://www.uscis.gov/working-united-states/temporary-workers/h-1b-specialty-occupations-and-fashion-models/h-1b-fiscal-year-fy-2015-cap-season.

44. Kiran Dhillon, "How Google, Facebook and Others Pay Their H-1B Employees," *Tech Crunch*, March 29, 2015, https://techcrunch.com/2015/03/29/how-google-facebook-and-others-pay-their-h-1b-employees/.

45. Daniel Costa and Ron Hira, "Major U.S. Firms—Not Just Outsourcing Companies—Pay Low Wages to Their H-1B Employees," *Economic Policy Institute*, May

4, 2020, https://www.epi.org/publication/h-1b-visas-and-prevailing-wage-levels/#major-us-firms.

46. "What U.S. Immigration Policies Mean to Google," *Google Blog*, June 6, 2007, https://googleblog.blogspot.com/2007/06/what-us-immigration-policies-mean-to.html.

47. Brendan Sasso, "Microsoft: Shortage of Tech Workers in the US Becoming 'Genuine Crisis,'" *Hill*, September 27, 2012, http://thehill.com/blogs/hillicon-valley/technology/258985-microsoft-lack-of-tech-workers-approaching-genuine-crisis.

48. Ibid.

49. House Committee on Science and Technology, Competitiveness and Innovation on the Committee's 50th Anniversary, with Bill Gates, Chairman of Microsoft: Hearing Before the Committee on Science and Technology, House of Representatives,110th Cong., 2nd sess., March 12, 2008, https://www.govinfo.gov/content/pkg/CHRG-110hhrg41066/pdf/CHRG-110hhrg41066.pdf.

50. Rani Molla, "Visa Approvals for Tech Workers Are on the Decline. That Won't Just Hurt Silicon Valley," *Vox*, February 28, 2019, https://www.vox.com/2019/2/28/18241522/trump-h1b-tech-work-jobs-overseas.

51. Adam Chandler, "Silicon Valley's Biggest Companies Denounce the Immigration Ban in Court," *Atlantic*, February 2, 2017, https://www.theatlantic.com/business/archive/2017/02/silicon-valley-immigration-ban/515802/.

52. Bethany Allen-Ebrahimian, "Former Google CEO and Others Call for U.S.-China Tech 'Bifurcation,'" *Axios*, January 26, 2021, https://www.axios.com/2021/01/26/scoop-former-google-ceo-and-others-call-for-us-china-tech-bifurcation.

53. China Strategy Group, "Asymmetric Competition: A Strategy for China and Technology," Fall 2020, https://s3.documentcloud.org/documents/20463382/final-memo-china-strategy-group-axios-1.pdf.

54. See US Government Accountability Office, H-1 Visa Program, *Reforms Are Needed to Minimize the Risks and Costs of Current Program*, GAO-11–26, January 2011, table 1, http://www.gao.gov/new.items/d1126.pdf, p. 12; Dhillon, "How Google, Facebook and Others Pay."

55. Costa and Hira, "H-1B Employees."

56. Biao Xiang, *Global Body Shopping* (Princeton: Princeton University Press, 2006), 6.

57. Ibid.

58. Braverman, *Labor and Monopoly Capital*, 58.

59. Daisuke Wakabayashi, "Google's Shadow Work Force: Temps Who Outnumber Full-Time Employees," *New York Times*, May 28, 2019, https://www.nytimes.com/2019/05/28/technology/google-temp-workers.html.

60. Daisuke Wakabayashi, "Google Rescinds Offers to Thousands of Contract Workers," *New York Times*, May 20, 2020, https://www.nytimes.com/2020/05/29/technology/google-rescinds-job-offers-to-contract-workers.html.

61. Wakabayashi, "Google's Shadow Work Force."

62. David Harvey, *Seventeen Contradictions and the End of Capitalism* (Oxford: Oxford University Press, 2014), 119–120.

63. Miranda Miller, "How Google Uses Human Raters in Organic Search," *Search Engine Watch*, March 2, 2012, http://searchenginewatch.com/article/2172154/How-Google-Uses-Human-Raters-in-Organic-Search.

64. "General Guidelines," Google, October 19, 2021, https://static.googleusercontent.com/media/guidelines.raterhub.com/en//searchqualityevaluatorguidelines.pdf.

65. "Improving Search with Rigorous Testing," Google Search, https://www.google.com/search/howsearchworks/how-search-works/rigorous-testing/.

66. Matt McGee, "An Interview with a Google Search Quality Rater," *Search Engine Land*, January 20, 2012, http://searchengineland.com/interview-google-search-quality-rater-108702.

67. Ibid.

68. Ibid.

69. "Working at Home for Lionbridge—Non-Phone Work," *Earn Money Online*, June 13, 2013, http://realwaystoearnmoneyonline.com/2013/06/working-at-home-for-lionbridge-non-phone-work.html.

70. Barry Schwartz, "Google Has Search Quality Raters in Tons of Countries," *Search Engine Roundtable*, January 16, 2017, https://www.seroundtable.com/google-has-search-quality-raters-globally-23260.html.

71. Mary L. Gray and Siddharth Suri, *Ghost Work: How to Stop Silicon Valley from Building a New Global Underclass* (Boston: Houghton Mifflin Harcourt, 2019).

72. Tarleton Gillespie, *Custodians of the Internet: Platforms, Content Moderation, and the Hidden Decisions That Shape Social Media* (New Haven, CT: Yale University Press, 2018).

73. Ursula Huws, "Logged Labour: A New Paradigm of Work Organisation?," *Work Organisation, Labour and Globalisation* 10, no. 1 (2016): 7–26, doi:10.13169/workorgalaboglob.10.1.0007.

74. David Harvey, "Neoliberalism Is a Political Project," *Jacobin*, July 23, 2016, https://www.jacobinmag.com/2016/07/david-harvey-neoliberalism-capitalism-labor-crisis-resistance/.

75. Kim Moody, *On New Terrain: How Capital Is Reshaping the Battleground of Class War* (Chicago: Haymarket, 2017), 13–19.

76. Ibid. While many believe that the "just-in-time" model began in Japan, it was actually rooted in the United States. Starting in the 1950s Toyota employed just-in-time manufacturing, borrowing the idea from the American supermarket supply system, to cope with financial distress and increase production without investing more capital. See Taiichi, Ohno, *Toyota Production System: Beyond Large-Scale Production* (Cambridge, MA: Productivity, 1988).

77. Kathleen Barker and Kathleen Christensen, "Controversy and Challenges Raised by Contingent Work Arrangements," in *Contingent Work: American Employment Relations in Transition*, ed. Kathleen Barker and Kathleen Christensen (Ithaca, NY: ILR, 1998), 1.

78. Annie Lowery, "Recovery Has Created Far More Low-Wage Jobs Than Better-Paid Ones," *New York Times*, April 17, 2014, https://www.nytimes.com/2014/04/28/business/economy/recovery-has-created-far-more-low-wage-jobs-than-better-paid-ones.html.

79. Martha Ross and Nicole Bateman, "Meet the Low-Wage Workforce," Brookings, November 7, 2019, https://www.brookings.edu/research/meet-the-low-wage-workforce/.

80. Ursula Huws, "Logged In," *Jacobin*, January 6, 2016, https://www.jacobinmag.com/2016/01/huws-sharing-economy-crowdsource-precarity-uber-workers.

81. "Amazon Lead Engineer Salary," Comparably, https://www.comparably.com/companies/amazon/salaries/lead-engineer.

82. "Amazon CEO Jassy Says He Wants to Improve Warehouse Safety," *AP Press*, April 14, 2022, https://apnews.com/article/technology-business-amazoncom-inc-jeff-bezos-labor-unions-955411f611617a63bf44180266e73392.

83. Michael Sainato, "'I'm not a Robot': Amazon Workers Condemn Unsafe, Grueling Conditions at Warehouse," *Guardian*, February 5, 2020, https://www.theguardian.com/technology/2020/feb/05/amazon-workers-protest-unsafe-grueling-conditions-warehouse.

84. Johan Moreno, "Google Follows a Growing Workplace Trend: Hiring More Contractors Than Employees," *Forbes*, May 31, 2019, https://www.forbes.com/sites/johanmoreno/2019/05/31/google-follows-a-growing-workplace-trend-hiring-more-contractors-than-employees/#32c0a4d1447f.

85. Janet Nguyen, "The US Government Is Becoming More Dependent on Contract Workers," *Market Place*, January 17, 2019, https://www.marketplace.org/2019/01/17/rise-federal-contractors/.

86. American Association of University Professors, *Background Facts on Contingent Faculty Positions*, https://www.aaup.org/issues/contingency/background-facts.

87. Paul Farhi, "At NPR, an Army of Temps Faces a Workplace of Anxiety and Insecurity," *Washington Post*, December 9, 2018, https://www.washingtonpost.com/lifestyle/style/at-npr-an-army-of-temps-resents-a-workplace-full-of-anxiety-and-insecurity/2018/12/07/32e49632-f35b-11e8–80d0-f7e1948d55f4_story.html.

88. R. Jamil Jonna and John Bellamy Foster, "Marx's Theory of Working-Class Precariousness," *Monthly Review*, April 1, 2016, https://monthlyreview.org/2016/04/01/marxs-theory-of-working-class-precariousness/.

89. Other works on free labor debates include Nick Dyer-Witheford, *Cyber-Marx: Cycles and Circuits of Struggle in High Technology Capitalism* (Chicago: University of Illinois Press, 1999); Mark Andrejevic, "The Work of Being Watched: Interactive Media and the Exploitation of Self-Discourse," *Critical Studies in Media Communication* 10, no. 2 (2002): 230–248; Trebor Scholz, "What the MySpace Generation Should Know About Working for Free," *Re-public,* April 27, 2007, https://www.republic.gr/en/?p=138.

90. Christian Fuchs, "Dallas Smythe Today: The Audience Commodity, the Digital Labor Debate, Marxist Political Economy and Critical Theory; Prolegomena to a

Digital Labor Theory of Value," *TripleC: Communication, Capitalism and Critique*, 10, no. 2 (2012): 692–674.

91. Adam Arvidsson and Elanor Colleoni, "Value in Informational Capitalism and on the Internet," *Information Society* 28, no. 3 (2012): 135–150.

92. Ursula Huws, *Labor in the Global Digital Economy: The Cybertariat Comes of Age* (New York: Monthly Review Press, 2014), 170–173.

93. Ibid., 171.

94. Robin Leidner, *Fast Food, Fast Talk: Service Work and the Routinization of Everyday Life* (Berkeley: University of California Press, 1993).

95. Lisa C. Tolbert, "The Aristocracy of the Market Basket: Self-Service Food Shopping in the New South," in *Food Chains: From Farmyard to Shopping Cart*, ed. Warren James Belasco and Roger Horowitz (Philadelphia: University of Pennsylvania Press, 2009), 180–189.

96. Tracey Deutsch, *Building a Housewife's Paradise: Gender, Politics, and American Grocery Stores in the Twentieth Century* (Chapel Hill: University of North Carolina Press, 2010), 52.

97. Nona Glazer, "Servants to Capital: Unpaid Domestic Labor and Paid Work," *Review of Radical Political Economics* 16, no. 1 (1984): 69.

98. Michael Palm, "Phoning It In: Self-Service, Telecommunications and New Consumer Labor" (PhD diss., University of North Carolina, 2010), 23.

99. Venus Green, *Race on the Line: Gender, Labor, and Technology in the Bell System, 1880–1980* (Durham, NC: Duke University Press, 2001).

100. Christopher Lovelock and Robert Young, "Look to Consumers to Increase Productivity," *Harvard Business Review* 57 (May–June 1979), http://hbr.org/1979/05/look-to-consumers-to-increase-productivity/ar/1.

101. Theodore Levitt, "Production-Line Approach to Service," *Harvard Business Review* 50, no. 5 (September 1972): 20–31; Theodore Levitt, "The Industrialization of Service," *Harvard Business Review*, 54, no. 5 (1976): 32–43.

102. Jeanne Boydston, *Home and Work: Housework, Wages, and the Ideology of Labor in the Early Republic* (New York: Oxford University Press, 1990), 137.

103. Chris Oakes, "The Distributed Yahoo! 'NewHoo,'" *Wired*, July 8, 1998, http://archive.wired.com/science/discoveries/news/1998/07/13625.

104. Karen Angel, *Inside Yahoo! Reinvention and the Road Ahead* (New York: Wiley, 2002), 142.

105. Chris Sherman, "Humans Do It Better Inside the Open Directory Project," *Online*, June 2000, http://www.infotoday.com/online/OL2000/sherman7.html; Angel, *Inside Yahoo!*, 143; Craig Bricknell, "Netscape Acquires NewHoo," *Wired*, November 18, 1998, https://www.wired.com/1998/11/netscape-acquires-newhoo/.

106. William Aspray and Paul E. Ceruzzi, *The Internet and American Business* (Cambridge, MA: MIT Press, 2008), 167.

107. Eric Mueller, "Mr. Bohnett Builds His Dream House," *Upside*, December 1997, 44–8.

108. Ibid., 44.

109. "Yahoo! Buys GeoCities," *CNN*, January 28,1999, http://money.cnn.com/1999/01/28/technology/yahoo_a/.

110. Elliot Zaret, "Volunteer Rebels Rock Web Community," *ZDnet*, April 14, 1999, http://www.zdnet.com/news/volunteer-rebels-rock-Web-community/102083; See Hector Postigo, "America Online Volunteers Lessons from an Early Co-Production Community," *International Journal of Cultural Studies* 12, no. 5 (2009): 419–431.

111. Michael Malone, "The Little People Vs. America Online," *Forbes*, February 19, 2011, http://www.forbes.com/asap/2001/0219/060_print.html.

112. Eliot Zaret, "AOL Drops Hundreds of Teen Volunteers," *ZDnet*, July 26, 1999, http://www.zdnet.com/news/aol-drops-hundreds-of-teen-volunteers/102876.

113. Malone, "Little People Vs. America Online."

114. David Raymond, "True Value," *Forbes*, February 19, 2001, http://www.forbes.com/asap/2001/0219/060s02.html.

115. Stefan Thomke and Eric von Hippel, "Customers as Innovators: A New Way to Create Value," *Harvard Business Review*, April 2002, https://hbr.org/2002/04/customers-as-innovators-a-new-way-to-create-value/ar/1.

116. C. K. Prahalad and Venkatram Ramaswamy, *The Future of Competition: Co-Creating Unique Value with Customers* (Boston: Harvard Business School Press, 2004), 12.

117. Tim O'Reilly, "What Is Web 2.0? Design Patterns and Business Models for the Next Generation of Software," *O'Reilly*, September 30, 2005, https://www.oreilly.com/pub/a/web2/archive/what-is-web-20.html?page=1.

118. "Google SEO News: Google Algorithm Updates," *Search Engine Land*, https://searchengineland.com/google-seo-news-google-algorithm-updates.

119. Matt Southern, "Google's Top Search Ranking Factors of 2016, According to Searchmetrics Study," *Search Engine Journal*, December 13, 2016, https://www.searchenginejournal.com/googles-top-search-ranking-factors-2016-according-searchmetrics-study/181157/.

120. Laura Ceci, "Hours of Video Uploaded to YouTube Every Minute as of February 2020," *Statista*, April 4, 2022, https://www.statista.com/statistics/259477/hours-of-video-uploaded-to-youtube-every-minute/.

121. "YouTube," Linkedin, https://www.linkedin.com/company/youtube/about/.

122. Chris O'Brien, "NYU Study: Facebook's Content Moderation Efforts Are 'Grossly Inadequate,'" *Venture Beat*, June 7, 2020, https://venturebeat.com/2020/06/07/nyu-study-facebooks-content-moderation-efforts-are-grossly-inadequate/.

123. Elizabeth Dwoskin, Jeanne Whalen, and Regine Cabato, "Content Moderators at YouTube, Facebook and Twitter See the Worst of the Web—and Suffer Silently," *Washington Post,* July 25, 2019, https://www.washingtonpost.com/technology/2019/07/25/social-media-companies-are-outsourcing-their-dirty-work-philippines-generation-workers-is-paying-price/.

124. Ben Quinn, "YouTube Staff Too Swamped to Filter out All Terror-Related Content," *Guardian*, January 28, 2015, http://www.theguardian.com/technology/2015/jan/28/youtube-too-swamped-to-filter-terror-content.

125. Alex Moazed, "YouTube Decides It Doesn't Want to Be Netflix," Inc., March 28, 2019, https://www.inc.com/alex-moazed/youtube-decides-it-doesnt-want-to-be-netflix.html.

126. "A Fresh Take on the Browser," *Google Official Blog*, September 1, 2008, http://googleblog.blogspot.com/2008/09/fresh-take-on-browser.html.

127. Jeff Jarvis, *What Would Google Do?* (New York: Collins Business, 2009), 93.

128. "What Is the Product Experts Program?," Google, https://support.google.com/communities/answer/9138806?hl=en.

129. "Google Help Communities Overview," Google, https://support.google.com/communities/answer/7424249?hl=en&ref_topic=7570485.

130. At the risk of overgeneralizing or oversimplifying, considering the complexity of figuring out what exactly is "unpaid" labor and what is "exchange" for use of Google's various services, one could perform a rough calculation to at least begin to conceptualize how Google's profit making could be impacted if it had to pay for its unpaid labor. Americans alone spend over fifty-seven billion hours per year on Google search (Chandra Steele, "Americans Spend Nearly 60 Billion Hours a Year on Google," *PC Magazine*, July 28, 2021, https://www.pcmag.com/news/americans-spend-nearly-60-billion-hours-a-year-on-google). Even if only 5 percent of those hours were unpaid labor, if one assumes a wage of $10 per hour, this labor would cost Google $5.7 billion per year. This would erode Google's net profit by perhaps 10 percent per year. If one were to add all of Google's various services—YouTube, Google Maps, Google Translate—this number would be much higher.

131. Joseph Johnson, "Annual Revenue of Alphabet from 2011 to 2021," *Statista*, February 7, 2022, https://www.statista.com/statistics/507742/alphabet-annual-global-revenue/.

Chapter 4. Digital Welfare Capitalism

1. Terina Allen, "Google to Employees: Work from Home for at Least 12 More Months," *Forbes*, July 27, 2020, https://www.forbes.com/sites/terinaallen/2020/07/27/google-to-employees-work-from-home-for-at-least-12-more-months/?sh=31c6073a47e5.

2. Frederick Winslow Taylor, *The Principles of Scientific Management* (New York: Norton, 1967).

3. Daniel Bell, *The Coming of Post-Industrial Society: A Venture in Social Forecasting* (New York: Basic Books, 1973); Alvin Toffler, *The Third Wave* (New York: Morrow, 1980).

4. Michael Piore and Charles Sabel, *The Second Industrial Divide* (New York: Basic Books, 1984); Larry Hirschhorn, *Beyond Mechanization* (Cambridge, MA: MIT Press, 1984); Shoshana Zuboff, *In the Age of the Smart Machine: The Future of Work and Power* (New York: Basic Books, 1988).

5. Gideon Kunda, *Engineering Culture Control and Commitment in a High-Tech Corporation* (Philadelphia: Temple University Press, 1992).

6. Luc Boltanski and Eve Chiapello, "The New Spirit of Capitalism," *International Journal of Politics, and Society* 18, nos. 3–4 (2005): 161–188.

7. "Google's '20 Percent Time' in Action," *Google Official Blog*, http://googleblog.blogspot.com/2006/05/googles-20-percent-time-in-action.html.

8. Jillian D'Onfro, "The Truth About Google's Famous '20% time' policy," *Business Insider*, April 17, 2015, https://www.businessinsider.com/google-20-percent-time-policy-2015–4.

9. Matthew Panzrino, "Apple Fires up Its Version of Google's '20 percent time,' Giving Some Employees 2 Weeks for Special Projects," *The Next Web*, November 12, 2012, http://thenextWeb.com/apple/2012/11/12/apple-fires-up-its-version-of-googles-20-time-giving-some-employees-2-weeks-for-special-projects/.

10. Chris Weller, "What You Need to Know About Egg-Freezing, the Hot New Perk at Google, Apple, and Facebook," *Business Insider*, September 17, 2017, https://www.businessinsider.com/egg-freezing-at-facebook-apple-google-hot-new-perk-2017–9.

11. Daniel Gross, "Goodbye, Pension. Goodbye, Health Insurance. Goodbye, Vacations," *Slate*, September 23, 2004, http://www.slate.com/articles/business/moneybox/2004/09/goodbye_pension_goodbye_health_insurance_goodbye_vacations.html.

12. James Green, *Death in the Haymarket: A Story of Chicago, the First Labor Movement, and the Bombing That Divided Gilded Age America* (New York: Anchor, 2007).

13. Ahmed White, *The Last Great Strike: Little Steel, the CIO, and the Struggle for Labor Rights in New Deal America* (Oakland: University of California Press, 2016).

14. Stuart Brandes, *American Welfare Capitalism, 1880–1940* (Chicago: University of Chicago Press, 1976), 1.

15. Some important works on the early years of welfare capitalism include Irving Bernstein, *The Lean Years: A History of the American Worker, 1920–1933* (Chicago: Haymarket Books, 2010); Stephen Meyer, *The Five Dollar Day: Labor Management and Social Control in the Ford Motor Company, 1908–1921* (Albany: State University of New York Press, 1981); Gerald Zahavi, *Workers, Managers, and Welfare Capitalism: The Shoe Workers and Tanners of Endicott Johnson, 1890–1950* (Urbana: University of Illinois Pres, 1988); Sanford Jacoby, *Modern Manors: Welfare Capitalism Since the New Deal* (Princeton, NJ: Princeton University Press, 1997); Nikki Mandell, *The Corporation as Family: The Gendering of Corporate Welfare, 1890–1930* (Chapel Hill: University of North Carolina Press, 2002).

16. Andrea Tone, *The Business of Benevolence: Industrial Paternalism in Progressive America* (Ithaca, NY: Cornell University Press, 1997), 7.

17. Bruce Kaufman, *Managing the Human Factor: The Early Years of Human Resource Management in American Industry* (Ithaca, NY: Cornell University Press, 2008), 69.

18. Daniel Nelson, *Managers and Workers: Origins of the Twentieth-Century Factory System in the United States, 1880–1920* (Madison: University of Wisconsin Press, 1995), 11–17.

19. Kaufman, *Managing the Human Factor*, 115.

20. Tone, *Business of Benevolence*, 11–12.

21. Nelson, *Managers and Workers*, 112–118.

22. Tone, *Business of Benevolence*, 53–55.

23. Krissy Clark, "America's Forgotten Forerunner to Silicon Valley," *BBC*, March 20, 2015, https://www.bbc.com/news/business-31989802.

24. Sanford Jacoby, *Employing Bureaucracy: Managers, Unions, and the Transformation of Work in the 20th Century* (Mahwah, NJ: Lawrence Erlbaum, 2004), 46–48.

25. Please see additional private and government surveys of welfare firms in the early twentieth century in Tone, *Business of Benevolence*, 44–45.

26. Elizabeth Lewis Otey, "Employers' Welfare Work," *Bulletin of the United States Bureau of Labor Statistics* 123 (May 15, 1913), 41–43.

27. Ibid.

28. Ibid.

29. Zahavi, *Welfare Capitalism*, 1492–1493.

30. Gerald Zahavi, "Welfare Capitalism" in *Encyclopedia of U.S. Labor and Working-Class History* ed. Eric Arneson (London:: Routledge, 2007) 1:1492.

31. Kaufman, *Managing the Human Factor*, 79–80.

32. Melvyn Dubofsky, *The Oxford Encyclopedia of American Business, Labor, and Economic History* (Oxford: Oxford University Press, 2013), 390.

33. Ibid.

34. David Montgomery, *The Fall of the House of Labor: The Workplace, the State, and American Labor Activism, 1865–1925* (Cambridge: Cambridge University Press, 1987), 236.

35. Robert Zieger, Timothy Minchin, and Gilbert Gall, *American Workers, American Unions: The Twentieth and Early Twenty-First Centuries* (Baltimore: Johns Hopkins University Press, 2014), 11.

36. Meyer, *Five Dollar Day,* 109–111.

37. Ibid.

38. Greg Grandin, *Fordlandia: The Rise and Fall of Henry Ford's Forgotten Jungle City* (New York: Picador, 2010), 38.

39. Meyer, *Five Dollar Day*, 96.

40. Richard Gillespie, *Manufacturing Knowledge* (Cambridge: Cambridge University Press, 1993), 18–19.

41. Please see chapter 5 in Kaufman, *Managing the Human Factor* for the evolution of the relationship between welfare capitalism and human resource management.

42. Gillespie, *Manufacturing Knowledge*, 36.

43. Ibid., 54–55.

44. Ibid, 2.

45. Ibid., 96.

46. Sean Dennis Cashman, *America Ascendant: From Theodore Roosevelt to FDR in the Century of American Power, 1901–1945* (New York: New York University Press, 1998), 237.

47. Ibid.

48. Gerald Zahavi, "Welfare Capitalism," in *Encyclopedia of U.S. Labor and Working-Class History*, ed. Eric Arneson (London: Routledge, 2007), 1:1493.

49. Paul Bernstein, *American Work Values: Their Origin and Development* (Albany: State University of New York Press, 1997), 195; Bernstein, *The Lean Years*, 88.

50. Jerold S. Auerbach, *Labor and Liberty: The La Follette Committee and the New Deal* (Indianapolis: Bobbs-Merrill, 1966).

51. David Brody, "The Rise and Decline of Welfare Capitalism," in *Workers in Industrial America*, ed. David Brody (New York: Oxford University Press, 1993), 48–81; Lizabeth Cohen, *Making a New Deal: Industrial Workers in Chicago, 1919–1939* (Cambridge: Cambridge University Press, 2008).

52. Jacoby, *Modern Manors*, 31.

53. Lizabeth Cohen, *Making a New Deal: Industrial Workers in Chicago, 1919–1939* (Cambridge: Cambridge University Press, 2014), 267.

54. Jacoby, *Modern Manors*, 34.

55. Ibid., 5.

56. David Bacon, "Social Justice Unions Claim Deep Roots in Silicon Valley," *Reimagine*, https://www.reimaginerpe.org/20-2/bacon-Valley-union-history.

57. Luc Boltanski and Eve Chiapello, *The New Spirit of Capitalism* (London: Verso, 2005), 14.

58. Ibid., 64.

59. Ibid., 76.

60. "Ten things we know to be true," Google, https://about.google/philosophy/.

61. Richard Edwards, *Contested Terrain: The Transformation of the Workplace in the Twentieth Century* (New York: Basic Books, 1979), 150.

62. Mandell, *Corporation as Family*, 23.

63. Stephanie Vozza, "Why Employees at Apple and Google Are More Productive," *Fast Company*, March 13, 2017, https://www.fastcompany.com/3068771/how-employees-at-apple-and-google-are-more-productive.

64. Susan Gargoyle, "How Employee Freedom Delivers Better Business," *CNN*, September 21, 2011, http://edition.cnn.com/2011/09/19/business/gargiulo-google-workplace-empowerment/.

65. Sara Kehaulani Goo, "At Google, Hours Are Long, But the Consommé Is Free," *Washington Post*, January 24, 2007, http://www.washingtonpost.com/wp-dyn/content/article/2007/01/23/AR2007012300334.html.

66. Juju Chan and Mary Marsh, "The Google Diet: Search Giant Overhauled Its Eating Options to 'Nudge' Healthy Choices," *ABC News*, http://abcnews.go.com/Health/google-diet-search-giant-overhauled-eating-options-nudge/story?id=18241908#.UUwJkRn1dyU.

67. Mandell, *Corporation as Family*, 23.

68. Joe Mont, "Here's the Real Reason Your Employer Loves Giving Perks," *Business Insider*, August 31, 2011, https://www.businessinsider.com.au/turns-out-employers-have-an-alternative-motive-for-providing-luxury-perks-2011-8.

69. James Manyika, "Google's View on the Future of Business: An Interview with CEO Eric Schmidt," *McKinsey Quarterly*, November 2008, 5.

70. Mike Swift, "Google's Growth Online Reflected by Expansion in Mountain View," *San Jose Mercury News*, November 21, 2010, https://web.archive.org/web/20150115181958/http://seattletimes.com/html/businesstechnology/2013485338_googlerealestate22.html.

71. Sarah Amelar, "Google Re-Envisions the Workplace at Its New Bay View Campus," *Architectural Record*, July 6, 2022, https://www.architecturalrecord.com/articles/15660-google-re-envisions-the-workplace-at-its-new-bay-view-campus.

72. Swift, "Google's Growth Online."

73. "A Vision for Housing and Community in East Whisman," Google, https://realestate.withgoogle.com/middlefieldpark/.

74. Kevin Forestieri, "Google's North Bayshore Megaproject Could Take 30 Years to Build," *Mountain View Voice*, November 23m 2021, https://www.mv-voice.com/news/2021/11/23/googles-north-bayshore-megaproject-could-take-30-years-to-build.

75. "A Neighborhood Vision for North Bayshore," Google, https://realestate.withgoogle.com/northbayshore/.

76. "Open Sourcing Google's HR Secrets," *Knowledge@Wharton*, February 26, 2016, http://knowledge.wharton.upenn.edu/article/open-sourcing-googles-hr-secrets/.

77. Ciara Bryne, "People Analytics: How Google Does HR by the Numbers," *Venture Beat*, September 20, 2011, http://venturebeat.com/2011/09/20/people-analytics-google-hr/.

78. Jennifer Kurkoski, "Hello Science—Meet HR," *Google Research Blog*, http://googleresearch.blogspot.com/2012/06/hello-sciencemeet-hr.html.

79. James Stewart, "Looking for a Lesson in Google's Perks," *New York Times*, March 15, 2013, http://www.nytimes.com/2013/03/16/business/at-google-a-place-to-work-and-play.html?pagewanted=all&_r=0.

80. Teresa Amabile and Steven Kramer, "Employee Happiness Matters More Than You Think," *Bloomberg Business News*, February 22, 2012, http://www.businessweek.com/debateroom/archives/2012/02/employee_happiness_matters_more_than_you_think.html.

81. Farhad Manjoo, "The Happiness Machine," *Slate*, January 21, 2013, http://www.slate.com/articles/technology/technology/2013/01/google_people_operations_the_secrets_of_the_world_s_most_scientific_human.single.html.

82. Ibid.

83. Steven Henn, "'Serendipitous Interaction' Key to Tech Firms' Workplace Design," *All Tech Considered*, March 13, 2013, http://www.npr.org/blogs/alltechconsidered/2013/03/13/174195695/serendipitous-interaction-key-to-tech-firms-workplace-design.

84. The term *Google by design* plays with David Noble's book *American by Design* (New York: Knopf, 1979), in which he documents the rise of science-based industry in the United States and how science and the engineering profession were subjugated by capital.

85. Cliff Kuang, "In the Cafeteria, Google Gets Healthy," *Fast Company*, March 19, 2012, http://www.fastcompany.com/1822516/cafeteria-google-gets-healthy.

84. Ibid.; Ceilia Kang, "Google Crunches Data on Munching in Office," *Washington Post*, September 1, 2003, https://www.washingtonpost.com/business/technology/google-crunches-data-on-munching-in-office/2013/09/01/3902b444-0e83-11e3-85b6-d27422650fd5_story.html.

85. John Blackstone, "Inside Google Workplaces, from Perks to Nap Pods," *CBS News*, January 22, 2013, https://www.cbsnews.com/news/inside-google-workplaces-from-perks-to-nap-pods/.

86. Scott Morrison, "Google Searches for Staffing Answers," *Wall Street Journal*, May 19, 2009, http://online.wsj.com/article/SB124269038041932531.html.

87. Ibid.

88. David Garvin, "How Google Sold Its Engineers on Management," *Harvard Business Review*, December 13, 2013, https://hbr.org/2013/12/how-google-sold-its-engineers-on-management.

89. Ibid.

90. Adam Bryant, "Google's Quest to Build a Better Boss," *New York Times*, March 12, 2011, https://www.nytimes.com/2011/03/13/business/13hire.html.

91. Joseph Walker, "School's in Session at Google," *Wall Street Journal*, July 5, 2012, http://online.wsj.com/article/SB10001424052702303410404577466852658514144.html.

92. Charles Duhigg, "What Google Learned from Its Quest to Build the Perfect Team," *New York Times*, February 25, 2016, https://www.nytimes.com/2016/02/28/magazine/what-google-learned-from-its-quest-to-build-the-perfect-team.html.

93. Julia Rozovsky, "The Five Keys to a Successful Google Team," *re:Work*, November 15, 2015, https://rework.withgoogle.com/blog/five-keys-to-a-successful-google-team/.

94. Tim Fernholz, "Inside Google's Culture of Relentless Self-Surveying," *Quartz*, June 26, 2013, https://qz.com/97731/inside-googles-culture-of-relentless-self-surveying/.

95. Julia Carrie Wong and Mario Koran, "Google Contract Workers in Pittsburgh Vote to form Union," *Guardian*, September 24, 2019, https://www.theguardian.com/technology/2019/sep/24/google-contract-workers-in-pittsburgh-vote-to-form-union.

96. David Bacon, "Land of the Open Shop: The Long Struggle to Organize Silicon Valley," *New Labor Forum* 20, no. 1 (February 2011): 73–80, https://doi.org/10.4179/NLF.201.0000011.

97. Shirin Ghaffary, "Google Employees Protest the Company's 'Attempt to Silence Workers,'" *Recode*, November 22, 2019, https://www.vox.com/recode/2019/11/22/20978537/google-workers-suspension-employee-activists-protest.

98. Josh Eidelson and Mark Bergen, "Google Urged the US to Limit Protection for Activist Workers," *Bloomberg*, January 24, 2019, https://hub.packtpub.com/google-is-secretly-urging-national-labor-relations-board-to-overturn-protection-for-activist-workers-bloomberg-reports/.

99. Shirin Ghaffary, "What Are You Legally Allowed to Say at Work? A Group of Fired Googlers Could Change the Rules," *Recode*, June 11, 2021, https://www.vox.com/recode/22528599/google-workers-nlrb-complaint-paul-duke-rebecca-rivers-sophie-waldman-activism-free-speech.

100. Tim De Chant, "Google Hired Union-Busting Consultants to Convince Employees 'Unions Suck,'" *Ars Technica*, January 11, 2020, https://arstechnica.com/tech-policy/2022/01/google-hired-union-busting-consultants-to-convince-employees-unions-suck/.

101. Ron Amadei, "Google's 80-Acre Megacampus Will Take over a Chunk of San Jose," *Ars Technica*, May 27, 2021, https://arstechnica.com/gadgets/2021/05/googles-san-jose-megacampus-will-be-a-mixed-use-neighborhood/.

102. Jacoby, *Modern Manors*, 262.

Chapter 5. Market Dynamics and Geopolitics

1. Dan Schiller, "Geopolitical-Economic Conflict and Network Infrastructures," *Chinese Journal of Communication* 1, no. 1 (2011), 90–107.

2. See Daniel Headrick, *The Invisible Weapon: Telecommunications and International Politics, 1851–1945* (New York: Oxford University Press, 1991); Jill Hills, *Telecommunications and Empire* (Urbana: University of Illinois Press, 2007); Dwayne Winseck and Robert Pike, *Communication and Empire: Media, Markets, and Globalization, 1860–1930* (Durham, NC: Duke University Press, 2007).

3. Winseck and Pike, *Communication and Empire*, xvii.

4. Ellen Wood, "Kosovo and the New Imperialism," *Monthly Review*, June 1, 1991, https://monthlyreview.org/1999/06/01/kosovo-and-the-new-imperialism/.

5. Ellen Wood, "Unhappy Families: Global Capitalism in a World of Nation-States," *Monthly Review*, July 1, 1999, https://monthlyreview.org/1999/07/01/unhappy-families/.

6. Jonathan Reed Winkler, *Nexus: Strategic Communications and American Security in World War* (Cambridge, MA: Harvard University Press, 2009).

7. Schiller, "Geopolitical-Economic Conflict," 93.

8. Simon Nora and Alain Minc, *The Computerization of Society: A Report to the President of France* (Cambridge, MA: MIT Press, 1980).

9. Kaarle Nordenstreng, "The New World Information and Communication Order: An Idea That Refuses to Die," in *The International Encyclopedia of Media Studies*, ed. John Nerone (Chichester, UK: Wiley-Blackwell, 2012), 1:477–499.

10. Herbert Schiller, *Communication and Cultural Domination* (White Plains, NY: International Arts and Sciences Press, 1976).

11. Victor Pickard, "Neoliberal Visions and Revisions in Global Communications Policy from NWICO to WSIS," *Journal of Communication Inquiry* 31, no. 2 (April 2007): 118–139. https://doi.org/10.1177/0196859906298162.

12. "Tunis Agenda for the Information Society," WSIS World Summit on the Information Society, November 18, 2005, https://www.itu.int/net/wsis/docs2/tunis/off/6rev1.html.

13. Paula Chakravartty, "Who Speaks for the Governed? World Summit on Information Society, Civil Society and the Limits of 'Multistakeholderism,'" *Economic and Political Weekly* 41, no. 3 (2006): 250–257.

14. Dan Schiller, *Digital Depression: Information Technology and Economic Crisis* (Urbana: University of Illinois Press), 188.

15. J. P. Singh, "Cultural Understandings and Contestations in the Global Governance of Information Technologies and Networks," in *Routledge Handbook of Science, Technology and Society*, ed. Daniel Lee Kleinman and Kelly Moore (Routledge/Taylor & Francis Group, 2014), 215.

16. The White House Office of the Press Secretary, "2011 Remarks by the President in State of Union Address," January 25, 2011, http://www.whitehouse.gov/the-press-office/2011/01/25/remarks-president-state-union-address.

17. Yuezhi Zhao, *Communication in China: Political Economy, Power, and Conflict* (Lanham, MD: Rowman & Littlefield, 2008); Yu Hong, *Labor, Class Formation, and China's Informationized Policy of Economic Development* (Lanham, MD: Lexington, 2011).

18. Hong, "China's Informationized Policy," 31.

19. "Promotion of Information Infrastructure Urged," *People's Daily*, July 27, 2002, http://china.org.cn/english/government/37832.htm.

20. Christopher Hughes and Gudrun Wacker, *China and the Internet: Politics of the Digital Leap Forward* (London: Routledge Curzon, 2003); Yu Zhou, *The Inside Story of China's High-Tech Industry: Making Silicon Valley in Beijing* (Lanham, MD: Rowman & Littlefield, 2008).

21. Min Tang, *Tencent: The Political Economy of China's Surging Internet Giant* (New York: Routledge, 2020), 60.

22. Zixiang Tan, William Foster, and Seymour Goodman, "China's State-Coordinated Internet Infrastructure," *Communications of the ACM* 42, no. 6 (1999), 52.

23. Yu Hong, "Distinctive Characteristics of China's Path of ICT Development: A Critical Analysis of Chinese Developmental Strategies in Light of the Eastern Asian Model," *International Journal of Communication* 2 (2008): 460–461.

24. *China Telecom Newsletter*, July 1995, 2.

25. Zhao, *Communication in China*, 152.

26. In the wake of its accession to the WTO in 2000, China established the regulatory framework for its telecommunication sectors and defined the categories of basic telecom service operators and value-added telecommunication services operating over the network such as email, Internet service providers, content providers, and online data processing. China purposefully relaxed its restrictions on foreign investment in value-added services such that foreign firms could take 50 percent ownership two years after WTO accession and 49 percent ownership for mobile and fixed-line services four and five years afterward, respectively.

27. Lutao Ning, "China's Leadership in the World ICT Industry a Successful Story of Its Attracting-In and Walking-Out Strategy? China's Outward and Inward Foreign Direct Investment Policies," *Pacific Affairs* 82, no. 1 (2009): 70.

28. Min Tang, "From 'Bring-In' to 'Going Out': Transnationalizing China's Internet Capital Through State Policies," *Chinese Journal of Communication* 13, no. 1 (2019): 27–47.

29. Ibid.

30. Steven White, Jian Gao, and Wei Zang, "Financing New Ventures in China: System Antecedents and Institutionalization," *Research Policy* 34, no. 6 (2005): 849–913.

31. Ibid., 901.

32. Ibid., 906.

33. Joy Shaw and Lisa Chow, "China's VIE Structure May Hold Hidden Risk," *Financial Times*, November 11, 2011, https://web.archive.org/web/20150708154942/http://www.ft.com/intl/cms/s/2/0a1e4d78-0bf6-11e1-9310-00144feabdc0.html.

34. Kathrin Hille, "Foreign Internet Presence in China to Face Scrutiny," *Financial Times*, September 1, 2011, http://www.ft.com/intl/cms/s/2/7f8645e2-d493-11e0-a42b-00144feab49a.html.

35. Kevin Rosier, "The Risks of China's Internet Companies on U.S. Stock Exchanges," U.S.-China Economic and Security Review Commission, September 12, 2014, https://www.uscc.gov/research/risks-chinas-internet-companies-us-stock-exchanges-addendum-added-september-12-2014.

36. Charles Cover, "China Proposes to Change Status of Foreign Stakes in Tech Sector," *Financial Times*, January 22, 2015, http://www.ft.com/intl/cms/s/0/dc6b479a-a211-11e4-aba2-00144feab7de.html#axzz3hK9N4An3.

37. "Beijing Overhauls Rules on Companies Seeking an Overseas IPO, Including Banning Any Listing Deemed a National Security Threat," *Bloomberg*, December 27, 2021, https://fortune.com/2021/12/27/china-overseas-ipo-rules-didi-vie-foreign-waiver/.

38. Zhao, *Communication in China*, 145.

39. David Barboza, "The Rise of Baidu," *New York Times*, September 17, 2006, http://www.nytimes.com/2006/09/17/business/yourmoney/17baidu.html?pagewanted=all.

40. Ibid.

41. *2010 Report to Congress of the US China Economic and Security Review Commission*, 100th Cong., 2nd sess. (Washington, DC: US Government Printing Office, 2010), 231, https://www.uscc.gov/sites/default/files/annual_reports/2010-Report-to-Congress.pdf.

42. "Google Acquires Sizeable Stake in Baidu," *China Daily*, June 16, 2004, http://www.china.org.cn/english/BAT/98325.htm.

43. Jennifer Pan, "How the Market for Social Media Shapes Strategies of Internet Censorship," in *Digital Media and Democratic Futures*, ed. Michael X. Delli Carpini (Philadelphia: University of Pennsylvania Press, 2019), 218.

44. Robin Wauters, "Baidu Acquires Dominant Stake in Online Video Firm iQiyi, Buys out Ex-Hulu Investor Providence," *NextWeb*, November 2, 2012, http://thenextWeb.com/asia/2012/11/02/baidu-acquires-majority-stake-in-online-video-firm-iqiyi-buys-out-ex-hulu-investor-providence/.

45. Matt Marshall, "Yahoo China to File Aggressive Suit against Qihoo Nemesis," *Venture Beat*, November 2, 2006, http://venturebeat.com/2006/11/03/yahoo-china-hits-back-at-qihoo-nemesis/.

46. Ellyne Phneah, "Baidu Takes Qihoo 360 to Court over Search Dispute," *ZDNet*, February 22, 2013, http://www.zdnet.com/cn/baidu-takes-qihoo-360-to-court-over-search-dispute-7000011649/.

47. Ibid.

48. Michael Kan, "China's Baidu and Qihoo 360 Sign Pact Meant to Resolve Dispute," *PC World*, November 2, 2012, http://www.pcworld.idg.com.au/article/440847/china_baidu_qihoo_360_sign_pact_meant_resolve_dispute.

49. Zhang Wenxian, Huiyao Wang, and Ilan Alon, *Entrepreneurial and Business Elites of China: The Chinese Returnees Who Have Shaped Modern China* (Bingley, UK: Emerald Group, 2011), 219.

50. Sarah Lacy, "What Valley Companies Should Know About Tencent," *Tech Crunch*, June 20, 2010, http://techcrunch.com/2010/06/20/what-valley-companies-should-know-about-tencent/.

51. Gregg Sterling, "Alibaba Creates Aliyun Search Engine to Challenge Baidu, Google in China," *Search Engine Land*, February 19, 2013, http://searchengineland.com/alibaba-creates-aliyun-search-engine-to-challenge-baidu-google-in-china-148992.

52. Josh Ong, "Alibaba's New Aliyun Search Engine Raises the Stakes in Its Feud with Google and Android," *NewWeb*, February 19, 2013, http://thenextWeb.com/asia/2013/02/19/alibabas-new-aliyun-search-engine-raises-the-stakes-in-its-feud-with-google-and-android/.

53. "ByteDance Launches New Search Engine in China," *Reuters*, August 12, 2019, https://www.reuters.com/article/us-china-bytedance/bytedance-launches-new-search-engine-in-china-idUSKCN1V20Z7.

54. Lianrui Jia and Dwayne Winseck, "The Political Economy of Chinese Internet Companies: Financialization, Concentration, and Capitalization," *International Communication Gazette* 80, no. 1 (January 2018): 30–59.

55. Shanhong Liu, "Artificial Intelligence (AI) Market Revenues Worldwide in 2020 and Forecasts for 2021 and 2024," *Statista*, April 22, 2021, https://www-statista-com.stanford.idm.oclc.org/statistics/694638/worldwide-cognitive-and-artificial-intelligence-revenues/.

56. François Candelon, Michael G. Jacobides, Stefano Brusoni, and Matthieu Gombeaud, "China's Business 'Ecosystems' Are Helping It Win the Global A.I. Race," *Fortune*, July 2, 2021, https://fortune.com/2021/07/02/china-artificial-intelligence-ai-business-ecosystems-tencent-baidu-alibaba/.

57. "Baidu Leads China in Artificial Intelligence Patents, Is Poised to Bring About Intelligent Transformation," *PR Newswire*, December 1, 2020, https://www.prnewswire.com/news-releases/baidu-leads-china-in-artificial-intelligence-patents-is-poised-to-bring-about-intelligent-transformation-301182591.html.

58. Yating Zhao, "Baidu's Lost Decade in International Markets," *Low Down*, August 22, 2018, https://thelowdown.momentum.asia/baidus-lost-decade-in-international-markets/.

59. "Baidu Research Establishes an Advisory Board, Holds 1st Board Meeting in Silicon Valley," *Baidu Research*, November 15, 2018, http://research.baidu.com/Blog/index-view?id=108.

60. Jane Lanhee Lee, Munsif Vengattil, "Baidu Gets California Nod for Testing Empty Self-Driving Cars," *Reuters*, January 27, 2021, https://www.reuters.com/article/us-baidu-autonomous/baidu-gets-california-nod-for-testing-empty-self-driving-cars-idUSKBN29W20T.

61. Sharon Gaudin, "Microsoft to Maintain China Operations, Report Says," *Computer World*, March 5, 2010, http://www.computerworld.com/s/article/9166738/Microsoft_to_maintain_China_operations_report_says.

62. David Pierson and David Sarno, "Bing Gets Foothold in China Market," *Los Angeles Times*, July 6, 2011, http://articles.latimes.com/2011/jul/06/business/la-fi-microsoft-baidu-20110706.

63. David Kirkpatrick, "Gates in China," *Fortune*, July 17, 2007, https://archive.fortune.com/magazines/fortune/fortune_archive/2007/07/23/100134488/.

64. "Microsoft Warns US Crackdown on China's Huawei Could Backfire," *Sputnik International*, May 28, 2019, https://sputniknews.com/business/201905281075407312-microsoft-us-china-huawei/.

65. Susan Li and Brian Womack, "Google China Business Grows, 'Continues to Thrive,' Alegre Says," *Bloomberg*, January 23, 2014, http://www.bloomberg.com/news/2012-01-24/google-china-business-grows-continues-to-thrive-alegre-says.html.

66. "A New Approach to China: An Update," *Google Blog*, March 22, 2010, http://googleblog.blogspot.com/2010/03/new-approach-to-china-update.html.

67. Li Yuan and Daisuke Wakabayashi, "Google, Seeking a Return to China, Is Said to Be Building a Censored Search Engine," *New York Times*, August 1, 2018, https://www.nytimes.com/2018/08/01/technology/china-google-censored-search-engine.html.

68. Melanie Lee, "Analysis: A Year after China Retreat, Google Plots New Growth," *Reuters*, January 13, 2011, https://www.reuters.com/article/us-google-china/analysis-a-year-after-china-retreat-google-plots-new-growth-idUSTRE70C1X820110113.

69. Mark Bergen, "Google CEO Sundar Pichai: 'We Want to Be in China Serving Chinese Users,'" *Recode*, June 1, 2016, http://www.recode.net/2016/6/1/11830654/google-ceo-sundar-pichai-china.

70. "Google AdWords Experience Center Settles in Tianjin," *China Daily*, October 17, 2017, https://govt.chinadaily.com.cn/s/201710/17/WS5b77fbaf498e855160e8a489/google-adwords-experience-center-settles-in-tianjin.html.

71. "Google Center to Aid Businesses," *Shanghai Daily*, May 17, 2016, http://www.shanghaidaily.com/district/songjiang/Google-center-to-aid-businesses/shdaily.shtml.

72. Alistair Barr, "Some Alphabet Units May Return to China Ahead of Others, Brin Says," *Wall Street Journal*, October 29, 2015, http://blogs.wsj.com/digits/2015/10/29/some-google-units-may-return-to-china-ahead-of-others-brin-says/.

73. Ryan Gallagher, "Google's Censored Search Would Help China 'Be More Open,' Said Ex-CEO Eric Schmidt," *Intercept*, May 14, 2019, https://theintercept.com/2019/05/14/google-search-china-eric-schmidt-comments/.

74. Yuezhi Zhao, "China's Pursuits of Indigenous Innovations in Information Technology Developments: Hopes, Follies and Uncertainties," *Chinese Journal of Communication* 3, no. 3 (2010): 266–289.

75. Gorden Lubold and Alex Leary, "Biden Expands Blacklist of Chinese Companies Banned from U.S. Investment," *Wall Street Journal*, June 2, 2021, https://www.wsj.com/articles/biden-expands-blacklist-of-chinese-companies-banned-from-u-s-investment-11622741711.

76. Ming Tang, "Not Yet the End of Transnational Digital Capitalism: A Communication Perspective of the U.S.–China Decoupling Rhetoric," *International Journal of Communication* 16 (2022): 1506–1531.

77. "Understanding U.S.–China Decoupling: Macro Trends and Industry Impacts," *U.S. Chamber of Commerce*, February 17, 2021, https://www.uschamber.com/report/understanding-us-china-decoupling-macro-trends-and-industry-impacts.

78. "Yellen Says U.S. May Decouple to Some Extent from China to Protect Security," *Reuters*, June 16, 2021, https://www.reuters.com/world/us/yellen-says-us-may-decouple-some-extent-china-protect-security-2021–06–16/.

79. "Asymmetric Competition: A Strategy for China and Technology," *China Strategy Group*, Fall 2020, https://archive.org/details/final-memo-china-strategy-group-axios-1.

80. "Emerging Technologies and Defense: Getting the Fundamentals Right," Before the Senate Committee on Armed Services, 117 Cong., February 23, 2021 (Dr. Eric E. Schmidt, Co-Founder, Schmidt Futures and Chair, National Security Commission on Artificial Intelligence), https://www.armed-services.senate.gov/imo/media/doc/Schmidt_02–23–21.pdf.

81. Nathaniel Taplin, "China's Tech Crackdown Could Backfire Badly," *Financial Times*, July 30, 2021, https://www.wsj.com/articles/chinas-tech-crackdown-could-backfire-badly-11627627273/.

82. "Trivium China Kendra Schaefer on China's Tech Crackdown," *Bloomberg*, July 12, 2021, https://finance.yahoo.com/video/trivium-china-kendra-schaefer-chinas-035412197.html.

83. Greg Ip, "China Wants Manufacturing—Not the Internet—to Lead the Economy," *Washington Post*, August 21, 2021, https://www.wsj.com/articles/china-wants-manufacturingnot-the-internetto-lead-the-economy-11628078155.

84. European Newspaper Publisher's Association, "Joint Industry Letter Against Google's Self-Preferencing," November 12, 2020, https://www.enpa.eu/policy-issues/joint-industry-letter-against-googles-self-preferencing.

85. "Attack of the Eurogoogle," *Economist*, March 9, 2006, http://www.economist.com/node/5571496.

86. Ibid.

87. Kevin O'Brien and Thomas Crampton, "Germany Quits Search Engine Project—Business—International Herald Tribune," *New York Times*, January 2, 2007, http://www.nytimes.com/2007/01/02/business/worldbusiness/02iht-search.4081237.html?_r=1&.

88. Ibid.

89. Ibid.

90. Ibid.

91. Ibid.

92. Federal Ministry of Economics and Technology (Germany), "The Theseus Research Program: New Technology for the Internet of Services," November 11, 2008, https://www.bmwi.de/Redaktion/EN/Publikationen/theseus-research-program.pdf?__blob=publicationFile&v=1.

93. Mathis Winker, "Germany Pulls away from Quaero Search-Engine Project," *Deutche Welle*, December 21, 2006, http://www.dw.de/germany-pulls-away-from-quaero-search-engine-project/a-2287489.

94. Federal Ministry of Economics and Technology (Germany), "The Theseus Research Program: New Technology for the Internet of Services," September 2011, https://www.digitale-technologien.de/DT/Redaktion/EN/Downloads/Publikation/theseus-forschungsprogramm-broschuere-en.pdf?__blob=publicationFile&v=2.

95. "Germany to Fund Rival to Google Search Engine," *Deutsche Welle*, July 20, 2007, http://www.dw.de/germany-to-fund-rival-to-google-search-engine/a-2698176.

96. Jean-Noël Jeanneney, *Google and the Myth of Universal Knowledge: A View from Europe* (Chicago: University of Chicago Press, 2008).

97. European Commission, "Commission Launches Five-Year Strategy to Boost the Digital Economy," European Union Press Release, June 1, 2005, http://europa.eu/rapid/press-release_IP-05-643_en.htm?locale=en.

98. Ibid.

99. Roland Parry, "France Accepts Google Role in Book Scanning," *Agence France Presse*, January 20, 2010, https://web.archive.org/web/20130426074722/http://www.google.com/hostednews/afp/article/ALeqM5gZPe-DbjkDNnuBOdOLWMQIt5vHSw.

100. Henry Samuel, "Nicolas Sarkozy Fights Google over Classic Books," *Telegraph*, December 14, 2009, http://www.telegraph.co.uk/technology/google/6811462/Sarkozy-fights-Google-over-classic-books.html.

101. Sophie Hardach, "France's Sarkozy Takes on Google in Books Dispute," *Globe and Mail* (Toronto), 2012, August 23, 2012, http://www.theglobeandmail.com/technology/frances-sarkozy-takes-on-google-in-books-dispute/article4295693/?service=mobile.

102. Samuel, "Nicolas Sarkozy Fights Google."

103. Lance Whitney, "France Planning Google Books Rival," *CNET*, January 13, 2010, http://www.cnet.com/news/france-planning-google-books-rival/.

104. "Googlisation of France," Unclassified US Cable, US Embassy, Paris, France, December 18, 2009, WikiLeaks Public Library of US Diplomacy, http://www.wikileaks.org/plusd/cables/09PARIS1729_a.html.

105. Scott Sayare, "France to Digitize Its Own Literary Works," *New York Times*, December 14, 2009, http://www.nytimes.com/2009/12/15/world/europe/15france.html.

106. "Googlisation of France."

107. Jenny Barchfield, "France Plans Its Own Rival to Google Books," *Boston.com*, January 12, 2010, http://www.boston.com/business/technology/articles/2010/01/12/france_plans_its_own_rival_to_google_books/.

108. Ben Hall, "Paris Threatens Google Over Book-Scanning," *Financial Times*, January 13, 2010, https://www.ft.com/content/4ef6dc08-ffaa-11de-921f-00144feabdc0.

109. "Google Book Scanning: Cultural Theft or Freedom of Information?," *CNN World*, February 8, 2020, http://edition.cnn.com/2010/WORLD/europe/02/08/google.livres.france/.

110. Primavera De Filippi, "Communia Condemns the Privatization of the Public Domain by the Bibliothèque Nationale de France," *Communia*, January 21, 2013, https://www.communia-association.org/2013/01/21/no-to-the-privatization-of-the-public-domain-by-the-bibliotheque-nationale-de-france/.

111. Dan Schiller and ShinJoung Yeo, "Powered by Google: Widening Access and Tightening Corporate Control," *Leonardo Electronic Almanac* 20, no. 1 (2014), http://www.leoalmanac.org/vol-20-no-1-red-art/.

112. Gregg Keizer, "Microsoft Not Fooling Anyone by Using FairSearch Front in Antitrust Complaint against Google," *Computer World*, April 9, 2013, http://www.computerworld.com/article/2496436/technology-law-regulation/microsoft-not-fooling-anyone-by-using-fairsearch-front-in-antitrust-compla.html.

113. Matt Rosoft, "US Firms Lead EU Lobbying League," *Business Insider*, September 1, 2015, http://www.businessinsider.com.au/european-lobbying-spend-by-american-tech-companies-2015-8.

114. Ibid.

115. Richard Waters and Nikki Tait, "Microsoft in Spotlight over Google Case," *Financial Times*, March 4, 2010, http://www.ft.com/intl/cms/s/2/ad1c2094-27bf-11df-863d-00144feabdc0.html#axzz3GcufcYWl.

116. Bill Rigby and Foo Yun Chee, "Microsoft Files EU Competition Complaint vs. Google," *Reuters*, March 31, 2011, https://www.reuters.com/article/idINIndia-56015620110331.

117. John Ribeiro, "EU Tells Google to Make More Concessions or Face Charges in Antitrust Dispute," *PC World*, September 23, 2014, http://www.pcworld.com/article/2687212/eu-tells-google-to-make-more-concessions-or-face-charges-in-antitrust-dispute.html.

118. "FairSearch: 'It Would Be Better to Do Nothing Than to Accept Google's Proposals' to the European Commission," *Fair Search*, June 23, 2015, https://fairsearch

.org/it-would-be-better-to-do-nothing-than-to-accept-googles-proposals-to-the-european-commission/.

119. Jeevan Vasagar, "The News Baron Battling Google," *Financial Times*, June 9, 2014, http://www.ft.com/intl/cms/s/0/beb7aeae-eb3d-11e3-bab6–00144feabdc0.html#axzz3BLT1fsMn.

120. Loek Essers, "Publishers Urge European Commission to Reject Google Antitrust Deal," *PC World*, September 4, 2014, http://www.pcworld.com/article/2602600/publishers-urge-european-commission-to-reject-google-antitrust-deal.html.

121. Alex Barker, James Fontanella-Khan, and Jeevan Vasagar, "Google Feels Political Wind Shift Against It in Europe," *Financial Times*, March 21, 2014, http://www.ft.com/intl/cms/s/2/7848572e-e0c1–11e3-a934–00144feabdc0.html#axzz3Aic8kphy.

122. Jeevan Vasagar, Richard Waters, and James Fontanella-Khan, "Europe Strikes Back," *Financial Times*, September 15, 2014, http://www.ft.com/intl/cms/s/0/37e363c2-3cc9-11e4-871d-00144feabdc0.html#axzz3GFQYly7h.

123. Dominic Rushe, "Yahoo $250,000 Daily Fine over NSA Data Refusal Was Set to Double Every Week," *Guardian*, http://www.theguardian.com/world/2014/sep/11/yahoo-nsa-lawsuit-documents-fine-user-data-refusal.

124. Claire Miller, "Revelations of N.S.A. Spying Cost US Tech Companies," *New York Times*, March 21, 2014, http://www.nytimes.com/2014/03/22/business/fallout-from-snowden-hurting-bottom-line-of-tech-companies.html?_r=0.

125. James Fontanella-Khan, "Microsoft to Shield Foreign Users' Data," *Financial Times*, January 22, 2014, http://www.ft.com/intl/cms/s/0/e14ddf70–8390–11e3-aa65–00144feab7de.html?siteedition=intl#ixzz2r9yJN1Qz.

126. Peter Judge, "Microsoft Puts Deutsche Telekom in Charge of German Data," *Data Center Dynamics*, November 25, 2015, http://www.datacenterdynamics.com/content-tracks/colo-cloud/microsoft-puts-deutsche-telekom-in-charge-of-german-data/95200.fullarticle.

127. Foo Yun Chee, "EU Antitrust Regulators open Third Front Against Google," *Reuters*, July 15, 2016, http://uk.reuters.com/article/uk-eu-google-antitrust-idUKKCN0ZU0YQ; Aleksandra Eriksson, "EU Files New Antitrust Case Against Google," *EU Observer*, July 14, 2016, https://euobserver.com/economic/134361.

128. Mark Bergen, "Microsoft Quietly Retreats from FairSearch, Watchdog Behind Google Antitrust Cases," *Vox*, January 22, 2016, https://www.vox.com/2016/1/22/11588992/microsoft-quietly-retreats-from-fairsearch-watchdog-behind-google.

129. Ibid.

130. Javier Espinoza and Sam Fleming, "Margrethe Vestager Examines Curbs on non-EU State-Backed Companies," *Financial Times*, December 16, 2019, https://www.ft.com/content/452d2c7a-1f0e-11ea-92da-f0c92e957a96.

131. "Annual Value of Completed M&A and Greenfield Investment Transactions from China in the EU-27 and UK from 2012 to 2021," *Statista*, May 5, 2022, https://www.statista.com/statistics/1306532/china-completed-manda-and-greenfield-investment-in-europe/.

132. Ibid.

133. Agatha Kratz, Max J. Zenglein, and Gregor Sebastian, "Chinese FDI in Europe: 2020," *Merics Report*, June 2021, https://merics.org/en/report/chinese-fdi-europe-2020-update#:~:text=China's%20FDI%20in%20Europe%20continued,to%20a%2010%2Dyear%20low.

134. Gwénaëlle Barzic, "Europe's 5G to Cost $62 Billion More if Chinese Vendors Banned: Telcos," *Reuters*, June 7, 2019, https://www.reuters.com/article/us-huawei-europe-gsma/europes-5g-to-cost-62-billion-more-if-chinese-vendors-banned-telcos-idUSKCN1T80Y3.

135. Ben Hall, "EU Needs Common Telecoms Rules to Thwart Huawei's 5G Threat," *Financial Times*, December 17, 2019, https://www.ft.com/content/9d95f576-20bd-11ea-92da-f0c92e957a96.

136. Stu Woo, "Beijing Shuns Ericsson, Nokia as the West Curbs Huawei," *Wall Street Journal*, August 3, 2021, https://www.wsj.com/articles/beijing-shuns-ericsson-nokia-as-the-west-curbs-huawei-11627982882.

137. Nick Wadhams, "Biden Putting Tech, Not Troops, at Core of U.S.-China Policy," *Bloomberg*, March 1, 2021, https://www.bloomberg.com/news/articles/2021-03-01/biden-putting-tech-not-troops-at-center-of-u-s-china-strategy.

138. "EU Makes Tech Alliance Offer to Biden Administration," *Science Business*, December 3, 2020, https://sciencebusiness.net/technology-strategy-board/news/eu-makes-tech-alliance-offer-biden-administration.

139. Madhumita Murgia, "Europe 'a Global Trendsetter on Tech Regulation,'" *Financial Times*, October 30, 2019, https://www.ft.com/content/e7b22230-fa32–11e9-a354-36acbbb0d9b6.

140. Sven Becker, "Google's Lobby Offensive: Internet Giant Builds Web of Influence in Berlin," *Spiegel Online International*, September 25, 2013, https://web.archive.org/web/20220619045630/https://www.spiegel.de/international/business/how-google-lobbies-german-government-over-internet-regulation-a-857654.html.

141. Ibid.

142. Javier Espinoza, "Internal Google Document Reveals Campaign Against EU Lawmakers," *Financial Times*, October 28, 2020, https://www.ft.com/content/d9d05b1e-45c0-44b8-a1ba-3aa6d0561bed.

143. Raphaël Kergueno, Nicholas Aiossa, Lucinda Pearson, Nuri Syed Corser, Vitor Teixeira, and Michiel van Hulten, "Deep Pockets, Open Doors: Big Tech Lobbying in Brussels," *Transparency International* (2021), https://transparency.eu/wp-content/uploads/2021/02/Deep_pockets_open_doors_report.pdf.

144. Ibid.

145. Adam Satariano and Matina Stevis-Gridneff, "Big Tech Turns Its Lobbyists Loose on Europe, Alarming Regulators," *New York Times*, December 14, 2020, https://www.nytimes.com/2020/12/14/technology/big-tech-lobbying-europe.html.

146. Mehreen Khan, "EU Floats Plan for €100bn Sovereign Wealth Fund," *Financial Times*, August 23, 2019, https://www.ft.com/content/033057a2-c504–11e9-a8e9-296ca66511c9.

147. "France, Germany Step up Effort to Build Rivals to US Cloud Firms," *Reuters*, October 23, 2019, https://www.reuters.com/article/us-france-germany-cloud/france-germany-step-up-effort-to-build-rivals-to-u-s-cloud-firms-idUSKBN1X81YO.

148. David Sanger, "Biden Defines His Underlying Challenge with China: 'Prove Democracy Works,'" *New York Times*, March 26, 2021, https://www.nytimes.com/2021/03/26/us/politics/biden-china-democracy.html.

Conclusion

1. Jon Swartz, "Former Google CEO: 'This is the first time as a species we have had to face the same problem as a planet,'" *Marketwatch*, April 8, 2020, https://www.marketwatch.com/story/former-google-ceo-this-is-the-first-time-as-a-species-we-have-had-to-face-the-same-problem-as-a-planet-2020-04-08.

2. Theodore Schleifer, "Google's Former CEO Hopes the Coronavirus Makes People More 'Grateful' for Big Tech," *Recode*, April 14, 2020, https://www.vox.com/recode/2020/4/14/21221141/coronavirus-eric-schmidt-google-big-tech-grateful.

3. Didi Rankovic, "Ex-Google CEO Eric Schmidt: Coronavirus Should Make People Grateful for Big Tech," *Reclaim the Net*, April 15, 2020, https://reclaimthenet.org/ex-google-ceo-eric-schmidt-grateful-big-tech/.

4. David Harvey, "The 'New' Imperialism: Accumulation by Dispossession," *Socialist Register* 40 (2004): 74.

5. Anwar Shaikh, *Capitalism: Competition, Conflict, Crises* (Oxford: Oxford University Press, 2016), 14.

6. Tom Wheeler, "Time for a U.S.—EU Digital Alliance," *Brookings*, January 21, 2021, https://www.brookings.edu/research/time-for-a-us-eu-digital-alliance/.

7. Vivek Chibber, "Why We Still Talk about the Working Class," *Jacobin*, March 15, 2017, https://www-jacobinmag-com.stanford.idm.oclc.org/2017/03/abcs-socialism-working-class-workers-capitalism-power-vivek-chibber/.

8. Johana Bhuiyan and Carly Olson, "Uber and Lyft Drivers Strike over Pay, Gig-Work Conditions," *Los Angeles Times*, July 21, 2021, https://www.latimes.com/business/story/2021–07–21/uber-and-lyft-rideshare-drivers-strike-rally-for-pro-act-union.

9. Achin Vanaik, "Farmers Are Leading India's Biggest Social Movement in a Generation," *Jacobin*, April 17, 2021, https://jacobinmag.com/2021/04/indian-farmers-strike-modi-bjp-social-movements-historical-struggles.

10. Jennifer Pedraza, "Colombia's Uprising Isn't About Duque. It's About Overturning Neoliberalism," *Jacobin*, June 8, 2021, https://www.jacobinmag.com/2021/06/colombia-ivan-duque-government-neoliberalism-protest-general-strike.

INDEX

ShinJoung Yeo is assistant professor of media studies at Queens College, City University of New York.

The Geopolitics of Information

Digital Depression: Information Technology and Economic Crisis *Dan Schiller*
Signal Traffic: Critical Studies of Media Infrastructures *Edited by Lisa Parks and Nicole Starosielski*
Media in New Turkey: The Origins of an Authoritarian Neoliberal State *Bilge Yesil*
Goodbye iSlave: A Manifesto for Digital Abolition *Jack Linchuan Qiu*
Networking China: The Digital Transformation of the Chinese Economy *Yu Hong*
The Media Commons: Globalization and Environmental Discourses *Patrick D. Murphy*
Media, Geopolitics, and Power: A View from the Global South *Herman Wasserman*
The Huawei Model: The Rise of China's Technology Giant *Yun Wen*
Television and the Afghan Culture Wars: Brought to You by Foreigners, Warlords, and Local Activists *Wazhmah Osman*
Behind the Search Box: Google and the Global Internet Industry *ShinJoung Yeo*

The University of Illinois Press
is a founding member of the
Association of University Presses.

University of Illinois Press
1325 South Oak Street
Champaign, IL 61820-6903
www.press.uillinois.edu